Mobilizing the Marginalized

The Other One Percent

Sanjoy Chakravorty, Devesh Kapur, and Nirvikar Singh

Social Justice through Inclusion

Francesca R. Jensenius

The Man Who Remade India

Vinay Sitapati

Business and Politics in India

Edited by Christophe Jaffrelot, Atul Kohli, and Kanta Murali

Mobilizing the Marginalized

Amit Ahuja

Mobilizing
the Marginalized

Ethnic Parties without Ethnic Movements

AMIT AHUJA

OXFORD
UNIVERSITY PRESS

OXFORD
UNIVERSITY PRESS

Oxford University Press is a department of the University of Oxford. It furthers
the University's objective of excellence in research, scholarship, and education
by publishing worldwide. Oxford is a registered trade mark of Oxford University
Press in the UK and certain other countries.

Published in the United States of America by Oxford University Press
198 Madison Avenue, New York, NY 10016, United States of America.

Library of Congress Cataloging-in-Publication Data
Names: Ahuja, Amit, author.
Title: Mobilizing the marginalized :
ethnic parties without ethnic movements / Amit Ahuja.
Description: New York, NY : Oxford University Press, [2018]
Identifiers: LCCN 2018018231 | ISBN 9780190916428 (hard cover) |
ISBN 9780190916435 (pbk.) | ISBN 9780190916442 (updf) |
ISBN 9780190916459 (epub)
Subjects: LCSH: Dalits—India—Social conditions. |
Dalits—Political activity—India. | Marginality, Social—Political aspects—India. |
Social movements—India. | Political parties—India. | India—Politics and government.
Classification: LCC DS422.C3 A64 2018 | DDC 324.254/08—dc23
LC record available at https://lccn.loc.gov/2018018231

1 3 5 7 9 8 6 4 2

Paperback printed by Sheridan Books, Inc., United States of America
Hardback printed by Bridgeport National Bindery, Inc., United States of America

In the loving memory of my father, whose steps I sense beside me every day of my life, and to the Ladies Ahuja—Mom, Anu, and Jane—who are the wonder women in my life.

CONTENTS

FIGURES, MAPS, AND TABLES

Figure

Maps

Tables

PREFACE

Writing on caste inequality in India, Myron Weiner observed, "Perhaps no other major society in recent history has known inequalities so gross, so long preserved, or so ideologically well entrenched."[1] Dalits, a name people formerly known as the untouchables give themselves, are the world's largest and longest discriminated group. They number more than 200 million and have been treated as outcastes for two millennia.[2] Dalits are among India's most marginalized citizens.

Humiliation has defined Dalits' relationship with the rest of Indian society. In some parts of India, members of untouchable castes were forced to string a broom around their waists to sweep over the ground they had polluted by merely walking on it. Others were required to hang an earthen pot around their necks so that their spit should not fall on the ground and pollute a caste Hindu who may unknowingly tread over it. In other parts of India, even the shadow of an untouchable was deemed polluting and, thus, untouchables were not allowed to use public paths and streets. Many untouchables were compelled to wear black bracelets to identify themselves. The caste system is a multilayered, hierarchical social order, in which members of every caste except the Dalits enjoys the privilege of kicking others ranked below them. Historically, as a people at the bottom of the caste pyramid, Dalits have been obliged to bow to the abuse heaped at

---

[1] See Myron Weiner, "The Struggle for Equality: Caste in Indian Politics," in Atul Kohli, ed., *The Success of India's Democracy* (New York: Cambridge University Press, 2001), p. 194.

[2] This system was codified in one well-known text, the *Manusmriti* ("Laws of Manu"), dated ca. 200 B.C.E.–200 C.E. More recently, scientists have used genetic evidence to trace the strict intragroup marriage practices associated with the caste system to at least 100 C.E. and possibly as early as 4200 C.E. SeePriya Moorjani, Kumarasamy Thangaraj, Nick Patterson, Mark Lipson, Po-Ru Loh, Priyasamy Govindaraj, Bonnie Berger, David Reich, and Lalji Singh, "Genetic Evidence for Recent Population Mixture in India," *The American Journal of Human Genetics*, vol. 93, no. 3 (2013), pp. 422–438.

them by everyone else. Untouchability has been the most powerful mechanism to enforce the exclusion of Dalits from the rest of society.

The Constitution of India outlawed the practice of untouchability in 1950; however, it and subsequent laws that punish the practice have been enforced only weakly. Although the practice of untouchability has declined gradually in the public domain in India, a recent countrywide study finds that it is still widely practiced in the private domain. Untouchability and its accompanying stigma have spawned a pattern of segregation—the Dalit/non-Dalit division—that is visible across housing settlements, marriage ties, employment, and every-day social interactions. Interactions between Dalits and non-Dalits are socially policed through the implicit and explicit threats of social boycotts, ostracism, and violence. Beyond the experience of untouchability, Dalits then also live under the threat of intimidation, violence, and social humiliation. This oppression is especially acute in rural areas, where most Dalits continue to live, and from where the worst acts of caste-based atrocities are still reported. This is not to say that time has stood still when it comes to exclusion of Dalits and their domination by other groups. Change has been slow to arrive, but materially, socially, and politically, the lives of Dalits have improved over the past seven decades of Indian independence. Yet, Dalits remain some of the most marginalized citizens of India.

While writing this book, I strove to see the world from the vantage point of Dalits. The India I grew up in hardly offered much preparation; the stories of Dalits, in principle Indian citizens like me, did not make it into my high school textbooks. There were no school trips to museums or memorials that commemorated Dalit struggles against oppression. Neither were Dalits present in the undergraduate economics curriculum of the University of Delhi in the 1990s. Later, in preparation for this project, secondary accounts and socioeconomic statistics on Dalits were helpful, but they gave me only a limited sense of the context that shapes Dalit politics. For this reason, I visited hundreds of Dalit localities in villages, towns, and cities across four of India's largest states that had experienced Dalit assertion—Uttar Pradesh, Bihar, Maharashtra, and Tamil Nadu—and spoke to countless Dalits myself.

In one of the first large villages we visited for focus group discussion and interviews in eastern Uttar Pradesh, my research assistant Ramesh and I got lost. A small boy did us the kindness of showing us the way to the Dalit part of the village. After I had gathered the people for the focus group discussion, I discovered that to some of the questions, no responses were forthcoming. There was silence. I was puzzled. But Ramesh picked up on it. He noticed that everyone was looking at the small boy who was still standing around out of curiosity. It turned out he was from a Thakur (a dominant caste) family in the village. Twelve grown-up men and women sat quietly petrified of talking in front of a seven-year-old boy.

Until he left, no one opened his or her mouth. It is one thing to read about sub-ordination, but it is an entirely different proposition to come face to face with it.

During interviews and focus group discussions, Dalits regularly complained about their ill treatment by members of higher-caste groups. For example, Dalits were intimidated and bullied, excluded from village commons and other castes' localities, and shut out of temples and common water sources.

Dalits overall expressed little faith in the laws enacted to protect them from atrocities and to guarantee their rights. One explanation given was that the implementation of these laws remains weak at best. The conviction rates for crimes charged under the different legal provisions created to protect Dalits remain low. Society marginalizes Dalits, and the state often fails them. In these conversations, Dalits sometimes reported that they approached the state administration and the courts for assistance. For most individuals, however, turning to the judicial system was not seen as a viable proposition. Interview subjects frequently pointed out that cases languished in the courts for many years and that the costs of fighting a case were prohibitively high. "Those with land and assets can use courts," said one man, "We cannot." "Going to the police is futile," reported another, "They don't register the complaints and, even when they do, they will not protect us from the reprisals." In poor Dalit localities, people reported that they had no control over the teachers in their schools, they were openly intimidated in police stations, they faced rampant neglect in health centers, and in government offices their petitions got put on the back burner.

We live in the age of anger, as commentators often remind us.[3] Dalits have much to be angry about. They are an electoral minority, albeit a sizable one, so their rage is rarely in a position to topple governments. They do not bomb theaters or highjack planes. Historically denied the opportunity to take up arms against their oppressors, they have seldom joined guerilla groups. Still, theirs is not a two-dimensional story of victimhood. Even under severe con-straints, they have developed their own culture and discourse, not to mention political beliefs. They have narrated their stories to themselves and to others. They have discovered their own heroes and celebrated them. Increasingly, they protest, and as enthusiastic voters, they make themselves count as dem-ocratic citizens.

The more I came face to face with the disdain and contempt that Dalits are held in, and the fear and humiliation they endure, the more remarkable I found their assertion. Dalits, for me personally, highlighted the possibility of democracy.

---

[3] See Pankaj Mishra, *Age of Anger: A History of the Present* (New York: Farrar, Straus and Giroux, 2017).

Their mobilization signified the redemption of the promise of democracy in a society that remains undemocratic.

What do the marginalized do in the face of dominance? In his remarkable book, *Weapons of the Weak*, James Scott taught us that as vulnerable citizens, the marginalized respond to routine dominance through hidden forms of resistance.[4] They drag their feet, pilfer, evade, gossip, and sabotage. But as I researched my own book, conducted the interviews, and returned to the transcripts later, my faith in that interpretation of the world of the marginalized ebbed away gradually. I found there just is very little freedom in powerlessness, even when it is aided by the crutches of covert resistance. The momentary restoration of self-worth, which is what hidden resistance is about, disappears when social discrimination, or state neglect, or both, are a regular feature of one's life. Beyond a doubt, there has existed a hidden transcript to Dalit resistance; however, over centuries, it did little to rob the caste system of its legitimacy. For that, Dalits had to organize. Dr. B. R. Ambedkar, the greatest Dalit civil rights leader and one of India's most formidable intellectuals, was right. Without organization, the weak just do not get taken seriously. Organization is their first weapon. It is the only way they stand any chance of getting a seat at the table. This is what drew me to Dalit mobilization. I wanted to study Dalit movements and parties.

In my conversations and numerous visits to Dalit localities, I discovered much that is common to the experience of being a Dalit across Indian states, and much that is different. Dalit assertion has been expressed socially as well as electorally. It has been sensitive to institutional conditions. In particular, the fragmenting party system over the twenty-five-year period between 1989 and 2014 lowered the threshold for electoral success for Dalit parties and enabled their emergence and survival. But Dalit parties are not the only form of Dalit assertion. In fact, they are not the predominant form. So much of Dalit everyday politics is close to the ground and informal. Early in my research, I viewed Dalit organizations as the primary representations of Dalit social mobilization. It was only after I began to visit Dalit localities and spent time in them that I discovered how Dalit social mobilization is structured. It does not find expression in large formal organizations with manifestos or lists of members. Instead, it is practiced within households and in localities; in stories elders tell children; in the writing and consumption of protest, theater, and music; and during festivals and prayer meetings. It is nurtured by local social entrepreneurs who bolster their own legitimacy by being involved in such activities. This close to the ground, locality-level informal politics has shifted broader social attitudes toward Dalits and their

---

[4] See James C. Scott, *Weapons of the Weak: Everyday Forms of Peasant Resistance* (New Haven: Yale University Press, 1985).

political inclusion slowly, often at glacial speed, but as this book will show, over time these effects have been profound.

Listening to Dalits also made me recognize that the long-surviving trope of Indian politics that voters vote their caste does not travel well across Indian states. One of the questions I began my research with was: Why do Dalits vote their caste with such regularity? I quickly realized that this was the wrong question to ask, because what was true for Dalits' interest in voting their caste in Uttar Pradesh in northern India was not as true for Dalits in Maharashtra in the West, or Tamil Nadu in the South. In fact, the question that came to guide this book was why Dalits were more interested in voting their caste in some states, but not in others.

Across the states, Dalit habitations were low-income localities, and during my fieldwork, I began to notice that in some states the work on public projects in Dalit localities and neighborhoods stalled and remained incomplete when governments changed, but in other states, despite government alternation, the work was completed. These observations forced me to reconsider the value of electoral solidarity for marginalized groups. Dr. B. R. Ambedkar's insistence on organization notwithstanding, group solidarity in elections, as I realized, is a double-edged sword. It lends a marginalized group political presence and a voice, not to mention a sense of efficacy, but at the same time, it can reduce the competition for the support of the group. Elections then become a lottery for the marginalized; if their party wins, the state shows up at their doorstep, but if their party loses, they are shutout of public programs.

Dalit mobilization has produced Dalit presidents, chief ministers, cabinet ministers, and members of parliament and state assemblies. The affirmative action policies and sustained economic expansion since the 1990s have generated a small Dalit urban middle class. The first Dalit Indian Chamber of Commerce was established in Maharashtra in 2005, and commentators have begun to document the rise of Dalit entrepreneurs.[5] At the same time, Dalits have begun to report fewer incidents of discrimination in the public sphere. In light of these changes, I wanted to inquire if upwardly mobile upper-middle-class Dalits were able to escape the shadow of stigma in the private sphere. When I interviewed them, I discovered that many among these Dalits placed their professional, educational, and class identity above their caste identity. But could others look past the Dalit identity? To find out, I studied the treatment of well-to-do, highly educated Dalit grooms by prospective brides belonging to different castes in the urban middle-class marriage market.

---

[5] See Devesh Kapur, D. Shyam Babu, and Chandra Bhan Prasad, *Defying the Odds: The Rise of Dalit Entrepreneurs* (Gurgaon: Random House India, 2014).

To the marginalized, democracy promises the opportunity to seek equality and inclusion through mobilization. Dalits have tested the democratic promise over the past seven decades in India by mobilizing socially and electorally. Through an in-depth exploration of Dalit mobilization, this book offers a close scrutiny of the opportunities and limitations of democratic assertion of the marginalized.

ACKNOWLEDGMENTS

It takes a village to produce a book. Below I introduce you to mine.

My book owes its greatest debt to the many people who agreed to participate in focus groups, interviews, and surveys. It is their contribution that breathed life into this project.

Ramesh, Ashok, Muragan, Ravi, Gopal, Puneet, Meena, Sampat, and Sanjana provided superb research assistance in the field. They adapted to a grueling schedule and demanding situations. Without their dedication, my research for this book could have been derailed on many occasions. It is thanks to them that I was able to navigate the often treacherous terrain in villages, towns, and cities across the length and breadth of India.

My research was made possible through the support of many institutions in India and in the United States. During my fieldwork, I benefited from the intellectual contributions and hospitality of the Madras Institute of Development Studies in Chennai, the Giri Institute of Development Studies and Sanatkadda in Lucknow, the Rajiv Gandhi Foundation in New Delhi, and the Department of Political Science in Savitribhai Phule University in Pune. The Center for the Study of Developing Societies became my home in India. The Lokniti Program there taught me much about survey research in India and shared its insights and data readily. I will never be able to thank Sanjay Kumar and Himanshu enough for the warmth and generosity they have shown me.

At the University of Michigan, fellowships from the International Institute, Rackham Graduate School, and Telluride Foundation, and at the University of California at Santa Barbara, a Faculty Enrichment Grant and a Senate Faculty Grant supported the various stages of this research. My work benefited from the suggestions and questions offered by participants in the Comparative Politics Workshop at the University of Michigan at Ann Arbor, the South Asian Politics Workshop at the University of California at Berkeley, the Indian Democracy Workshop at Brown University, India's Political

Economy Workshop at the Center for the Advanced Study of India at the University of Pennsylvania, the race and ethnicity series at the University of California at Los Angeles, and the Global Studies Workshop at the University of California at Santa Barbara.

Shyam Babu, Gopal Guru, Chandra Bhan Prasad, Sudha Pai, Yogendra Yadav, Sanjay Kumar, Suhas Palshikar, the late M.S.S. Pandian, Ghanshyam Shah, Ashis Nandy, Dilip Menon, Jagpal Singh, Farzand Ahmed, S. Visvanathan, Srikanth, and Mahesh Rangarajan offered invaluable guidance and advice at the early stage of the project.

Mark Sawyer, Irfan Nooruddin, Francesca Jensenius, Adnan Naseemullah, and Devesh Kapur read and commented on parts of the manuscript. To them and my anonymous reviewers, I am deeply indebted.

Kanti Bajpai in Delhi and Mushtaq Khan in London were my early role models. At the University of Michigan, Elizabeth Anderson, Edie Goldenberg, Ronald Inglehart, Ken Colman, Vincent Hutchings, and Anna Grzymala Busse offered immense support and advice. At the University of California at Santa Barbara, friends and colleagues, including Kate Bruhn, Cynthia Kaplan, Pei-te Lien, Heather Stoll, Aashish Mehta, Paige Digeser, Hahrie Han, and Kum-Kum Bhavnani, provided constant encouragement. As department chairs, John Woolley, Eric Smith, and Bruce Bimber were good shepherds during my time as a junior faculty member. I also owe special thanks to Emily Mackenzie at Oxford University Press for steering the book through the publication process and to Rachel Digiambattista for expertly managing the edits.

Gaurav, Amit, Vivek, Bahar, Kim, Aleks, Massimo, Dann, Susan, Radhika, and Aparna gave unconditional warmth and affection, and their belief in me has been relentless. Anu has been my guardian angel. She kept the faith even on those days when I lost mine. In Jane, my book had the best friend. She has been its harshest critic and its strongest champion. Without her I would not have written this book. Writing is a solitary enterprise. Simon, Sophie, and Tashi were my companions at different stages. On good days and bad ones, I was much comforted by my furry friends.

I owe unpayable debts to Pradeep Chhibber, Ashutosh Varshney, and Allen Hicken for suffering different iterations of the book's main argument. I was most fortunate to have thoughtful and generous mentors in them. They, more than anyone else, have taught me the meaning of being an academic. I will try to pay these debts forward for the rest of my life. No words will ever capture the gratitude I feel toward them.

Very early in life, my parents instilled in me an ethos—never let blindness come in the way of things you want to accomplish. Dr. Anil Wilson at St. Stephen's College reinforced the same. "Even if you are going to miss the bus," he would say, "make sure you miss it running." So I ran. I wish my father and Dr. Wilson had lived to hold this book in their hands.

ABBREVIATIONS

AIADMK	All India Anna Dravida Munnetra Kazhagam
BAMCEF	All-India Backward and Minority Communities Employees' Federation
BBM	Bharipa Bahujan Mahasangh
BC	Backward Caste
BJP	Bharatiya Janata Party
BSP	Bahujan Samaj Party
DMDK	Desiya Murpokku Dravida Kazhagam
DMK	Dravida Munnetra Kazhagam
DPI	Dalit Panthers of India
DS4	Dalit Soshit Samaj Sangharsh Sanghatan
EVR	E. V. Ramaswamy Naikar/"Periyar"
IHDS	India Human Development Survey
INC	Indian National Congress
JD	Janata Dal
JD(U)	Janata Dal (United)
LJP	Lok Janshakti Party
MLA	Member of the Legislative Assembly
NCP	Nationalist Congress Party
NDA	National Democratic Alliance
NES	Indian National Election Studies
OBC	Other Backward Caste
PT	Puthiya Tamilagam
RJD	Rashtriya Janata Dal
RPI	Republican Party of India
RSS	Rashtriya Swayamsevak Sangh

SC	Scheduled Caste
SCF	Scheduled Caste Federation
SP	Samajwadi Party
ST	Scheduled Tribe
VCK	Viduthalai Chiruthaikal Katchi

ABOUT THE COMPANION WEBSITE

http://global.oup.com/us/companion.websites/9780190900656/

Oxford has created a Web site to accompany the titles in the Modern South Asia Series. Material that cannot be made available in a book, namely series editor information and submission guidelines are provided here. The reader is encouraged to consult this resource if they would like to find out more about the books in this series.

Mobilizing the Marginalized

1

Introduction

On the 26th of January 1950, we are going to enter into a life of contradictions. In politics we will have equality and in social and economic life we
will have inequality. In politics we will be recognizing the principle of one
man one vote and one vote one value. In our social and economic life, we
shall, by reason of our social and economic structure, continue to deny
the principle of one man one value. How long shall we continue to live
this life of contradictions? How long shall we continue to deny equality
in our social and economic life? If we continue to deny it for long, we will
do so only by putting our political democracy in peril. We must remove
this contradiction at the earliest possible moment or else those who suffer
from inequality will blow up the structure of political democracy which
this Assembly has so laboriously built up.
—Dr. Bhimrao Ramji Ambedkar, Chairman of the Drafting Committee
of the Indian Constitution and a Dalit[1]

Democracy rests on the tantalizing prospect that political equality can be
leveraged to remedy social and economic inequality. This prospect has cer-
tainly inspired the mass mobilization of Dalits in India, an ethnic group once
referred to as "outcastes" or "untouchables" that comprises nearly 17% of the
country's total population.[2] Dalits have organized themselves through social

[1] These remarks were made before the Constituent Assembly on November 25, 1949, while introducing the Constitution of India for approval. They are recorded in Volume XI of the proceedings
and are available online at http://parliamentofindia.nic.in/ls/debates/vol11p11.htm. The date the
Constitution entered into effect (January 26, 1950) is celebrated annually as Republic Day. Dr. B. R.
Ambedkar (b. 1891–d. 1956) is the premier Dalit ideologue and icon.

[2] Caste is regarded as an ethnic identity because of its descent-based attributes. See Kanchan
Chandra, "What Is Ethnic Identity and What Does It Matter?" *Annual Review of Political Science*,
vol. 9 (2006), pp. 397–424; Kanchan Chandra and Steven Wilkinson, "Measuring the Effect of
Ethnicity," *Comparative Political Studies*, vol. 41, nos. 4–5 (2008), pp. 515–563. Caste, as an ascriptive
identity, also satisfies Fredrik Barth's criteria for ethnic identity: "a categorical ascription is an ethnic
ascription when it classifies a person in terms of his basic, most general identity, presumptively determined by his origin and background" (p. 13). See Fredrik Barth, "Introduction," in Fredrik Barth, ed.,
Ethnic Groups and Boundaries: The Social Organization of Culture Difference (Boston: Little, Brown,
and Company, 1969), pp. 9–38.

1

movements and political parties to confront the two-thousand-year-old Hindu caste system and improve their circumstances. This revolution from below, while uneven and incomplete, has been hailed as a major achievement of Indian democracy.

The Puzzle

This book's inquiry into Dalit mobilization is motivated by an empirical puzzle: Dalits' ethnic parties have performed poorly in elections in Indian states where their historical social mobilization has been strong and sustained, yet Dalits' ethnic parties have performed well in elections in states where their historical social mobilization has been absent or weak. For Dalits, collective action in the social sphere appears to undermine rather than enable collective action in the electoral sphere.

This runs counter to expectations. Social movements are widely believed to produce resources, including finances, dedicated manpower, skilled leadership, popular symbols and discourses, and, frequently, allies, that can be transferred. Given favorable institutional conditions in a first-past-the-post electoral system, such as free and fair elections and a fragmented party system, we would expect emergent political parties to be electorally successful. Indeed, there are notable examples of social movements generating successful political parties. Some cases include the environmental movement and Green parties in Germany, France, and New Zealand; workers' rights movements and labor and social democratic parties in Britain, Scandinavia, and Australia; Christian sects and confessional parties in Europe; the coca growers' movement and the Movement for Socialism (MAS) Party in Bolivia; the Islamist movement and the Justice and Development (AK) Party in Turkey; and the Hindu nationalist movement and the Bharatiya Janata Party (BJP) in India. Movements have generated single-issue parties, class-based parties, and ethnic parties. In the case of movement-driven ethnic parties, these have represented both majority and minority groups inside polities.

Prompted by the Dalit mobilization paradox, this book explores three sets of interrelated questions:

- Why is Dalit mobilization distinct? What factors shape the nature and the prospects of a marginalized group's mobilization?
- What is the relationship between Dalit social and electoral mobilization? How do social movements affect political parties?

- Why do Dalits in some places in India vote on the basis of their ethnicity while others do not? When does ethnic identity influence voting?

The Argument

Recognizing status inequality among ethnic groups matters. Dalits differ fundamentally from many other ethnic groups because they are marginalized. I identify a marginalized ethnic group using two criteria: (1) it is stigmatized by others, and (2) it is disproportionately poor. These criteria are self-reinforcing and produce substantial intergroup disparities over time. Dalits are the largest marginalized ethnic group in the world; their total population in India is above 200 million.[3] Some other marginalized ethnic groups include African-origin populations in Brazil and the United States, indigenous peoples in Latin America and Australia, the Roma in Europe, and groups such as the Burakumin in Japan and Al-Akhdam in Yemen that are also characterized by untouchability.

A marginalized group can mobilize socially as well as electorally. When a marginalized group self-organizes in everyday life for the purpose of demanding social equality and equal access to public resources, I view it as social mobilization; it is directed toward both society and the state. By contrast, electoral mobilization is usually time-bound and restricted to those activities that have to do with the group's participation in elections. Political parties that mobilize marginalized groups can be ethnic or multiethnic. I recognize a political party as an ethnic party when the majority of its electoral support at the state level is provided by a particular ethnic group and when the party is disproportionately committed to advancing the welfare of that ethnic group. Multiethnic parties may represent the select interests of an amalgamation of ethnic groups or they may be ideological.

The sequencing of a marginalized group's mobilization is consequential. The mobilization of the marginalized can take the form of an ethnic social movement, an ethnic political party, or both. The threshold for the success of an ethnic party is higher than that of a social movement because ethnic party success requires an additional electoral opportunity and bloc voting. As a result, movements of the marginalized can precede their ethnic parties. When a marginalized ethnic group's social mobilization precedes its electoral mobilization, marginalized ethnic parties' electoral success will be curtailed. This is because any inclusion won

[3] See Census of India, 2011.

by a marginalized group's movement weakens the ethnic bloc voting required by its ethnic political party to be electorally successful.

Two processes are at work. First, social movements generate *mobilizers*: these are entrepreneurial activists working at the grass-roots level for the marginalized ethnic group. Political parties have incentives to recruit these individuals to improve their competitiveness with one another in a multiparty system. Mobilizers also have incentives to align with parties as they compete among themselves for standing. Second, social movements produce *mobilization frames*, popular symbols and discourses rooted in culture.[4] Parties have incentives to incorporate these to improve their credibility with marginalized voters. Together, both processes increase competition for marginalized votes at the local level and reduce the utility of a marginalized ethnic identity for differentiating among parties. Ethnically-inclined voters are then compelled to alter their rationales for choosing parties. They may be persuaded by programmatic promises or the charisma of specific party leaders. These dynamics between voters and parties are self-reinforcing and shift a party's emphasis from the provision of symbolic goods to material goods. As marginalized ethnic voters split their preferences across multiple parties and adopt multiple decision-making rationales, their ethnic bloc voting remains weak. Marginalized ethnic group parties cannot succeed under these conditions.

By contrast, where a marginalized group's social mobilization is absent or weak, the party system is deprived of its mobilizers and mobilization frames. Marginalized voters are unmobilized or undermobilized in these circumstances. Significant potential remains for them to be unified into an electoral bloc because mobilizers retain a first-mover advantage to select and frame the group's popular symbols and discourses. Marginalized ethnic group parties are much more likely to succeed under these conditions.

The experience of Dalits typifies the mobilization of a marginalized ethnic group in a diverse society in a developing country, but patterns in Dalits' mobilization are instructive for general theories of ethnic politics and ethnic identity.

Mobilization of the marginalized matters. It shapes how the marginalized are included in democratic politics and how political parties acknowledge and respond to their social as well as material needs. For long, we have assessed the relationship of the marginalized with India's democracy by focusing on their participation in elections. Numerous studies have highlighted the high rates in which the marginalized show up to vote.[5] But participation does not imply mobilization.

[4] See Sidney Tarrow, *Power in Movement: Social Movements and Contentious Politics*, 3rd Edition (Cambridge: Cambridge University Press, 2011).
[5] See Yogendra Yadav, "Understanding the Second Democratic Upsurge: Trends of Bahujan Participation in Electoral Politics in the 1990s," in Francine R. Frankel, Zoya Hasan, Rajeev Bhargava, and Balveer Arora, eds., *Transforming India: Social and Political Dynamics of Democracy*

Just because the marginalized vote in large numbers does not necessarily mean that their demands for inclusion are acknowledged in electoral politics. A shift in the focus from participation to mobilization is therefore necessary to evaluate the agency of the marginalized in their relationship with democratic politics.

In hierarchical societies, electoral assertion of the marginalized through bloc voting represents the redemption of the promise of democracy that allows the socially powerless to convert their numbers into electoral power. But, bloc voting is also said to have far-reaching perverse effects for distributional politics and how voters hold parties and their representatives accountable.[6] To reconcile the promise of democracy for the marginalized with the unintended consequences of their mobilization, then, we have to explore the relationship between the forms of mobilization and democratic accountability.

It is also essential to comprehend the varied relationships between social and electoral mobilization. Electoral outcomes remain the focus of democratic politics, with vote share of political parties and their relationship with electoral rules and the nature of party system holding center stage in academic and popular discussions. However, this emphasis can sometimes eclipse the significance of political activities that take place in-between elections, which besides shaping voter attitudes, produce mobilization resources for political parties, including entrepreneurs, ideological discourse, and iconic symbols. Agitations, protests, and other movement-related activities represent such politics, and as compared to electoral mobilization, their lower threshold for organization presents a viable avenue for the assertion of the marginalized.

Ethnicity has been the basis for social exclusion across many societies. Even as societies historically ordered by hierarchical or ranked relationships between groups come to be governed democratically, members of excluded groups continue to struggle to access the full panoply of their legal, political, and social rights.[7] Political parties and social movements that represent such

---

(New Delhi: Oxford University Press, 2000), pp. 120–145; Javeed Alam, *Who Wants Democracy?* (New Delhi: Orient Longman, 2004); Sanjai Kumar, "Patterns of Political Participation: Trends and Perspective," *Economic and Political Weekly*, vol. 44, no. 39 (2009), pp. 47–51; Mukulika Banerjee, *Why India Votes* (New Delhi: Routledge India, 2014); Amit Ahuja and Pradeep Chhibber, "Why the Poor Vote in India: 'If I Don't Vote, I Am Dead to the State,'" *Studies in Comparative International Development*, vol. 47, no. 4 (2012), pp. 389–410.

[6] When voters vote their identity, voter choices for parties and candidates are motivated by fear of other groups, or issues related to group pride, and not necessarily pocketbook concerns. See Paul Collier, *Wars, Guns, and Votes: Democracy in Dangerous Places* (New York: Harper, 2009).

[7] As described by Horowitz, an ideal type of ranked system has an acknowledged absence of an upper class belonging to the subordinate group, a ritualized mode of hierarchy, and a leadership of the subordinates that necessarily has to enjoy the approval of the dominant groups. See Donald Horowitz, *Ethnic Groups in Conflict* (Berkeley: University of California Press, 1985).

historically marginalized groups are then an important category of collective action to study since they mobilize citizens with both low levels of political efficacy and either inaccessible or ineffective avenues of representation outside the electoral arena.

The Distinctness of the Ethnic Mobilization of the Marginalized

Ethnic diversity does not necessarily imply ethnic difference; it also manifests in ethnic disparity. In fact, it is critical to acknowledge the distinction between marginalized groups and other groups because ethnicity-based explanations for a variety of outcomes oftentimes actually rely on the properties associated with ethnicity rather than on the ethnic identity itself.[8] For such explanations to be complete, these properties and their effects must be identified.

The mobilization of marginalized ethnic groups, when it occurs, is qualitatively distinct in the goals it espouses and the forms it takes. Consider two types of collective action. On the one hand, we have the mobilization of dominant groups against marginalized groups, as in the mobilization of European far-right groups against immigrants in European countries; the mobilization of the Ku Klux Klan against African Americans in the American South; the Hindu nationalist mobilization against Indian Muslims, as well as the mobilization of India's upper castes against the country's lower castes; and the mobilization of some Muslims against certain sects, especially Ahmadiyyas, in Pakistan. On the other hand, and in sharp contrast, we have the mobilization of marginalized groups such as India's Dalits, Japan's Burakumin, and Europe's Roma, in addition to Afro-Brazilians, African Americans, aboriginal groups in Australia and New Zealand, and indigenous groups in Latin America.

The mobilization of dominant ethnic groups can often take the form of a "politics of othering," which involves the identification and vilification of an out-group. Dominant ethnic groups mobilize for the purpose of preserving their privileged status with respect to the rest of society. By contrast, marginalized ethnic groups seek the end of exclusion, and their mobilization is directed at

---

[8] Chandra has argued that the largest number of explanatory claims about ethnicity rest on properties that are not intrinsic to ethnic identities in general, such as fixedness, a common culture, and territorial concentration. She suggests, "As such, they cannot be taken as claims about the effect of ethnic identities in general . . . Rather than reading them to mean that ethnicity is associated with some dependent variable Y, we should read them to mean either that a particular subset of ethnic identities are associated with dependent variable Y or that ethnicity, along with some other variable X, is associated with the dependent variable Y." I treat historic marginalization as that associated variable X. See Chandra, "What Is Ethnic Identity and What Does It Matter?" p. 419.

the state and the rest of the society. Members of a marginalized group mobilize in order to claim their rightful space, both in society and in politics. Therefore, the mobilization of a marginalized group takes the form of a "politics of self" by building collective respect through the process of organization. Both types of collective action represent ethnic mobilization, but they are different in fundamental ways. Thus, an observational equivalence of the two types of mobilization should not be mistaken for their similarity.

Parties, Movements, and the Puzzle of Dalit Mobilization

The relationship between political parties and social movements and their combined influence on public policy has remained under-explored because of disciplinary boundaries. Political scientists who examine electoral and party mobilization pay little attention to social mobilization, while sociologists who study social movements often neglect political parties.[9] Research on Dalit mobilization reflects this gap. A large scholarship exists on Dalit social mobilization.[10] Dalit electoral mobilization has also been studied

---

[9] See Paul Burstein, Rachel L. Einwohner, and Jocelyn A. Hollander, "The Success of Political Movements: A Bargaining Perspective," in J. Craig Jenkins and Bert Klandermans, eds., *The Politics of Social Protest* (Minneapolis: University of Minnesota Press, 1995), pp. 275–295; Doug McAdam and Karina Kloos, *Deeply Divided: Racial Politics and Social Movements in Postwar America* (New York: Oxford University Press, 2014).

[10] Outside the confines of political science, a large body of scholarship has appeared on the social mobilization of Dalits. A limited selection of this writing includes Owen M. Lynch, *The Politics of Untouchability: Social Mobility and Social Change in a City of India* (New York: Columbia University Press, 1969); Rosalind O'Hanlon, *Caste, Conflict, and Ideology: Mahatma Jotirao Phule and Low-Caste Protest in Nineteenth-Century Western India* (Cambridge: Cambridge University Press, 1985); D. R. Nagaraj, *The Flaming Feet: A Study of the Dalit Movement in India* (Bangalore: South Forum, 1993); Simon Charsley, "'Untouchable': What Is in a Name?" *Journal of the Royal Anthropological Institute*, vol. 2, no. 1 (1996), pp. 1–23; Lata Murugkar, *The Dalit Panther Movement in Maharashtra: A Sociological Appraisal* (Bombay: Popular Prakashan, 1991); Eleanor Zelliot, "Learning the Use of Political Means: The Mahars of Maharashtra," in Rajni Kothari, ed., *Caste in Indian Politics* (New Delhi: Orient Longman, 1970), pp. 29–69; Oliver Mendelsohn and Marika Vicziany, *The Untouchables: Subordination, Poverty, and the State in Modern India* (Cambridge: Cambridge University Press, 1998); Gail Omvedt, *Dalit Visions: The Anti-caste Movement and the Construction of an Indian Identity* (New Delhi: Orient Longman, 1995); Hugo Gorringe, *Untouchable Citizens: Dalit Movements and Democratization in Tamil Nadu* (Thousand Oaks: Sage, 2005); Gyanendra Pandey, *A History of Prejudice: Race, Caste, and Difference in India and the United States* (Cambridge: Cambridge University Press, 2013); Rupa Viswanath, *The Pariah Problem: Caste, Religion, and the Social in Modern India* (New York City: Columbia University Press, 2014); Eva-Maria Hardtmann, *The Dalit Movement in India: Local Practices, Global Connections* (New Delhi: Oxford University Press, 2009);

extensively.[11] But, how Dalit social mobilization influences Dalit electoral mobilization is a question that has escaped systematic scrutiny.[12] The conventional wisdom on movements and parties holds that the strength of a social movement is reflected in the strong electoral performance of an allied political party, and that each of these forms of collective action is able to draw on the success of the other.[13] And yet, this state of affairs does not appear to apply to the case of Dalit mobilization.

A more complicated view of the relationship between social movements and allied political parties emerges from research showing that the relationship between movements and parties is not necessarily symbiotic, regardless of whether the alliance between a movement and a party rests on shared principles or plays out more pragmatically on the ground. For instance, relationships between social movements and political parties on the Left in Mexico and

Nicolas Jaoul, "The 'Righteous Anger' of the Powerless: Investigating Dalit Outrage over Caste Violence," *South Asia Multidisciplinary Academic Journal*, vol. 2 (2008), pp. 2–28; V. Geetha and S. V. Rajadurai, *Towards a Non-Brahmin Millennium: From Iyothee Thass to Periyar* (Calcutta: Samya, 1998); Badri Narayan, *The Making of the Dalit Public in North India: Uttar Pradesh, 1950–Present* (New Delhi: Oxford University Press, 2011); Anupama Rao, *The Caste Question: Dalits and the Politics of Modern India* (Berkeley: University of California Press, 2009); Ramnarayan S. Rawat, *Reconsidering Untouchability: Chamars and Dalit History in North India* (Bloomington: Indiana University Press, 2011).

[11] And within the field of political science, researchers have focused their attention on the electoral mobilization of Dalits, as in Pushpendra, "Dalit Assertion through Electoral Politics," *Economic and Political Weekly*, vol. 34, no. 36 (1999), pp. 2609–2618; Ian Duncan, "Dalits and Politics in Rural North India: The Bahujan Samaj Party in Uttar Pradesh," *Journal of Peasant Studies*, vol. 27, no. 1 (1999), pp. 35–60; Yogendra Yadav, "Understanding the Second Democratic Upsurge," pp. 120–145; Sudha Pai, *Dalit Assertion and the Unfinished Democratic Revolution: The Bahujan Samaj Party in Uttar Pradesh* (New Delhi: Sage, 2002); Christophe Jaffrelot, *India's Silent Revolution: The Rise of the Lower Castes* (New York: Columbia University Press, 2003); Kanchan Chandra, *Why Ethnic Parties Succeed: Patronage and Ethnic Head Counts in India* (Cambridge: Cambridge University Press, 2004).

[12] An exception is thoughtful ethnographic work on the Dalit movement and its relationship with the BSP in Maharashtra. See Suryakant Waghmore, *Civility against Caste: Dalit Politics and Citizenship in Western India* (Thousand Oaks: Sage, 2013).

[13] For example, when institutional opportunities opened up in Latin American countries, indigenous people's movements became the building blocks for political parties; see Donna Lee Van Cott, *From Movements to Parties in Latin America: The Evolution of Ethnic Politics* (Cambridge: Cambridge University Press, 2005). Similarly, the appearance of the Green Movement in European countries led to the emergence of the Green Parties in these countries. And in India, likewise, a strong Hindu nationalist movement is understood to enhance the electoral success of the Hindu nationalist Bharatiya Janata Party (BJP). In this connection, see Thomas Blom Hansen, *The Saffron Wave: Democracy and Hindu Nationalism in Modern India* (Princeton: Princeton University Press, 1999); Amrita Basu, "The Dialectics of Hindu Nationalism," in Atul Kohli, ed., *The Success of India's Democracy* (Cambridge: Cambridge University Press, 2001), pp. 163–190.

Brazil are not always mutually supportive, nor do the movements and parties always have the same agendas and concerns, and a movement organization is not unwilling to oppose its own governing party if that stance will serve the organization's interests.[14] Similarly, in some European countries, political differences between the Catholic Church and the rising confessional parties have not prevented the Church from pursuing its own interests through alliances with those parties, nor have political differences stood in the way of pragmatic alliances between confessional parties and other, secular parties.[15] The experience of the movement-party relationship in the United States suggests that even when movements and parties represent the same social group, an alliance between the two is not guaranteed. Motivated by electoral performance, parties are hard-nosed about when to ally with social movements. When gatekeepers within the party believe that an alliance will make election victory more likely, only then a movement and a party are more likely to partner.[16] In India, contrary to popular belief, the expanding Hindu nationalist movement and its electoral affiliate the BJP do not always see eye-to-eye and actually disagree on a number of policy issues.[17] This book adds to the general insights produced by the research emphasizing the links between the two forms of collective action represented by social movements and political parties.[18]

As for the extant research on political parties in India, it has focused in large part on the role of the elite organizing class.[19] But voter attitudes do not necessarily bend to the whims of the political elite on demand. Besides, voters form an equally

---

[14] See Kathleen Bruhn, *Urban Protest in Mexico and Brazil* (Cambridge: Cambridge University Press, 2008).

[15] See Stathis N. Kalyvas, *The Rise of Christian Democracy in Europe* (Ithaca: Cornell University Press, 1996).

[16] See Daniel Schlozman, *When Movements Anchor Parties: Electoral Alignments in American History* (Princeton: Princeton University Press, 2015).

[17] See Walter Andersen and Shridhar Damle, *The RSS: A View to the Inside* (Delhi: Penguin India, 2018).

[18] See Jack A. Goldstone, ed., *States, Parties, and Social Movements* (New York: Cambridge University Press, 2003); Van Cott, *From Movements to Parties in Latin America*; Bruhn, *Urban Protest in Mexico and Brazil*; Adrienne LeBas, *From Protest to Parties: Party-Building and Democratization in Africa* (Oxford: Oxford University Press, 2011); McAdam and Kloos, *Deeply Divided*; Schlozman, *When Movements Anchor Parties*.

[19] See Pradeep Chhibber, *Democracy without Associations: Transformation of Party Systems and Social Cleavages in India* (Ann Arbor: University of Michigan Press, 1999); Pai, *Dalit Assertion and the Unfinished Democratic Revolution*; Chandra, *Why Ethnic Parties Succeed*; Andrew Wyatt, *Party System Change in South India: Political Entrepreneurs, Patterns, and Processes* (Abingdon: Routledge, 2010); Tariq Thachil, "Elite Parties and Poor Voters: Theory and Evidence from India," *American Political Science Review*, vol. 108, no. 2 (2014), pp. 454–477.

important component of the process of electoral mobilization. The emergence of a political party does not after all guarantee its popularity with voters.

Many accounts of electoral mobilization point to how party elites produce consent among poor voters. Some point to the elite's promise of state patronage[20] or provision of services by nonstate actors.[21] Others highlight the use of ideology by the elite in shaping the common sense of poor voters.[22] This book uncovers the role that marginalized voters themselves play in the elites' production of consent, for even among the marginalized, there exists significant variation in patterns of mobilization as well as in the gains that mobilization brings. By focusing on Dalits' self-mobilization at the local level, the book substantiates the agency that one marginalized group has had in its own electoral mobilization.

Moreover, despite substantial scholarship on the voting patterns of caste groups in general and Dalits in particular, there remains much for us to learn about the sources of variation in Dalits' opinions and political behavior. The book offers new insights by exploring and explaining that variation across states, within the group of Dalits in a particular state, and between Dalits and other groups. In addition, by approaching the process of mobilization from the standpoint of the voter, the book adds a new set of questions and explanations to the literature. In the process, it shows how the Dalit mobilization experience challenges the conventional wisdom surrounding the link between social movements and political parties and clarifies the roles that social movements and political parties play in providing a consistent stream of public goods and other resources to a society's most marginalized citizens.

The Dalits

Dalit means "ground down" or "broken to pieces" in Marathi, a regional language from Western India. Dalits have claimed this term as a name for themselves. The Indian government calls the group "Scheduled Castes (SCs)," a legacy of the British colonial census project that listed social groups by their purported occupations.[23] Dalits number over 200 million and are distributed across the country (see Map 1.1).

---

[20] See Chandra, *Why Ethnic Parties Succeed.*

[21] See Thachil, "Elite Parties and Poor Voters," pp. 454–477.

[22] Pradeep K. Chhibber and Rahul Verma, *Ideology and Identity: The Changing Party Systems of India* (New York: Oxford University Press, 2018).

[23] For a description of this process, see Nicholas Dirks, *Castes of Mind: Colonialism and the Making of Modern India* (Princeton: Princeton University Press, 2001). State recognition was fundamental to the construction of caste identity as we understand it today; however, the state did not construct these identities out of thin air. These identities were rooted in and reflected social realities.

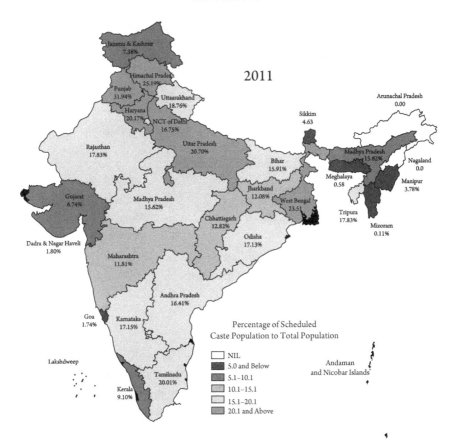

Jammu & Kashmir
7.38%

Himachal Pradesh
25.19%

Punjab
31.94%

Uttaarakhand
18.76%

Haryana
20.17%

NCT of Delhi
16.75%

Arunachal Pradesh
0.00

Sikkim
4.63

2011

Rajasthan
17.83%

Uttar Pradesh
20.70%

Madhya Pradesh
15.62%

Nagaland
0.0

Bihar
15.91%

Meghalaya
0.58

Manipur
3.78%

Gujarat
6.74%

Madhya Pradesh
15.62%

Jharkhand
12.08%

West Bengal
23.51%

Tripura
17.83%

Mizoram
0.11%

Chhattisgarh
12.82%

Dadra & Nagar Haveli
1.80%

Maharashtra
11.81%

Odisha
17.13%

Andhra Pradesh
16.41%

Goa
1.74%

Karnataka
17.15%

Lakshdweep

Tamilnadu
20.01%

Kerala
9.10%

Percentage of Scheduled
Caste Population to Total Population

NIL

5.0 and Below

5.1–10.1

10.1–15.1

15.1–20.1

20.1 and Above

Andaman
and Nicobar Islands

Map 1.1 Percentage of Dalit population in Indian states *Source*: Map outline from the Global Administrative Areas version 2.8 (GADMv2.8; www.gadm.org) and Primary Census Abstract for Total Population, Scheduled Castes and Scheduled Tribes, 2011. Office of the Registrar General & Census Commissioner, India. Map does not include disputed territory in Kashmir.

Dalits' ethnic identity has been constructed on the basis of the Hindu caste system. The Hindu social order divides society into five groups on the basis of ritual purity (see Table 1.1). Four groups—*Brahmins, Kshatriyas, Vaishyas,* and *Shudras*—have different levels of ritual purity. One group—the *Adi-Shudras* or the untouchables—does not have any ritual purity. Ritual purity is determined by occupation, inherited across generations, and preserved through endogamy. Broad social groups are *castes* or *varnas* while individual occupations serve as subcastes, also known as *jatis*.

Castes are often described in terms of their social ranks as "upper" or "lower." The upper castes include Brahmins, Kshatriyas, and Vaishyas. The lower castes include Shudras and Adi-Shudras. The Indian state has also made an effort to differentiate among lower castes; this has resulted in Shudras being described as "Other Backward Castes (OBCs)."

Table 1.1. **The Hindu caste system and terminology describing it**

	Hindu Caste Group	*Associated Occupations*	*Other Names*
Upper Castes	Brahmins	Priests, scholars	—
	Kshatriyas	Nobles, warriors	—
	Vaishyas	Merchants, traders	—
Lower Castes	Shudras	Laborers, peasants, artisans, craftsmen	Other Backward Castes (OBCs) Backward Castes Intermediate castes
	Adi-Shudras	Barbers, leatherworkers, scavengers, sweepers, toilet cleaners	Scheduled Castes (SCs) Dalits

The defining characteristic of Adi-Shudras has been untouchability. This group's ritual impurity was framed as so severe that it could contaminate other people and objects, in some instances by touch and in others by proximity alone. Hindus thus developed regulations to protect ritual purity by excluding untouchables almost entirely from public spaces and social life. The practice transcended Hinduism; Indian Muslims, Christians, and Sikhs also observed similar caste distinctions. Today, this relationship between caste identity and occupational status has largely broken down, yet Dalits' economic position mirrors their social status, and Dalits comprise a disproportionate share of India's poor.[24]

In 2010, based on health-, education-, and living-standards-related indicators, the United Nations Human Development Report estimated that 65.8% of Dalits were poor in comparison to just 55% of all Indians.[25] The disparities between the upper castes and Dalits are the sharpest. The 2004–2005 round of the India Human Development Survey (IHDS) finds that Dalits have less land, attend fewer years of school, report less income, and have weaker social networks, and (despite controlling for income and parental educational attainment)

[24] Ashwini Deshpande, "Does Caste Still Define Disparity? A Look at Inequality in Kerala, India," *American Economic Review*, vol. 90, no. 2 (2000), pp. 322–325.

[25] See Jeni Klugman, *Human Development Report 2010: The Real Wealth of Nations: Pathways to Human Development*, 20th edition (New York: Palgrave Macmillan, 2010).

Dalit children learn fewer skills at school.[26] Rapid economic growth since 1991 has reduced poverty in India; however, its impact has been felt differently by upper castes and Dalits, especially in rural India where 76% of Dalits still live.[27] Analysis of panel data from the two waves of IHDS, 2004–2005 and 2011–2012, suggests that within this period, 75% of upper castes in the rural areas were lifted out of poverty, but only 66% of Dalits reported the same economic progress. Additionally, while 20% of Dalits were more likely to fall into poverty, only 13% of the upper castes reported similar outcomes.[28]

Dalits lack conventional ethnic markers such as race, language, and descent from a common ancestor (tribe). They are similar in appearance and everyday behavior to other Indians. Instead, Dalits are primarily identified through two mechanisms: (1) shared local knowledge, and (2) regional naming practices that often use subcastes as surnames.

The British colonial state took the first steps toward the formalizing of caste categories. The colonial government recognized the caste system through practices such as the enumeration of castes in the census.[29] Begun in the late nineteenth century, these practices collapsed the various subcastes of untouchables into a single category first referred to as the Depressed Classes and, later in 1935, as the "Scheduled Castes." This bureaucratic nomenclature survives to date.[30]

When it was adopted in 1950, the Indian Constitution took a number of steps to empower Dalits and end their marginalization. It formally abolished the practice of untouchability, created institutions to monitor Dalits' welfare, and established penalties for caste-based discrimination. It guaranteed Dalits' political representation by reserving certain electoral districts at the state and national levels for Dalit candidates alone; this practice was later expanded to the local level. It sought to support a Dalit middle class by establishing quotas for Dalits in higher education and government employment. These comprehensive efforts have yielded disappointing results. Separate representation for Dalits has not benefitted their human development in reserved districts, and Dalits remain

---

[26] These findings appear in Sonalde Desai and Amaresh Dubey, "Caste in 21st Century India: Competing Narratives," *Economic and Political Weekly*, vol. 46, no. 11 (2012), pp. 40–49. The survey measures social networks with state, medical, and educational officials.

[27] According to the 2011 Indian census, Dalits are more rural as compared to the rest of the population. Whereas 68.84% of Indians live in rural areas, 76.39% of Dalits are rural residents.

[28] See Amit Thorat, Sonal Desai, Reeve Vanneman, and Amaresh Dubey, "Caste and Escape from Poverty in India 2005–2012," paper presented at the annual meeting of Population Association of America, Boston, 2014. http://paa2014.princeton.edu/papers/141967.

[29] For a description of this process, see Dirks, *Castes of Mind*.

[30] It refers to a list of untouchable castes that was prepared by the British government in 1935 and attached to the Order-in-Council issued under the Government of India Act of 1935.

largely invisible in public life outside of politics.[31] Dalits face challenges in filing police reports, states have a poor record of prosecuting those who target Dalits, and the Indian parliament has been slow to review reports from national-level monitoring institutions.[32] The vast majority of Dalits do not pursue higher education and so cannot take advantage of affirmative action policies for their group in universities. Dalits have benefitted from quotas in government employment, but they have tended to qualify in numbers for only the most menial, low-salary positions.[33] Government employment-driven economic progress has been slow. Thus, it has proven difficult to remedy Dalits' social and economic inequality through a variety of political approaches.

The practice of untouchability has diminished, but not disappeared. The IHDS (2011–2012) found untouchability was practiced in 27% of all Indian households. It was practiced across religions: Hindus (30%), Sikhs (23%), and Muslims (18%). This gives additional credence to what Mendelsohn and Vicziany observed: "[T]here is indeed something of a 'hard bar' separating Untouchables from the rest of Indian society, and Untouchables themselves have come to see that bar as the basis for a certain amount of common consciousness and action."[34]

[31] In electoral districts where the percentage of Dalits is high, the district is reserved for a Dalit candidate. In studies of reserved parliamentary districts, Alistair McMillan and Francesca Jensenius show that having a Dalit representative has not improved the economic status of Dalits in these reserved districts. See McMillan, *Standing at the Margins*; Francesca R. Jensenius, *Social Justice through Inclusion* (New York: Oxford University Press, 2017). Another study finds that reservation of electoral districts at the local panchayat level does not result in any additional welfare benefits for Dalits. See Thad Dunning and Janhavi Nilekani, "Ethnic Quotas and Political Mobilization: Caste, Parties, and Distribution in Indian Village Councils," *American Political Science Review*, vol. 107, no. 1 (2013), pp. 35–56. The policy of reserved districts has improved treatment of Dalits by others. See Simon Chauchard, *Why Representation Matters: The Meaning of Ethnic Quotas in Rural India* (Cambridge: Cambridge University Press, 2017). It has also produced a Dalit political elite. See Jensenius, *Social Justice through Inclusion*.

[32] See Human Rights Watch, *Hidden Apartheid: Caste Discrimination against India's "Untouchables"* (2007).

[33] These positions are classified as Class IV positions. Class IV (Group D) employees are manual workers who do not supervise others. They work as janitors, canteen staff, drivers, electricians, mechanics, and minor clerks.

[34] See Mendelsohn and Vicziany, *The Untouchables*, p. 18. In many ways, Dalits face the same constraints against upward mobility as do other poor citizens, but the added disadvantage of social exclusion for low income Dalits makes their escape from poverty that much harder.

The Institutional Context for Dalit
Electoral Mobilization

The caste system is common to all of India. Moreover, each broad caste category has a presence across the country, and no one caste enjoys a majority in any electoral district. As for Dalits, they, like the members of every other caste, are spread across all the major Indian states, and in those states, the Dalit population is dispersed over different electoral districts. But Dalits also comprise some four hundred subcastes, which means that they are divided linguistically across the states, as well as by subcaste differences within the states. Notwithstanding this diversity, successful Dalit parties do attempt to mobilize Dalits across subcaste differences within a particular state.[35] Be that as it may, there is a riddle at the heart of Dalit mobilization, and it turns on an incontrovertible fact—namely, that in those Indian states where Dalit social mobilization has been and remains strong (what I call *movement states*), the electoral performance of Dalit parties has been weak; and, conversely, the electoral performance of Dalit parties has been strong in states where Dalit social movements have been weak or entirely absent (what I call *non-movement states*).

Consider two examples. The Bahujan Samaj Party (BSP), India's premier Dalit-based political party, has produced strong electoral performances over time in the non-movement state of Uttar Pradesh, the most populous state in India, where Dalits make up 20% of the body politic. Moreover, the BSP in Uttar Pradesh expanded its vote share in elections since 1989, to the point of having garnered 80% of the Dalit vote in the 2009 parliamentary elections. Contrast the situation in Uttar Pradesh with that in the movement state of Tamil Nadu, India's sixth most populous state, where Dalits likewise make up 20% of the citizenry: in Tamil Nadu, the Dalit party known as Viduthalai Chiruthaikal Katchi (VCK), or the *Liberation Panthers Party*, has been unable to attract Dalits to its fold in the same numbers; in fact, its vote share among Dalits has not touched even 10%.

This is a puzzling state of affairs, at least from the perspective of the conventional wisdom about the relationship between ethnic social movements and allied ethnic parties. From that perspective, Tamil Nadu—as the center of an anticaste movement and with a longer history of Dalit social mobilization than that of Uttar Pradesh—could reasonably be expected to be a virtual incubator of successful Dalit political parties.[36] Before we get into what might explain this

---

[35] That said, these parties have to capture the vote of the largest Dalit subcaste in order to be successful.

[36] According to my count in 2009, Tamil Nadu had eighty-seven active social organizations working on Dalit rights, as opposed to forty-one in Uttar Pradesh, and in Tamil Nadu, as compared to

apparent anomaly, it is important to understand the institutional context in which the marginalized mobilize in India.

The Opportunity Structure for Electoral Mobilization

The presence of a historically marginalized ethnic group is not necessarily enough to produce the emergence of an allied political party, much less a successful one. And even when there is a clear reason for the group's social mobilization, its electoral mobilization depends on a favorable opportunity structure. A marginalized ethnic group's electoral mobilization depends on the group's possession of franchise and ability to vote freely. In other words, the right to vote is necessary but not sufficient, since voters who belong to the group can be obstructed in their exercise of the franchise.

At the time of India's independence, Dalits were invested with the right to vote, as were all other Indian citizens. But in the first few decades after independence, Dalits were not always able to avail themselves of this freedom. In some instances, they voted under instructions from the landlords for whom they worked, when they were not entirely prevented from casting their ballots.[37] In other words, Dalits did not always have to be overtly coerced into voting for a particular party or candidate, but their exercise of the right to vote reflected their dependence on a dominant caste whose influence directed the Dalit vote to parties and candidates of the dominant caste's choosing.

Gradual changes in the social structure, along with institutional interventions on the part of the state, have altered the situation for Dalits. Relationships between landowners and laborers have undergone a qualitative shift, with feudal arrangements gradually giving way to contractual agreements. Change overall has resulted from a variety of factors, including landownership sealing laws, fragmentation of landholdings, increased mechanization, rural to urban labor migration and availability of remittances from migrant family members, and diversification of the rural economy.[38] Such modifications have broken the hold that the landowning castes exerted on Dalits.[39] In addition, unprecedented

---

Uttar Pradesh, more Dalit localities observe Dalit movement-related events, and more Dalits are able to recognize movement symbols. Nevertheless, the Dalit party in Tamil Nadu has been unable to attain electoral success.

[37] See Harold Gould, "Sanskritisation and Westernzation: A Dynamic View," *Economic Weekly*, vol. 13, no. 24 (1961), pp. 945–950.

[38] See Dipankar Gupta, "Caste and Politics: Identity over System," *Annual Review of Anthropology*, vol. 34 (2005), pp. 409–427.

[39] See Francine R. Frankel and M. S. A. Rao, eds., *Dominance and State Power in Modern India: Decline of a Social Order*, vol. 1 (New Delhi: Oxford University Press, 1989).

security arrangements have been established to remove the threat of intimidation during the election process. In states known for electoral violence or fraud, elections are now staggered over many days to allow for the movement of security forces between different areas, and complaints of electoral malpractice are taken seriously and widely reported in the mass media.

The freedom to vote and free and fair elections support Dalits' electoral mobilization, but Dalits' ethnic parties require additional institutional opportunities for their success. Dalit parties, since they rely for their core support on a single ethnic group, emerge as small parties. Small parties are more likely to succeed in a first-past-the-post electoral system when the party system has fragmented. Party system fragmentation can split the votes among multiple parties, thereby lowering the threshold vote share that a party needs to win an election. Party system fragmentation also results in the appearance of coalition governments. Coalition politics provides leverage to small parties. By joining coalition governments, small parties get access to state resources to sustain and grow their vote shares. By 1989, the Indian party system began to fragment significantly, and thus it offered small political parties, including Dalit ethnic parties, the opportunity to become competitive within the system. The success of some of these parties further fragmented the party system at the national and state levels.

To be successful, a Dalit party has to first capture a substantial share of the ethnic vote. In other words, a Dalit electoral bloc is a prerequisite for Dalit party success. In a fragmenting party system, a substantial ethnic bloc allows an emergent ethnic party to attract strong candidates from within and outside the ethnic group, encourages co-ethnic voters to switch from other parties to the ethnic party, and enables the ethnic party to demand more seats in pre-poll alliances.

Party System Fragmentation in India

In the first twenty years of India's democratic life, the Congress Party was the country's most electorally successful party at both the state and the national level, and so India came to be seen as dominated by a single party. The Congress Party owed its dominance to its stature as the face of the freedom movement, its relatively well-developed organizational structure, and the preeminence of its leadership. Moreover, the Congress Party's control over the national and state governments was not strongly challenged during that initial twenty-year phase, for the party actively used the strategy of co-opting different movements.[40] By 1967,

---

[40] Those movements involved various ethnic, religious, and class-based interests. The Congress Party was the quintessential catch-all party. Its attempt to represent all aspirations showed its intention to mean the largest number of things to the largest number of people.

Table 1.2. **The erosion of the Congress Party vote share in Lok Sabha (parliamentary) elections**

Year	Congress Party Vote Share	National Parties Vote Share Overall	State Parties Vote Share Overall
1951	44.99%	76.00%	8.10%
1967	40.78%	76.13%	9.69%
1991	36.32%	80.65%	12.97%
1996	28.80%	69.08%	22.43%
2004	26.53%	62.89%	28.90%
2009	28.55%	63.58%	36.42%

Source: Election Commission of India, "Statistical Reports of Lok Sabha and State Assembly Elections."

however, those enabling circumstances had begun to fade away. For the first time, the Congress Party was losing elections to opposition parties across many states. In the following decades, the leader-centric party suffered two significant setbacks with respect to its leadership—the assassination of Indira Gandhi in 1984, and that of Rajiv Gandhi in 1991—and the early 1990s saw the unraveling of the Congress Party system.

In 1951, Congress vote share at the national level stood at 45%. By 1967, it had shrunk to 41% and, by 1996, to 28.8% (see Table 1.2).

Three distinct trends accompanied Congress's decline: (1) the number of political parties increased, (2) coalition governance replaced single-party majority governance, and (3) electoral politics became more competitive. In the wake of the party's decline, other national and state-based parties made electoral gains.[41] As shown in Table 1.3, while the number of national parties shrank from 14 in 1951, to 9 in 1991, to 7 in 2009, the number of state-based parties increased from 39 in 1951, to 136 in 1991, to 356 in 2009.[42]

[41] The Congress Party's declining vote share is evident in statistical reports published by the Election Commission for parliamentary elections over a period of five-and-a-half decades. In the 1951 elections, the Congress Party's vote share was roughly 45%, with an overall share of about 8% for state parties. In 1971, the Congress Party's vote share had dropped slightly, to roughly 44%, while the state parties showed a modest gain, with an overall vote share of about 10%. The Congress Party's vote share rose to 49% in 1984, but the influence of the state parties also continued to grow, as shown in their overall vote share of about 12%. But by 1989, the Congress Party's vote share had dropped to slightly below 27%, with the state parties winning an overall vote share of about 29%.

[42] Number of state-based parties = number of recognized state parties + number of registered (unrecognized) parties. The logic of federalism ensures that coalition governance at the national and

Table 1.3. **Party proliferation in India**

Year	Number of National Parties	Number of Recognized State Parties	Number of Registered (Unrecognized) Parties
1951	14	39	
1991	9	27	109
1996	8	30	171
2009	7	34	322
2014	6	39	419

Source: Election Commission of India.

Table 1.4. **Number of states with coalition governments**

Year	Number
1951	0
1995	4
2006	18
2014	7

Source: Election Commission of India.

With party system fragmentation in the 1990s, coalition politics became the order of the day at the national level. A similar pattern occurred in many states. Between 1989 and 2014, all nine national governments were coalition governments, and the number of states being ruled by coalition governments increased from zero in 1951, to four in 1995, to eighteen in 2006 (see Table 1.4). In the states where regional party systems replaced Congress earlier, these party systems also experienced fragmentation.

Before 1989, the level of party competition was lower than during the coalition phase. Between 1951 and 1984, the effective number of parties, as measured through vote share, ranged from 3.40 to 5.19; when measured using seat share in parliament, the range was 1.69 to 3.16. The corresponding ranges for the effective number of parties for the period 1989–2014 were 4.80 and 7.98, and

state levels creates more opportunities for small parties to receive access to public resources, thereby incentivizing the emergence of state-based parties.

Table 1.5. **Effective number of parties in Lok Sabha elections**

Year	Effective Number of Parties (Votes)	Effective Number of Parties (Seats)
1951	4.53	1.80
1957	3.98	1.76
1962	4.40	1.85
1967	5.19	3.16
1971	4.63	2.12
1977	3.40	2.63
1980	4.25	2.28
1984	3.99	1.69
1989	4.80	4.35
1991	5.10	3.70
1996	7.11	5.83
1998	6.91	5.28
1999	6.74	5.87
2004	7.60	6.50
2009	7.98	5.01
2014	7.06	3.50

Source: Adnan Farooqui and E. Sridharan, "Can Umbrella Parties
Survive? The Decline of the Indian National Congress," *Commonwealth &
Comparative Politics*, vol. 54, no. 3 (2016), pp. 331–361.

3.50 and 6.50, respectively (see Table 1.5).[43] These effects of party system fragmentation are likely to persist in the 2019 parliamentary elections encouraging the emergence and survival of small state-based parties.[44]

As we have seen, India has a first-past-the-: post electoral system, and caste groups are dispersed across electoral districts. Together, these two factors should

---

[43] After the 2014 parliamentary election, a single party, the Bharatiya Janata Party, attained a parliamentary majority after a gap of thirty years. The BJP was in power in seventeen out of India's twenty-nine states at the end of 2018. It remains to be seen if this outcome marks the end of political opportunity for emergent parties' success. There is ample evidence to suggest the persistence of a fragmented party system. For example, the effective number of parties (ENP) by vote share in the 2014 election stood at 7.06, which was higher than it had been for all the elections during the period of the Congress Party's hegemony, which came to an end in 1989, and during which the highest value for ENP, 5.2, was recorded for the 1967 election.

[44] See Prannoy Roy and Dorab R. Sopariwala, *The Verdict: Decoding India's Elections* (New Delhi: Penguin India, 2019).

incentivize a smaller party to increase its vote share by engaging in catch-all or multiethnic mobilization rather than ethnic mobilization. As such, that system should typically discourage the success of an ethnic party allied with a single group. And yet we know that Dalit parties have been overwhelmingly attractive to Dalit voters in the non-movement Indian states of Uttar Pradesh and Bihar. This is a phenomenon that requires explanation.

Research Design

Three factors make India a favorable site for the comparative study of mobilization of marginalized ethnic groups. First, India's federal form of governance generates many cases for comparative study, given the country's common electoral rules; its common set of social cleavages, including caste differences; and its similar party systems. Such control variables offer a unique opportunity for scholars of comparative politics to explain divergent patterns and outcomes across the different realms of politics.[45] Subnational analysis becomes viable as well, since the federal system grants many powers to the states in India, thus making state politics a contentious terrain.

Second, India, more than many other countries, is instructive for newly democratized states because suffrage in India, by contrast with the situation in the advanced industrial democracies, did not evolve in phases or through protracted struggle.[46] Instead, universal adult suffrage came at the moment of independence in 1947, when civil, political, and social rights were granted all at once. For that very reason, however, the institutionalization of social rights has been weak, and one consequence has been the coexistence of political equality with social inequality. Many citizens have been left with an incomplete version of the social contract, one made up of the state's unfulfilled commitments.

---

[45] A number of scholars have made use of controlled comparisons. See Atul Kohli, *Democracy and Discontent: India's Growing Crisis of Governability* (Cambridge: Cambridge University Press, 1990); Ashutosh Varshney, *Ethnic Conflict and Civic Life: Hindus and Muslims in India* (New Haven: Yale University Press, 2002); Chandra, *Why Ethnic Parties Succeed*; Aseema Sinha, *The Regional Roots of Developmental Politics in India: A Divided Leviathan* (Bloomington: Indiana University Press, 2005); Subrata Kumar Mitra, *The Puzzle of India's Governance: Culture, Context, and Comparative Theory* (London: Routledge, 2006); Sunila S. Kale, *Electrifying India: Regional Political Economies of Development* (Stanford: Stanford University Press, 2014); Rina Agarwala, *Informal Labor, Formal Politics, and Dignified Discontent* (New York: Cambridge University Press, 2013). Indeed, the opportunity to conduct controlled comparisons has led to India's characterization as a laboratory of democracy; see Rob Jenkins, "Introduction," in Rob Jenkins, ed., *Regional Reflections: Comparing Politics across India's States* (New York: Oxford University Press, 2014), pp. 1–25.

[46] For the history of citizenship, see Niraja Gopal Jayal, *Citizenship and Its Discontents: An Indian History* (Cambridge: Harvard University Press, 2013), and for a case of how social rights evolved in the West, see Theda Skocpol, *Protecting Soldiers and Mothers: The Political Origins of Social Policy in the United States* (Cambridge: Belknap Press of Harvard University Press, 1995).

And, third, the nationwide weakening of the formerly dominant Congress Party over the past decades, and the appearance of coalition politics in the aftermath of that weakening, created a window of opportunity for small parties, including ethnic parties, to be competitive. The variation in the performance of those parties has produced a variety of cases that can be compared across time and space.

The research design for this book takes advantage of the fact that the social mobilization of Dalits made an early appearance in certain Indian states—as early as the colonial period in the nineteenth century, in some cases—but not in other states. Another notable fact is that, at the moment of opportunity marked by the fragmentation of the party system across all the states, Dalit parties in different states have achieved varying degrees of success. These two facts are precisely what have enabled my exploration of the effects that historical Dalit movements have exerted on the electoral prospects of Dalit parties.

For this comparative study, I selected the states of Tamil Nadu and Maharashtra, on the one hand, and Uttar Pradesh and Bihar, on the other, and did so for several reasons. To begin with, all four states are large and politically important, and together they elect 40% of the Indian parliament. Which is to say that the parties in these states that enjoy significant electoral support are likely not only to have an impact on local politics, but also to play an important role at the national level (see Map 1.2).[47] In addition, all four states have offered an environment favorable to the electoral success of ethnic parties—that is, they have experienced party system fragmentation, and between 1989 and 2014 they were ruled either continuously or periodically by coalition governments. Moreover, two of the states—Tamil Nadu and Maharashtra—are home to the most prominent of the historical movements that have opposed the principle of caste hierarchy and demanded social equality, whereas such movements were absent from Bihar and confined to small pockets in Uttar Pradesh.[48]

Dalits in the four states are 43% of all Indian Dalits; Dalit politics in these states is consequential for Dalit politics nationally (see Table 1.6).

In three of the four states, the majority of the Dalit population is concentrated in a single subcaste. These include Adi-Dravidas in Tamil Nadu, Mahars in Maharashtra, and Chamars or Jatavs in Uttar Pradesh.[49] This internal unity should facilitate Dalit mobilization and, given bloc voting, provide a foundation for an emergent Dalit ethnic party (see Table 1.7). In Bihar, Dusadhs do not

---

[47] Among India's twenty-nine states and seven union territories, these four states alone have sent a total of 208 members to the 543-member Lok Sabha (parliament).

[48] See Pai, *Dalit Assertion and the Unfinished Democratic Revolution*.

[49] In each state, I study the mobilization of the most politically and socially organized caste, but for the sake of simplicity I largely refer to them as Dalits.

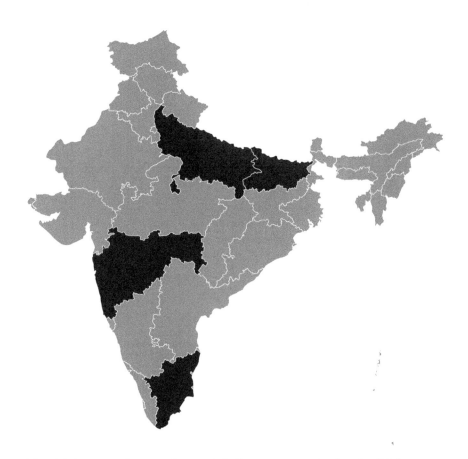

Map 1.2 Location of case-study states in India *Source*: Map outline from the Global Administrative Areas version 2.8 (GADMv2.8; www.gadm.org). Map does not include disputed territory in Kashmir.

Table 1.6. **Scheduled Caste (Dalit) population across case-study states**

	Percentage SC Population	*Total SC Population*	*Total Population*
Tamil Nadu	20	14,438, 445	72,147,030
Maharashtra	12	13,275,898	112,374,333
Uttar Pradesh	21	41,357,608	199,812,341
Bihar	16	16,567,325	104,099,452
India	17	201,378,372	1,210,569,573

Source: Census of India, 2011.

Table 1.7. **Profiles of the major Dalit subcaste in each case-study state**

	Tamil Nadu	Maharashtra	Uttar Pradesh	Bihar
Jati	Adi-Dravidas (Paraiyars)	Mahars	Chamars (Jatavs)	Dusadhs (Paswans)
Associated occupation(s)	Drummers	Village watchmen, repairers of boundary walls, street sweepers, removers and processors of animal carcasses	Tanning of animal hides, leatherwork	Palanquin bearers, village watchmen
Percentage of state's Dalit population	61.3	57.5	56.3	30.9

Source: Census of India, 2001. Data Highlights: The Scheduled Castes. State Reports.

form the majority of the Dalit population (no subcaste does), but are characterized by especially high levels of bloc voting.[50]

Finally, and what is most important for the purposes of this book, Dalit-based parties have competed in elections across each of the four states under favorable institutional conditions, and yet they have done so with divergent levels of success, as I show by juxtaposing the electoral performance of Dalit-based parties in the movement states of Tamil Nadu and Maharashtra with the electoral performance of Dalit-based parties in the non-movement states of Uttar Pradesh and Bihar. Within my case studies, my analysis focuses on four Dalit ethnic parties, each of which attempts to draw on the major Dalit subcaste in its state as an ethnic voting bloc. These parties are the *Viduthalai Chiruthaigal Katchi* (VCK) in Tamil Nadu, the *Bahujan Samaj Party* ("Common People's Party"; BSP) in Maharashtra, the BSP in Uttar Pradesh, and the *Lok Janshakti Party* ("People's Power Party"; LJP) in Bihar (see Table 1.8).

In movement states, Dalit ethnic parties have performed poorly in elections in the period of party system fragmentation. Their vote shares among Dalits have been low. In Tamil Nadu, the VCK has garnered less than 10% of Dalit votes. In Maharashtra, the BSP's Dalit vote share has fluctuated, but the party has never won a single seat in state assembly or parliamentary elections.

---

[50] Chamars are the largest Dalit jati (subcaste) in Bihar; they are 31.3% of the state's Dalit population. Chamars have not yet cohered as an ethnic electoral bloc to the same degree as Dusadhs.

Table 1.8. **The major Dalit ethnic party competing in each case-study state**

Movement states	Tamil Nadu	*Viduthalai Chiruthaigal Katchi* (VCK)
	Maharashtra	*Bahujan Samaj Party* (BSP)
Non-movement states	Uttar Pradesh	*Bahujan Samaj Party* (BSP)
	Bihar	*Lok Janshakti Party* (LJP)

In the same period, in non-movement states, Dalit ethnic parties were electorally more successful. Beginning in 1995, the BSP in Uttar Pradesh was a partner in coalition governments, and its party leader, Mayawati, was chief minister of the state on four occasions. She was even touted by the Indian press at various times as a possible candidate for prime minister. In Bihar, at the point of party system fragmentation, there was no Dalit ethnic party. Dalits were mobilized as part of a lower-caste ethnic alliance under the banner of the *Janata Dal* ("People's Group"; JD) in the 1990 state assembly elections. The JD split, however, and Dalits and Yadavs (a large OBC subcaste) shifted their allegiance to a new party, the *Rashtriya Janata Dal* ("National People's Group"; RJD), in the 2000 state assembly elections. The RJD itself then split, and Dalits switched to another new party, the *Lok Janshakti Party* ("People's Power Party"; LJP), in the 2005 state assembly elections. The LJP has primarily appealed to Dalits, especially Dusadhs, and allied with other parties instrumentally. Ram Vilas Paswan, the leader of the LJP, has effectively leveraged his small party's performance in Bihar at the national level; he has directed a series of critical national ministries since the mid-1990s.[51]

The analysis in this book relies on both within-case process tracing and controlled cross-case comparisons.[52] The controlled cross-case comparisons involved the manipulation of a cause—namely, the presence or absence of social mobilization across four cases. Since all cases were drawn from India, their common set of features allowed me to use controlled cross-case comparisons with a greater degree of confidence. I rely on the mechanism-process approach to explain the pattern of Dalit mobilization.[53] My aim is to unearth the process of

---

[51] Paswan has been Minister of Railways (1996–1998), Minister of Communications and Information Technology (1999–2001), Minister of Mines (2001–2002), Minister of Chemicals and Fertilizers (2004–2009), and Minister of Consumer Affairs, Food, and Public Distribution (2014–present). He has held these various positions in coalition governments led by two much larger but rival parties, the BJP and the Congress.

[52] These two methods have facilitated both the identification of mechanisms and the establishment of their validity; see Alexander L. George and Andrew Bennett, *Case Studies and Theory Development in the Social Sciences* (Cambridge: MIT Press, 2005).

[53] Mechanism- and process-based accounts explain salient features of episodes, or significant differences among them, by identifying robust mechanisms of relatively general scope within those

mobilization of a marginalized group and its constituent mechanisms. I do not propose a covering law, but rather in building a theory, my objective is to establish that the mechanisms are not only plausible but also amenable to empirical confirmation. Broadly speaking, in explaining the behavior of Dalit voters, I develop a context-driven explanation. I view ethnic or multiethnic party success in a particular state, and at a particular juncture, as a product of the wider social and political context of that state. In order to understand the relevant temporal constructs, such as the sequence of social and electoral mobilization in particular states, I process-traced the mobilization of Dalits within all four of the cases presented in this book.

Data and Sources

The theory elaborated in the chapters to come is based on multiple forms of evidence. Although I drew on survey data gathered by Indian National Election Studies (NES), Census of India, the India Human Development Study (IHDS), and the National Sample Survey Organization (NSSO) surveys, I relied primarily on extensive fieldwork conducted in Tamil Nadu, Maharashtra, Uttar Pradesh, and Bihar between 2004 and 2014.

The explanations offered in this book emerged from observation of social and electoral mobilization at the level of the neighborhood and the locality. A marginalized group's relative concentration in a particular locality has consequences for the prospects of the group's mobilization. Although states and electoral districts have mixed-caste populations, caste-based segregation in residential patterns means that neighborhoods and localities tend to be more homogeneous—and homogeneity, scholars tell us, enables collective action by ensuring easier communication of ideas, a sense of security and trust among co-ethnics, and shared interests with respect to public services. Therefore, the constraints that work against a marginalized group's mobilization are weakest at the local level.

To understand the context for Dalit politics at the local level, I investigated voter attitudes and party mobilization at the locality level. In 2004, I conducted focus groups and interviews in Tamil Nadu, Maharashtra, Uttar Pradesh, and Bihar. This fieldwork involved twenty focus groups in each of the four states, for a total of eighty groups with 1,100 participants. I specifically chose electoral districts

episodes; see Charles Tilly, "Mechanisms in Political Processes," *Annual Review of Political Science*, vol. 4, no. 1 (2001), pp. 21–41. See also Henry E. Brady, "Models of Causal Inference: Going beyond the Neyman-Rubin-Holland Theory," paper presented at the annual meeting of the Midwest Political Science Association, Chicago, 2003; in this approach, according to Brady, causation can be thought of as a process involving the mechanisms and capacities that lead from a cause to an effect.

with sizable Dalit populations because Dalit parties were active in those districts. To generate the information needed for this study, interaction with the focus group participants was confined to moderated discussion of selected questions.[54] To supplement and cross-check information gathered through the focus groups, I also conducted a total of 409 long semi-structured interviews with voters across all localities.[55] For a detailed discussion of the focus groups and follow-up interviews, see Appendix A.

We know very little about how political parties mobilize ethnic groups at the local level, and relatedly, how parties compete for the votes of a particular group. This is the other reason I studied electoral mobilization at the locality level. Across all four states discussed in this book, party competition was high, since the party system had fragmented, but initial observations appeared to suggest that a high number of competitive parties would not necessarily translate into an increase in the number of parties campaigning in all neighborhoods or localities, especially where the party system had fragmented along lines of ethnic cleavage. Therefore, to assess how Dalits were being mobilized by political parties, it was necessary to observe the parties' electoral campaigning at the level of the neighborhood and the locality. I observed and surveyed electoral campaigns conducted just before the 2009 parliamentary elections. Almost seven hundred voters were interviewed in electoral districts within the states of Tamil Nadu, Maharashtra, Uttar Pradesh, and Bihar, with the objectives of determining the number of political parties that were visiting localities dominated by different caste groups, discovering the types of appeals that ethnic as well as multiethnic parties were making to voters, and probing voters' attitudes regarding caste-based voting. For a detailed description of the electoral campaign surveys, see Appendix B.

During fieldwork, I also interviewed the district-level officeholders of the Dalit and multiethnic parties, party workers, and Dalit party state leadership. In the localities and neighborhoods I worked in, I identified Dalit notables and party workers, and inquired about their social and electoral mobilization activities. I draw on this evidence to trace the process of Dalit mobilization across the cases.

To compliment the evidence gathered during fieldwork, I turn to different rounds of the National Election Study conducted by Lokniti, housed at the

---

[54] The use of focus groups, as opposed to a method such as participant observation, also allowed me to replicate the questions across different areas and to test for the robustness of my findings; see David L. Morgan, *Focus Groups as Qualitative Research* (Thousand Oaks: Sage, 1997). In observing a representative sample of the participants as they shared and compared their views with respect to their support for political parties, I was keen to contrast individual opinions with the participants' consensus view or with sets of distinct opinions. Although I tabulated the responses of all the participants, I report only modal responses in the chapters to come.

[55] Some of my subjects spoke to me on the condition of anonymity, whereas many others did not. Still, for the most part, throughout the book, I do not identify any interview subject by name.

Center for the Study of Developing Societies, New Delhi. The NES, the only data source of its kind, provides information about the political participation and attitudes of voters belonging to different social groups.[56] In particular, I draw on the NES for 2004 parliamentary elections for two reasons: (1) it had a sample size of Dalit respondents large enough to allow for comparisons across states, and (2) it asked a number of questions on caste-related political as well as social attitudes. Additionally, the NES is more reliable for comparing voter attitudes across states than state election studies. The NES is administered across all Indian states during the same period proximate to a parliamentary election. In contrast to the election to the national parliament, state elections in India have come to be staggered. Since state election studies track state election schedules, these public opinion surveys are administered in their respective states at different points in time, and are therefore less useful for making cross-state comparisons. I interpret the NES data in light of responses gathered from voters during the focus groups and interviews.

In order to compare Dalit petition activities across movement and non-movement states, in 2006, I observed Dalit petitioning behavior at two different locations in each of my four case-study states. In each place, I observed a district collector's office, a member of the state legislative assembly's office, and the headquarters of a Dalit political party for two days. I tracked the issues Dalits raised and, in the government contexts, how Dalits were treated by government officials. Additionally, I systematically tracked reports of Dalit protest activity in English-language and vernacular newspapers in each of my four case-study states for six months between 2008 and 2009. Given their marginalization, I expected Dalit protests to occur at low levels, and for the press to report them more infrequently as compared to the activities of other groups. The total number of protests detected was low, but there was marked variation between movement and non-movement states. To track how welfare indicators have changed across movement and non-movement states, especially as they relate to the gap between Dalits and the rest of the population, I turn to the different rounds of the NSSO survey and the Indian census.

In this book, I not only explore the choices of identities available to Dalits in the public sphere (through social and political mobilization), but also examine the choice of social identities available to Dalits in the private sphere (through socioeconomic mobility). To understand the power of stigma, and how it traps Dalits in their caste identity in the private sphere, I turned to the marriage market. I compared the behavior of women in the marriage market toward potential

---

[56] The NES selects electoral districts through random sampling based on probability proportional to state and community size and to the number of polling booths. Similarly, NES respondents are selected through a stratified random sample using voter lists.

grooms of different castes in 2012 and 2013. For centuries, marriage has been an important mechanism through which the hierarchical caste system has reproduced itself. Individuals are born into a caste, generally marry someone within their own group, and then go on to have children who do the same. Openness to intercaste marriage signals the weakening of caste boundaries, for this reason, I designed a correspondence-based, semi-experimental study that included more than 2,000 Dalit, Backward-Caste, and upper-caste participants seeking marriage partners through three prominent Indian matrimonial websites. It was a study aimed at assessing the strength of caste boundaries in a modern, urban setting—the place where they are likely to be lowest. This project is discussed at length in Appendix C.

Democratic Politics and the Mobilization of the Marginalized

The existence of an ethnic group does not necessarily guarantee the success of its mobilization by its ethnic parties. Why, then, ethnic mobilization succeeds in some cases but not in others is an important question to answer.

Scholars of race politics, for example, have suggested that the shared experience of exclusion can forge both social and electoral solidarity. They find that African Americans are brought to the polling booth by a strong experience of in-group affinity and a sense of group purpose. According to this view, the salience of African Americans' racial identity and the emotional and social importance of their "blackness" are a resource that matters for their mobilization.[57] Theorists of social cleavage have argued that social cleavages form the basis of political cleavages.[58] For example, Donald Horowitz sees political parties as turning social cleavages into political cleavages.[59] He argues that ethnic elites form political parties to fulfill their particular interests, and since ethnic identity is ascriptive, ethnic elites know that once their ethnic constituency is captured, they can count on its support. Thus, an election becomes a kind of ethnic census, with the party's supporters voting on the basis of

---

[57] In this connection, see Michael C. Dawson, *Behind the Mule: Race and Class in African-American Politics* (Princeton: Princeton University Press, 1994); Lawrence Bobo and Franklin D. Gilliam Jr., "Race, Sociopolitical Participation, and Black Empowerment," *American Political Science Review*, vol. 84, no. 2 (1990), pp. 377–393; Carole J. Uhlaner, "Rational Turnout: The Neglected Role of Groups," *American Journal of Political Science*, vol. 33, no. 2 (1989), pp. 390–422.

[58] See Seymour Martin Lipset and Stein Rokkan, "Cleavage Structures, Party Systems, and Voter Alignments," in Peter Mair, ed., *The West European Party System* (Oxford: Oxford University Press, 1990), pp. 91–138.

[59] See Horowitz, *Ethnic Groups in Conflict*.

their ethnicity. Further, the members of an ethnic group, perceiving their shared interests as well as their shared sense of competition with other groups in the polity, form an ethnic party both to represent the identity of their own group and to respond to competing identity-based interests.

In the Indian context, Pradeep Chhibber has argued that political parties are primarily responsible for converting social cleavages into political cleavages.[60] Kanchan Chandra relates successful ethnic mobilization to the promise of patronage.[61] Chandra argues that in India the visibility of caste makes it a salient factor in elections—politicians and political parties distribute patronage to caste collectives, and Indians, when they go to the polls, are believed not just to cast their votes but to do so on the basis of their caste.[62] This book will show that the ability of Dalit parties to turn social cleavages into electoral cleavages varies between states. It will also show that in-group affinity is not enough to produce bloc voting; Dalits do not always vote their caste. In fact, their interest in voting with fellow caste members differs across states.

An organizational perspective on ethnic party performance is also centered on elite preferences. Parties are able to recruit and retain elites, according to these explanations, when elites see a path of upward mobility in the party organization. In her book, Kanchan Chandra points to the lack of opportunities for the Dalit elite to rise within the Congress Party. But for the voter on the ground, often the co-ethnic party worker, not the co-ethnic elite, is the face of the party. And yet, surprisingly, the different parties' mass mobilization of Dalits, in particular their recruitment of Dalit party workers, has remained relatively understudied.[63]

As for explanations rooted in resource-mobilization theory, Sudha Pai turns to this causal logic in her groundbreaking work on the rise of the Bahujan Samaj Party (BSP) in Uttar Pradesh.[64] According to Pai, ethnic consciousness among Dalits in Uttar Pradesh has increased as a result of the growth in literacy among Dalits and the appearance of a small Dalit middle class, thanks to the Indian state's policies of affirmative action for Dalits, and so the success of the Dalit-based BSP is an outcome of higher self-awareness among Dalits as a community.

---

[60] See Chhibber, *Democracy without Associations*.

[61] See Chandra, *Why Ethnic Parties Succeed*.

[62] Patronage-politics-based explanations are deeply problematic in the Indian context. They are rarely supported by systematic empirical evidence. In fact, field observations suggest that even when voters receive bribes from parties and candidates, either through policies or direct payments, they do not necessarily vote for them. Bribe-giving candidates and parties, on their part, cannot monitor voter behavior. Additionally, the promise of state jobs cannot sway elections. An anemic Indian state has few jobs to dole out; less than 3% of the labor force is employed by the state. See Chandra, *Why Ethnic Parties Succeed*.

[63] See Chandra, *Why Ethnic Parties Succeed*.

[64] See Pai, *Dalit Assertion and the Unfinished Democratic Revolution*.

Nevertheless, Sudha Pai's work is centered on Uttar Pradesh, and her intuitions are unable to account neither for the experience of Dalit mobilization in other states, where the prevalence of higher caste consciousness has not caused Dalit parties to flourish, nor for the counterintuitive outcomes reported in this book, with Dalit-based parties performing most poorly in precisely those states that have relatively higher rates of literacy and greater access to mass media.

Democratic politics, broadly defined, opens up a space for marginalized citizens to define themselves. Therefore, it should come as no surprise that wherever and whenever Dalits have been able to organize themselves into social movements, their reason for doing so has been to restore dignity to their identity and to contest their lowly status and social exclusion. Most important, for reasons discussed at length in the chapters to come, the mobilization of Dalits has varied and continues to vary across Indian states, notwithstanding Dalits' shared experience of discrimination and stigmatization. Nor do Dalits constitute a caste-based voting bloc across Indian states, and they exhibit great variance in their desire to vote with fellow caste members as well as in their consideration of caste as a basis for supporting a political party—a conceptualization of Dalits' self-mobilization that stands in sharp contrast to arguments explaining social and electoral mobilization on the basis of race politics, social cleavages, patronage, elite blockage, and resource mobilization.

Book Organization

Short summaries of eight additional chapters follow and provide a context for Dalits' social and electoral mobilization, the details of these processes, and their broader implications for Dalit welfare and identity formation.

Chapter 2—*Mobilization and the Marginalized*—describes how marginalization influences the processes of mobilization and clarifies the relationship between two common forms of mobilization: social movements and political parties.

Chapter 3—*Historical Dalit Social Mobilization*—explains how and why Dalit social movements emerged and gained strength in Tamil Nadu and Maharashtra but remained weak in Uttar Pradesh and Bihar.

Chapter 4—*The Effects of Historical Dalit Social Mobilization*—develops a set of indicators to measure the effects of Dalits' social mobilization on Dalits and non-Dalits. These, I show, vary between movement and non-movement states.

Chapter 5—*Dalit Party Performance and Bloc Voting*—outlines the electoral performance of Dalit ethnic parties. In non-movement states, Dalit ethnic party vote shares have been higher and Dalits have won more seats in state assembly and parliamentary elections than Dalit ethnic parties in movement states. Dalits' ethnic party performance is explained by Dalits' attitudes toward bloc voting, and importantly, these attitudes vary significantly across movement and non-movement states.

Chapter 6—*Dalit Social Mobilization and Bloc Voting*—illustrates how Dalits' historical social mobilization weakens bloc voting. Dalit social movements generate mobilizers and mobilization symbols that increase competition for Dalit votes at the locality-level, lower the utility of caste for differentiating among parties, shift the emphasis to material goods over symbolic goods, and split Dalit voters' party preferences.

Chapter 7—*How Mobilization Type Shapes Dalit Welfare*—argues variation in welfare provision at the state-level turns on a distinction in types of mobilization. When Dalits act collectively as a bloc, this has different consequences in the social sphere and the electoral sphere. In the social sphere, bloc behavior articulates demands, pressurizes bureaucrats and politicians, and monitors the quality of goods and services provided by the state. Democratic accountability is increased. In the electoral sphere, however, bloc behavior has two especially negative effects: (1) it transforms Dalits into weak clients; and (2) it increases the probability welfare schemes will be disrupted or dismantled with electoral transfers of power. Democratic accountability is decreased.

Chapter 8—*The Identity Trap*—argues Dalits' ability to adopt new social identities is highly constrained. This is because Dalits' social exclusion and material deprivation are self-reinforcing, and Dalits' limited choices of alternate identities are not recognized by other groups. It is difficult for a marginalized ethnic group to leverage political equality to remedy social inequality. Marginalized ethnic identities are very slow to change.

Chapter 9—*Conclusion: Whither Dalit Politics?*—reflects on the future prospects of Dalits' social and electoral mobilization in India and considers how the Dalit case informs a larger research agenda on mobilization of marginalized groups, ethnic politics, social movements, and political parties.

2

Mobilization and the Marginalized

This chapter begins to explore how, given an electoral opportunity in a multiethnic democracy, a marginalized group comes to be mobilized by ethnic parties in some cases and by multiethnic parties in others.

Mobilization and the Marginalized Ethnic Group

Ethnic mobilization is the process by which groups organize around some feature of ethnic identity, for example, skin color, language, or customs, in pursuit of collective ends.[1] Marginalized groups can mobilize on the basis of ethnicity, but they may also organize in other ways, at different times, through distinct forms, and for the sake of achieving multiple ends. For instance, a socially excluded group may mobilize to seek inclusion, as opposed to a dominant or privileged group, which may mobilize to exclude other groups.

When a marginalized ethnic group mobilizes, it can do so in the civic space, as a social movement (social mobilization), and in the electoral arena, as an ethnic bloc in a multiethnic party or as an ethnic party (electoral mobilization). The group's social mobilization, which depends on members' ability to come together for the purpose of demanding social equality and equal access to public resources, is directed toward both society and the state, whereas its electoral mobilization is restricted to participation in elections and the activities associated with them. Political parties as well as social movements represent distinct forms of collective action.

A movement and a political party both represent the mobilization of a group, and they share prerequisites for their emergence. But there remains a fundamental

[1] See Susan Olzak, "Contemporary Ethnic Mobilization," *Annual Review of Sociology,* vol. 9, no.1 (1983), pp. 355–374, where the author defines ethnic mobilization as "the process by which groups organize around some feature of ethnic identity (for example, skin color, language, customs) in pursuit of collective ends," p. 355.

difference between the two: a political party, unlike a movement, depends on an electoral opportunity for its success. Movements can remain autonomous of political parties, join a party, or turn themselves into a political party.[2] A party emerges from a movement in the presence of electoral opportunity, which in turn is determined by the electoral system as well as the fragmentation of the party system. When electoral opportunity is absent, a movement, instead of turning into a party, can alter the behavior of existing parties (for example, by diffusing the movement's message, symbols, and activists into the existing system of competitive parties). Recall that even when opportunity shifts enable the mobilization of a marginalized group by way of a social movement, an additional opportunity must exist in order for the group's mobilization to take the form of a successful ethnic party: namely, the electoral opportunity structure must allow for the success of small parties. Typically, a proportional representation (PR) system provides such structure; conversely, in a single-member-district plurality (SMDP), or first-past-the-post system, this type of opportunity is not available unless coalition governance has become common practice because of fragmentation in the party system. Movements can sometimes turn themselves into protest parties in the absence of electoral opportunity. In such instances, sustained electoral success is unlikely because deprived of political power, a protest party will eventually lose its voters to other political parties.

To comprehend fully how marginalized groups mobilize to engage the democratic process, it is essential to understand not only the influence of exclusion on the objectives of mobilization and the constraints that exclusion poses, but also the opportunity shifts that are needed in order for those constraints to be overcome.

Exclusion, Objectives, and Constraints

For a marginalized group, the objectives of mobilization are shaped by the group's experience of exclusion and its associated disadvantages. Exclusion is a product of social design rather than the outcome of some natural order, and so its termination requires that the discrimination-based design and its underlying principles be called into question. Consequently, when the opportunity to mobilize appears, group mobilization among the marginalized is motivated by the need both to gain political recognition and to end social exclusion. In this respect, democratic politics holds the possibility for marginalized citizens to mobilize and prompt the state to address the disadvantages rooted in lower

---

[2] Robert A. Dahl, *Pluralist Democracy in the United States: Conflict and Consent* (Chicago: Rand McNally, 1967).

social status. At the same time, marginalization and its related disadvantages constrain the ability of a marginalized group to mobilize.

Members of a marginalized group face a specific set of external and internal constraints on their mobilization. Structural domination—the political, economic, and social control of the marginalized ethnic group by another group— poses a fundamental challenge in that it prevents the marginalized group both from mobilizing itself and from being fully mobilized by outside organizations such as political parties. These relations of subordination imply the threat of coercion from the dominant group if the subordinate group challenges the relationship. But the group also faces internal resource constraints. Ethnic mobilization requires leadership and organization as well as material and cultural resources.[3]

The literature on ethnic politics often assumes that a reservoir of resources already exists for an ethnic group to use in its political mobilization. This may be true for many ethnic groups, but such resources may not exist for a marginalized ethnic group, and even if they do exist, they may not be easily deployed—a group that can be described as marginalized is, by definition, either entirely without an elite class or in possession of only a small organizing class in proportion to its population.[4] As for cultural resources, the group's exclusion is mirrored in mainstream historical accounts. Its own histories are often unrecorded, and its myths and symbols, while locally recognized, do not have universal recognition even within the group. This type of cultural material is important to the process of mobilization, since the existence of universally acknowledged symbols that exert a force on the group can be used to coordinate group action.[5]

[3] See also John D. McCarthy and Mayer N. Zald, *The Trend of Social Movements in America: Professionalization and Resource Mobilization* (Morristown: General Learning, 1973); J. Craig Jenkins, "Resource Mobilization Theory and the Study of Social Movements," *Annual Review of Sociology*, vol. 9, no. 1 (1983), pp. 527–553; Zoltan Barany, *The East European Gypsies: Regime Change, Marginality, and Ethnopolitics* (Cambridge: Cambridge University Press, 2002).

[4] On the lack of an elite class, see Donald Horowitz, *Ethnic Groups in Conflict* (Berkeley: University of California Press, 1985).

[5] It has been argued that the process of mobilization breathes meaning into symbols; see Kanchan Chandra, "What Is Ethnic Identity and Does It Matter?" *Annual Review of Political Science*, vol. 9 (2006), pp. 397–424. I agree with this argument, but it does presume the prior existence of universally recognized cultural material that can later be invested with meaning, and a historically marginalized group often lacks even such basic building blocks. On symbols and coordinated group action, see David D. Laitin, *Hegemony and Culture: Politics and Religious Change among the Yoruba* (Chicago: University of Chicago Press, 1986); Evelyn M. Simien, *Historic Firsts: How Symbolic Empowerment Changes U.S. Politics* (New York: Oxford University Press, 2015); Marc Howard Ross, *Cultural Contestation in Ethnic Conflict* (Cambridge: Cambridge University Press, 2007).

Opportunity Shifts

To mobilize successfully, a marginalized ethnic group must be exposed to opportunities that enable it to overcome external and internal constraints.[6] In the presence of external as well as internal constraints, no mobilization will be possible. Even when external constraints have weakened, the persistence of internal constraints will continue to prevent the group's mobilization. A situation in which external constraints persist while internal constraints have weakened is rare, but still rules out mobilization. In short, unless the marginalized group can overcome both types of constraints, it will not be able to mobilize (see Table 2.1).[7]

A variety of exogenous changes can trigger shifts in opportunity and create conditions for the closing of the power gap between the marginalized ethnic group and other groups in society. For instance, in the wake of an economic or political crisis or a state intervention, a sudden decline in the fortunes of a dominant group—in the form, say, of limits on the size of landowners' holdings—will have an effect on the level and type of control that members of the dominant group are able to exercise over the subordinate group. Or the relationship of interdependence between the dominant and subordinate groups may weaken; for example, the mechanization of agriculture across many developing societies made the role of the subordinate groups redundant, diminished the subordinate groups' value to the dominant groups, and eliminated the need for active control of the subordinate groups.[8] A marginalized group may also migrate out of dominant/subordinate social relations; in the United States, for instance, African American mobilization is linked to migration from the rural South to cities in the North.[9] Structural domination will stifle any type of mobilization, whether

Table 2.1 **Mobilization of a marginalized group: Constraints and possibilities**

	Internal Constraints Present	Internal Constraints Absent
External Constraints Present	Mobilization impossible	Mobilization unlikely
External Constraints Absent	Mobilization unlikely	Mobilization possible

[6] See Doug McAdam, John D. McCarthy, and Mayer N. Zald, eds., *Comparative Perspectives on Social Movements: Political Opportunities, Mobilizing Structures, and Cultural Framings* (Cambridge: Cambridge University Press, 1996).

[7] A corollary here is that marginalized groups often mobilize later than other groups in a society, since a marginalized group must overcome two sets of constraints on mobilization.

[8] James C. Scott, *Weapons of the Weak: Everyday Forms of Peasant Resistance* (New Haven: Yale University Press, 1985).

[9] See Frances Fox Piven and Richard A. Cloward, *Poor People's Movements: Why They Succeed, How They Fail* (New York: Pantheon, 1977). Although African Americans' migration did not end

electoral or social. At the same time, the weakening of external constraints does not guarantee the mobilization of a marginalized group, since the group must also overcome internal constraints in order for mobilization to occur. But the weakening of structural or external domination is often accelerated by the development of internal capacity within the marginalized group.

The opportunity shift most likely to enhance the internal capacity of a marginalized group involves access to education and to economic resources sufficient to assist in building the group's organizational capacity and enabling its mobilization. Sometimes the acquisition of these resources occurs as a result of affirmative action policies established by the state on behalf of the marginalized group. In this scenario, an educated class within the group goes on to assume roles as the group's organizers and mobilization leaders.[10] State-initiated policies, such as land redistribution or recruitment of marginalized individuals in sectors previously closed to the marginalized group (the military, for example), also contribute to the group's empowerment. Other institutional opportunities include affirmative action policies aimed at diversity in the legislatures and in government employment.[11] In addition, leadership resources within a marginalized group can be generated when power is decentralized to the level where there is a larger concentration of marginalized groups. For example, the mobilization of indigenous people in Latin America has been spurred by institutional change, with decentralization resulting in the appearance of groups of organizers

their social exclusion, it did create the conditions for their mobilization by removing them from the environment of everyday domination in the American South, and it turned them into a constituency for the Democratic Party. Increasing rural-to-urban migration over the past three decades has produced similar opportunities for Dalits in India. In fact, as long ago as the 1930s, Dr. B. R. Ambedkar (1891–1956), the renowned Dalit social reformer, was asking Dalits to leave their villages for urban areas; in Dr. B. R. Ambedkar's view, urban areas presented more opportunities to escape both the control of the dominant castes and the stigma of untouchability. Still, even as rural-to-urban migration has expanded with economic growth in urban India, fewer Dalits than members of other groups have migrated out of rural areas.

[10] It has been argued, for example, that the appearance of Dalit parties in the North Indian state of Uttar Pradesh corresponds with a rise in the number of literate Dalits; see Sudha Pai, *Dalit Assertion and the Unfinished Democratic Revolution: The Bahujan Samaj Party in Uttar Pradesh* (New Delhi: Sage, 2002); Kanchan Chandra, *Why Ethnic Parties Succeed: Patronage and Ethnic Head Counts in India* (Cambridge: Cambridge University Press, 2004). These findings resemble the account of African American mobilization, which also gained momentum as mobilization resources rose within the community; see Aldon D. Morris, *The Origins of the Civil Rights Movement: Black Communities Organizing for Change* (New York: Free Press, 1984).

[11] Research across fifteen Latin American countries suggests that representatives who appeared as a result of inclusive quotas were seldom accountable to their underrepresented constituency, and these groups remained underserved. See Mala Htun, *Inclusion Without Representation in Latin America: Gender Quotas and Ethnic Reservations* (New York: Cambridge University Press, 2016).

and leaders from within indigenous communities.[12] These types of opportunity shifts enhance a marginalized group's internal capacity to mobilize.

In addition to structural opportunity and availability of cultural resources, the presence of mobilization structures also aids the process of mobilization.[13] Mobilization structures are collectives of the group including unions, religious congregations, and community associations, which may not have been created to support group assertion, but can be galvanized to promote social and political mobilization when the circumstances are propitious. The black church, for example, played a critical role in mobilizing support from within the black community during the civil rights movement.[14] Such mobilization structures may not be available for all marginalized groups, and even when they are, their membership may be limited.

What Does a Social Movement Accomplish?

The social and/or ethnic movement of a marginalized group produces voice effects, facilitative effects, and coordinative effects. These have consequences for the group's electoral mobilization.

Voice effects have to do with the movement's expansion of the group's consciousness.[15] The movement frames the group's latent demands for social equality and creates symbols that exert their force on the entire ethnic group. In short, the movement represents the group's collective strength. By organizing the group, the movement also announces the group's agency to the rest of society, including political parties. In addition, by defining and giving voice to the marginalized group's grievances, the movement alters the behavior of parties with respect to the group. Parties relying on the group's support are thus obliged to respond to the group's mobilization. In a competitive party system, a lack of response from the party could drive members of the group to a competitor.

A marginalized group's movement also lays the groundwork for future mobilization in multiple arenas and, over time, creates *facilitative effects*.[16] In other words,

---

[12] See Donna Lee Van Cott, *From Movements to Parties in Latin America: The Evolution of Ethnic Politics* (Cambridge: Cambridge University Press, 2005).

[13] See McAdam, McCarthy, and Zald, eds., *Comparative Perspectives on Social Movements*.

[14] See Michael C. Dawson, Ronald E. Brown, and Richard L. Allen, "Racial Belief Systems, Religious Guidance, and African-American Political Participation," *National Political Science Review*, vol. 2 (1990), pp. 22–44.; Allison Calhoun-Brown, "African American Churches and Political Mobilization: The Psychological Impact of Organizational Resources," *The Journal of Politics*, vol. 58, no. 4 (1996), pp. 935–953.

[15] See S. Laurel Weldon, *When Protest Makes Policy: How Social Movements Represent Disadvantaged Groups* (Ann Arbor: The University of Michigan Press, 2011).

[16] See Doug McAdam, *Political Process and the Development of Black Insurgency, 1930–1970* (Chicago: University of Chicago Press, 1982).

the movement reduces the power imbalance between an insurgent marginalized group and its opponents, thereby raising the probability that the group will be able to mount successful social protests in the future. The movement makes repression of the insurgent group more expensive, and in this way it improves the group's bargaining position with respect both to other groups and the state.[17] These effects accumulate to undermine the norms of exclusion and hierarchy, thereby easing social resistance to the marginalized group's inclusion and integration.

This is not to say that, in the immediate short run, the movement will not provoke counter mobilization by dominant groups or repression on the part of the state. In this sense, the process of mobilization is dynamic.[18] Nevertheless, in democratic conditions, countermobilization by dominant groups and repression by the state are difficult to sustain over time. In addition, if a political party supports the repression of an insurgent but electorally relevant group, or remains silent about it, it can alienate the group from itself—a costly outcome for that party in a competitive multiparty system. Moreover, if the insurgent group's actions are peaceful, other state institutions, such as the courts and civil society organizations, may intervene on its side.

As the leaders and events associated with an insurgent group's mobilization gain symbolic value for the group, the movement's *coordinative effects* come into play. These human and temporal symbols, because of their immense significance to the group, assist in coordinating the group's actions.[19] Further, once these symbols are established in the public sphere, they become readily available to political parties, which can incorporate them in efforts to mobilize the group for electoral purposes.

Social mobilization, then, produces a group of community-level mobilization entrepreneurs; these are individuals who come together around the group's issues, facilitate the processes of spreading ethnic consciousness and organizing the group, and make the group's social mobilization consequential for its electoral mobilization by political parties. The group's social mobilization performs a signaling function, too, since it makes parties aware of the need to mobilize the group directly and enables them to adopt and identify with the marginalized group's symbols and demands.[20] Finally, at the level of the neighborhood and locality, the group's social mobilization solves the collective action problem for political parties.

---

[17] Elisabeth Jean Wood, *Insurgent Collective Action and Civil War in El Salvador* (New York: Cambridge University Press, 2003).

[18] McAdam, *Political Process and the Development of Black Insurgency.*

[19] James Johnson, "How Conceptual Problems Migrate: Rational Choice, Interpretation, and the Hazards of Pluralism," *Annual Review of Political Science*, vol. 5 (2002), pp. 223–248; Ross, *Cultural Contestation in Ethnic Conflict.*

[20] David Q. Gillion, *The Political Power of Protest: Minority Activism and Shifts in Public Policy* (Cambridge: Cambridge University Press, 2013).

Social Movements and Political Parties

Traditionally, scholars have regarded social movements as modes of challenge and protest.[21] Others have suggested that movements are potential rivals to the system of political representation.[22] According to these views, the activities of social movements lie outside institutions, whereas the actual levers of power lie within.[23] These narrow interpretations of the role of movements have been widely contested, however. An alternate view of movements is that they shape the workings of what we understand to be the formal institutional space of politics, which comprises political parties, elections, legislatures, and the judiciary.[24] It has even been suggested that social movements are "extra-institutional."[25] Indeed, scholars who hold this view argue that institutions do not operate in a vacuum, and that their behavior is often shaped by the social forces that surround them. Most notably, the importance of movement activity for political parties has been highlighted.[26]

As outsiders, the marginalized turn to movements to improve their access to institutional politics. Since social mobilization has a lower threshold for successful collective action, initially the marginalized are more likely to choose the path of movements over parties. But ultimately, parties are the ones that govern, so social movements will often seek to influence political parties.

[21] William A. Gamson, *The Strategy of Social Protest* (Belmont: Wadsworth, 1990).

[22] J. Craig Jenkins and Bert Klandermans, eds., *The Politics of Social Protest* (Minneapolis: University of Minnesota Press, 1995).

[23] Charles Tilly, *From Mobilization to Revolution* (Reading: Addison-Wesley, 1978).

[24] Paul Burstein, "Interest Organizations, Political Parties, and the Study of Democratic Politics," in Anne N. Costain and Andrew S. McFarland, eds., *Social Movements and American Political Institutions* (Lanham: Rowman & Littlefield, 1998), pp. 39–56; Sidney G. Tarrow, *Power in Movement: Social Movements and Contentious Politics* (Cambridge: Cambridge University Press, 1998); Kathleen Bruhn, *Urban Protest in Mexico and Brazil* (Cambridge: Cambridge University Press, 2008).

[25] Mary Fainsod Katzenstein, *Faithful and Fearless: Moving Feminist Protest Inside the Church and Military* (Princeton: Princeton University Press, 1998).

[26] Stathis N. Kalyvas, *The Rise of Christian Democracy in Europe* (Ithaca: Cornell University Press, 1996); Amrita Basu, "The Dialectics of Hindu Nationalism," in Atul Kohli, ed., *The Success of India's Democracy* (Cambridge: Cambridge University Press, 2001), pp. 163–190; Jack A. Goldstone, ed., *States, Parties, and Social Movements* (New York: Cambridge University Press, 2003); Van Cott, *From Movements to Parties in Latin America*; Bruhn, *Urban Protest in Mexico and Brazil*; Daniel Schlozman, *When Movements Anchor Parties: Electoral Alignments in American History* (Princeton: Princeton University Press, 2015); Rina Agarwala, *Informal Labor, Formal Politics, and Dignified Discontent in India* (New York: Cambridge University Press, 2013); Nancy Bermeo and Deborah J. Yashar, "Parties, Movements, and the Making of Democracy," in Nancy Bermeo and Deborah J. Yashar, eds., *Parties, Movements, and Democracy in the Developing World* (New York: Cambridge University Press, 2016), pp. 1–27.

Political parties are regarded as intermediaries between the state and its citizens. As we have seen, a marginalized ethnic group has the capacity to form a social movement only when the group is able to overcome external as well as internal constraints on such mobilization. How, then, does it happen that a political party is sometimes able to gain electoral support from a marginalized ethnic group that lacks a voice?

It is widely assumed that a multiethnic or catch-all party, when it is able to mobilize multiple groups within a polity, equally mobilizes all of them. In a ranked or hierarchical system, however, the question of whether the party can directly mobilize a marginalized group may be irrelevant to the party's ability to gain the group's electoral support, since the party's direct mobilization of the group is not necessary when the group is in a relationship of subordination to and controlled by another dominant group. In this situation, as represented by row 1 of Table 2.2, the party can obtain the marginalized group's votes through members of the dominant group, who act as intermediaries. If the marginalized

Table 2.2. **Electoral outcomes for a multiethnic party as a function of a marginalized ethnic group's prior social mobilization**

Constraints on Marginalized Ethnic Group's Social Mobilization	*Prospects for Marginalized Ethnic Group's Electoral Mobilization by a Multiethnic Party*	*Electoral Outcome for a Multiethnic Party*
External and internal constraints present	Direct mobilization impossible	*No mobilization:* Party can gain support from marginalized group controlled by a dominant group
External constraints weakened; internal constraints persist	Direct mobilization possible, but mobilization will be incomplete	*Undermobilization:* Party can gain support from some members of marginalized group but neglects group's social exclusion and cannot gain group's full electoral support
External and internal constraints weakened	Direct mobilization possible, including potential for full mobilization	*Potential for full mobilization:* Party is attentive to marginalized group's social exclusion and may be able to gain group's full electoral support

group has no possibility of coming out from under the dominant group's control, then the party has no incentive to mobilize the marginalized group directly
and can take its loyalty for granted. Without the threat of exit, the loyalty of the
marginalized group is assured.[27]

When members of the marginalized ethnic group are no longer under the
control of the dominant group but still lack the capacity to mobilize, a given
party may be able to begin mobilizing the group directly. But the party will
also continue to determine the issues around which the marginalized group is
mobilized, precisely because the group has not socially mobilized, a situation in
which the party is free not to acknowledge the entire set of issues affecting the
group; most particularly, the party can neglect the issue of social exclusion, the
very issue most salient to the marginalized group. In this case, the outcome will
be the party's undermobilization of the group, as represented by row 2 of Table
2.2. It is only when the marginalized ethnic group has overcome internal as well
as external constraints on social mobilization, to the point where it has raised
ethnic consciousness and voiced its exclusion-related grievances, that the group
can be fully mobilized by a multiethnic party, as represented by row 3 of Table
2.2. The party relies for its success on the group's electoral support, and so, it has
to alter its relationship with the group by acknowledging the group's demands
and using inclusive mobilization strategies. In a competitive party system, the
social mobilization of the group also signals the group's independence from the
control of any dominant group, and it opens the possibility for multiple parties
to seek the group's support and attempt to mobilize the group for electoral purposes. It must be stressed, however, that this process of inclusion does not occur
in the space of one election. Rather, it is gradual with the change taking hold
over multiple elections.

In an ethnically diverse society, a multiethnic party, then, is compelled to
seek the full electoral mobilization of a marginalized group only when the members of that group are already free to vote and have already managed to mobilize
themselves. In the absence of these two prerequisites, the multiethnic party will
either not directly mobilize the group, or undermobilize it. Thus the question of
whether a multiethnic party can mobilize a marginalized ethnic group is insepa-
rable from the question of whether the group has already mobilized itself—and,
as we will see, the latter question also has crucial implications for the electoral
prospects of an ethnic party.

A multiethnic party feels the pressure to respond to the social mobilization of a marginalized group especially when it is in competition with other

[27] Albert O. Hirschman, *Exit, Voice, and Loyalty: Responses to Decline in Firms, Organizations, and
States* (Cambridge: Harvard University Press, 1970).

parties for the support of a marginalized group. In a competitive party system, a party will hurt its electoral prospects by not including the group.[28] Party competition incentivizes (1) the recruitment of party workers and mobilization entrepreneurs from the marginalized group, and (2) incorporation of marginalized group symbols and demands. Multiparty competition incentivizes this inclusion more strongly than a two-party system.[29]

How Multiethnic and Ethnic Parties Succeed—or Fail

Multiethnic and ethnic parties alike can make ethnic appeals to voters, but ethnicity is not the only attribute through which a voter self-identifies in a competitive party system. A voter can also self-identify as a supporter of a particular party. This connection with a party can be based on a number of possible factors—the appeal of the party's leader, a salient issue that arises during an electoral campaign, or promises made by the party, for example. In addition, as a supporter of the party, the voter may share interests and aspirations with members of other ethnic groups. As a result, a voter's ethnic identity can come to compete in the electoral arena with the voter's party affiliation.

Strategies for Electoral Mobilization

In a first-past-the-post electoral system, a political party is inclined to build a multigroup coalition when the electoral district is made up of multiple groups and none of them constitutes a majority. Therefore, the multiethnic party faces a dilemma: on the one hand, existing cleavages offer a ready-made instrument for mobilizing voters; on the other hand, in a situation that includes competitive

---

[28] A number of scholars have reiterated this insight. See V. O. Key Jr., *Southern Politics: In State and Nation* (New York: Vintage Books, 1949); and Robert A. Dahl, *Who Governs?: Democracy and Power in an American City* (New Haven, CT: Yale University Press, 1961). Rina Agarwala in her work on organized labor in the Indian urban informal sector shows that labor benefits much more from democratic politics when parties compete for its vote than when this is not the case. See Agarwala, *Informal Labor, Formal Politics, and Dignified Discontent in India.* The literature on racial politics in the United States takes a skeptical view of the benefits of party competition for marginalized groups. Among other scholars, Paul Frymer suggests that a competitive two-party system in the United States has not improved the inclusion of African Americans. See Paul Frymer, "Race, Parties, and Democratic Inclusion," in Christina Wolbrecht, Rodney E. Hero, Peri E. Arnold, and Alvin B. Tillery, eds., *Politics of Democratic Inclusion* (Philadelphia: Temple University Press, 2005), pp. 122–142.

[29] In fact, Frymer suggests that a multiparty system under the SMDP rules or a PR system would have produced more inclusion. See Frymer, "Race, Parties, and Democratic Inclusion," pp. 122–142.

groups, ethnic mobilization may import intergroup conflict into the party organization. One way to avoid this mobilization dilemma is for the multiethnic party to rely on cross-group appeals to mobilize voters.

A multiethnic party must build a coalition of voters that draws from different groups. To do so, the party can use one or both of two mobilization strategies. First, it can choose to make a cross-group appeal; in this case, it will build a multiethnic coalition by mobilizing voters from multiple groups, but those voters will not be mobilized along lines created by ethnic cleavages. Second, the multiethnic party can indeed mobilize groups along ethnic cleavages and thus build a coalition made up of ethnic blocs. A multiethnic party will often mobilize voters by using a combination of these two strategies.[30]

When the party is able to use one or both strategies to mobilize a marginalized group of voters, the party can give the group's members access to political affiliations in the electoral arena. By entering the group's localities and neighborhoods, the party can create opportunities for the marginalized group to join larger political communities. Moreover, by recognizing the group's demand for social equality, and by honoring the group's symbols, the party can reduce the uncertainty in its relationship with the group. Party workers are the face of the party in neighborhoods and localities. Voters develop affiliations with the party through the party's workers and through its electoral campaigns. This is why recognition of a marginalized ethnic group, by having party workers in the group's locality, is essential to the process of mobilization. Even when an electoral district is ethnically mixed, its localities and neighborhoods tend to be more ethnically homogeneous. But within a particular locality, especially during elections, party affiliations can crosscut through ethnic ties when multiple parties are represented through their workers.

An ethnic party, by contrast, even when it operates in an environment where small parties are able to succeed, will not be successful unless it can mobilize the allied ethnic group as a voting bloc; an ethnic party relies on the ethnic appeal. In addition, if such a bloc already exists, its voters must choose the ethnic party over any other available multiethnic parties. In order to compete, then, the ethnic party must use the ethnic appeal with the broadest possible resonance within the group.[31] It must also appear as the most credible representation of group aspirations.

---

[30] In a multiethnic society, the success of multiethnic parties also means the failure of ethnic parties, and vice versa. The risk of building multiethnic coalitions by mobilizing multiple groups along ethnic cleavages may be reduced if the groups are territorially concentrated.

[31] The scholarship on voter-party linkages provides the microfoundations for theories about party systems and parties' success, and it explains what connects voters to parties. Some of that work (for example, Horowitz, *Ethnic Groups in Conflict*) sees voters' support for ethnic parties in terms of two kinds of expected effects: improved access to material benefits (mainly through improved

Effects of Prior Social Mobilization on Electoral
Mobilization in a Competitive Party System

If a marginalized ethnic group has already mobilized socially, the existence of that mobilization signals the group's ability to organize and mobilize itself, and this signal in turn invites attention from political parties interested in mobilizing the group in the electoral arena. Parties need to either recruit mobilization entrepreneurs from the group, or get endorsed by them. The group's self-assertion challenges its prescribed place in the social hierarchy. Self-mobilization, then, also undermines social hierarchy in the public sphere, and it creates alternate forms of ethnic representation outside the electoral arena. These extra-electoral forms of ethnic representation appear as changes take place within the group that involve the rejection of social hierarchy, and as group assertion occurs not only in the political sphere but also in the cultural sphere. As a result, symbols that represent the group's grievances and aspirations gradually diffuse into the party system. In addition, as multiethnic parties appropriate and honor the group's symbols, the intensity of self-esteem-based needs is reduced for marginalized voters in the electoral arena, since the related psychological benefits already accrue from multiple sources.

When voters can self-mobilize and are able to turn to different political parties, the relative salience of ethnicity diminishes, and voter-party relations become less dependent on ethnicity. Competition for the group's vote makes parties even more attentive to the investment in the voter-party relation, and as a result, the marginalized group's voters receive material as well as psychic benefits. When ethnic appeals are used across different parties, such appeals begin to lose their effectiveness and are no longer enough to mobilize voters. Parties, then, turn to other appeals, and the importance of ethnicity in the selection of a party is lowered because voters are driven by multiple considerations. With a party's gradual inclusion of the marginalized group as an equal participant in a larger political community, the group's members develop an attachment to the

access to the state) and enhanced self-esteem (through the enhanced status of the allied ethnic group). In essence, Horowitz's approach, which describes an exchange relationship between party and voter, combines the materialist and social-psychological approaches to ethnicity. On the materialist approach, see Robert H. Bates, *Ethnicity in Contemporary Africa* (Syracuse: Program of Eastern African Studies, Syracuse University, 1973); Albert Breton, "The Economics of Nationalism," *Journal of Political Economy*, vol. 72, no. 4 (1964), pp. 376–386; Russell Hardin, *One for All: The Logic of Group Conflict* (Princeton: Princeton University Press, 1995). On the social-psychological, self-esteem–based approach, see Henri Tajfel, "Experiments in Intergroup Discrimination," *Scientific American*, vol. 223, no. 5 (1970), pp. 96–102. It has also been suggested that ethnic voters in India turn to their own ethnic parties in search of patronage and psychic benefits; see Chandra, *Why Ethnic Parties Succeed*. This is a useful framework for understanding citizens' aspirations in relation to their support of political parties.

party. These attachments may be confined to the period of elections and may change from one election to the other, but that does not make them less consequential to the process of selecting parties.

Thus it happens that where a marginalized ethnic group's social mobilization has been and remains strong, an ethnic party will face two challenges to its potential success. First, of course, is a marginalized group's lower inclination toward ethnic bloc voting. When members of a marginalized group begin to affiliate with different parties, their impulse to stand behind a single party as an ethnic bloc diminishes. Second, once the marginalized group's members have grown accustomed to multiethnic parties' inclusive strategies of recognition and mobilization, such appeals lose their distinguishing power, and voters who belong to the group become less responsive to recognition-based appeals from ethnic parties. As a result, these voters become less likely to choose a party based on psychic benefits alone as other factors, including material considerations, come to matter more in the selection process. Both factors then prevent the party from building a voting bloc from among the members of the allied ethnic group.

Where a marginalized ethnic group has not socially mobilized, the group's members are either tied to one or more parties through intermediaries, and thus the group's mobilization, when it occurs, is motivated from outside the group. Here, even in a competitive party system, the marginalized group remains undermobilized. Multiethnic parties do not recruit party workers in the group's neighborhood and localities, relying instead on outsiders to secure the group's vote. Even if the multiethnic parties begin to recruit party workers from among the marginalized, the group is not acknowledged as a political equal, nor do multiethnic parties incorporate and honor the group's symbols.

In these conditions, voter-party relations are uncertain and capricious. The marginalized group's voters, dependent on the party or parties to which they are tied to, are undersupplied with material as well as psychic benefits, and so the group's need for recognition and dignity remains unaddressed. For these voters, their party affiliations remain weak. These are precisely the conditions that will benefit an emergent ethnic party at the moment of electoral opportunity. In the absence of social mobilization, marginalized and undermobilized groups of voters will place high value on the self-esteem–related benefits of supporting an ethnic political party. These voters' psychological needs are overwhelmingly defined by their desire for dignity, for social recognition, and for the removal of the stigma associated with their ethnic identity, and they typically support an ethnic party because of its promise to restore dignity and respect to their collective identity. In these conditions, an ethnic party also constitutes a rare public embodiment of the group's identity in the space of the larger society. As a result, marginalized voters respond positively to the ethnic party's attempts to mobilize them, even without guarantees that their support will be rewarded with material benefits.[32]

By recruiting party workers from localities and neighborhoods of the marginalized for the first time, the ethnic party develops credibility with marginalized voters. The ethnic party creates and introduces the group to new symbols of pride. All in all, an ethnic party's efforts at mobilization around the issue of social inclusion will resonate with marginalized voters because of the group's historical experience of indignity, its strong sense of exclusion, and the absence of public recognition of the group's identity.[33] The higher salience of ethnicity in the electoral arena makes it easier for the party to mobilize the marginalized ethnic group as a voting bloc. The party draws its rank and file from the group, establishes its presence in the group's neighborhood and localities, and creates the ethnic appeal for the group's mobilization by articulating the group's demands, as well as by identifying and popularizing the group's symbols. For these marginalized voters, then, ethnicity retains its importance in the selection of a political party, and the preference for voting with co-ethnics is also reinforced.

And so we return to the three definitive questions related to a marginalized group's mobilization that were presented in the first chapter: whether there is something distinctive about the mobilization of a marginalized ethnic group, whether the group's capacity for social mobilization has an effect on the group's

---

[32] Opportunity shifts permitting, social exclusion can actually assist the mobilization of a marginalized group by becoming a cause around which members of the group come together. By contrast with the mobilization of other ethnic groups, the sustained movement of a marginalized ethnic group does not depend on constant reframing of issues so as to ensure their salience, since the day-to-day experience of social indignity and exclusion provides a ready context for the framing of issues; see William A. Gamson, *Talking Politics* (Cambridge: Cambridge University Press, 1992); and Melissa Harris-Lacewell, *Barbershops, Bibles, and BET: Everyday Talk and Black Political Thought* (Princeton: Princeton University Press, 2006). Moreover, for the members of a marginalized ethnic group, participation in costly collective action, while remaining strategic (that is, sensitive to opportunity), is not contingent on materially based instrumentalist returns. In El Salvador, for instance, peasants who participated in high-risk collective action were motivated by nonmaterial returns (the opportunity to participate in an activity of social value, to defy their oppressors, and to acquire agency) despite the threat of violence, which is to say that their preferences were shaped by the experience of marginalization; see Wood, *Insurgent Collective Action and Civil War in El Salvador*.

[33] $V = (a)M + (b)P$, where V = total benefits derived from voting, M = material benefits derived from voting, and P = psychic benefits derived from voting; a and b are, respectively, the weights assigned by the voter to the two types of benefits $(a + b = 1)$. The absence of social mobilization increases the weight that voters assign to psychic benefits, and the value of b is higher than when social mobilization is strong. At the moment of electoral opportunity, then, all else being equal, the presence and strength of a social movement will cause the marginalized voter's choice of a political party to be driven by the material benefits that the voter expects to derive from voting, whereas the absence or weakness of a social movement will give psychic benefits more influence over the marginalized voter's choice of a political party.

mobilization in the electoral arena, and why it is that the group's members vote their ethnicity in some instances but not in others.

In the case of Dalits, we see that there is indeed a distinct feature of their mobilization. For Dalits, as for other marginalized ethnic groups, the aims of mobilization are both social (in terms of addressing the group's social exclusion) and political (in terms of gaining access to the state and its benefits). In addition, Dalits, like other marginalized groups, must overcome two types of constraints—external and internal—before mobilization of any kind becomes possible.

As for the possible effects of an existing social movement on the electoral mobilization of a marginalized ethnic group, we have examined a number of reasons that, at the moment of electoral opportunity, the group's prior social mobilization is likely, contrary to conventional expectations, to curtail the success of an ethnic party—and why the absence or weakness of social mobilization is likely to enable the creation and preservation of ethnic voting blocs. The following two chapters look more closely at social mobilization among Dalits and how its strength varies across states. Based on the strength of historical social mobilization, I classify these states as movement and non-movement states.

3

Historical Dalit Social Mobilization

Across colonial India, Dalit exposure to social movements varied. Social movements began earliest and gained their greatest strength in Maharashtra and Tamil Nadu, then administered as the Bombay and Madras Presidencies, respectively. Inland, in the areas of Uttar Pradesh and Bihar that were part of the United Provinces and the Bengal Presidency, respectively, Dalit mobilization arrived later and was sporadic and restricted to a few pockets. A variety of factors were responsible for the difference in the strength, influence, and goals of social movements in the two pairings of states.

Owing to sea trade and geography, peninsular India, including Maharashtra and Tamil Nadu, was the first area to come in contact with Western influences during the colonial period. The British, Portuguese, and French each established port settlements. Their presence disrupted the caste system in two ways. First, Christian missionaries brought with them the desire to find converts and popularize the ideal of social equality. Second, the relatively wider spread of overland trade and industrialization activity in the two peninsular presidencies brought Dalits in rural areas to urban settlements in larger numbers than was the case in the northern states. The urban environment proved to be far more conducive to movement activity than the rural one. But rural India was and is where most Dalits live. The two distinct land tenure systems that the colonial government institutionalized in the peninsular states and the northern states created different environments for urban movements to spread their influence into the rural hinterland.

Dalit social mobilization, when it appeared, was directed at caste Hindu society to demand an end to discrimination and social exclusion. It also targeted the British colonial state to obtain more resources, guarantee a minimum level of political representation, and recategorize caste groups in bureaucratic undertakings such as the census. The effects of the early mobilization of Dalits persist in the movement states of Maharashtra and Tamil Nadu.

Social Mobilization in Tamil Nadu and Maharashtra

Prior to independence from British colonial rule in 1947, the Madras and Bombay Presidencies witnessed a number of movements among lower castes, including Dalits. The influence of Christian missionaries and military service were pivotal to the emergence of Dalit movements.

Given the extent of the exclusion of untouchables, Christian missionaries were initially drawn to them in search of converts. But over time, their engagement with the community became much deeper. Protestant missionaries were the early advocates for untouchable emancipation. In this alliance, untouchables were not mere beneficiaries of missionary benevolence; instead they played an active role in it. They approached missionaries to intervene on their behalf.[1] Missionaries made it possible for untouchables to be treated fairly at the local levels of the state's administrative structure. In alliance with missionaries, then, untouchables transformed their villages from theaters of oppression to sites of struggle. The missionary presence brought rural bondage to the attention of the colonial officials. Missionaries were also heavily involved in spreading literacy among Dalits at a time when the community was barred from attending schools.

Christian missionaries were the first to introduce untouchables to Orientalist ideas that described Brahmins as Aryan conquerors who had subjugated the natives through the caste system. Looked at this way, Brahmins were outsiders ruling over the racially distinct race of Dravidas (inhabitants of South India). Since the Dalits were at the bottom of the caste hierarchy, they represented the "original inhabitants" of the land; Adi-Dravidas (original Dravidas was the new name they adopted for themselves).[2] In the Bombay Presidency also, Christian missionaries educated untouchables, although to a lesser extent than was the case in the Madras Presidency. Their ideational influence, however, was substantial. Here again, Orientalist ideas shaped the challenge to the caste hierarchy.[3]

---

[1] See Rupa Viswanath, *The Pariah Problem: Caste, Religion, and the Social in Modern India* (New York: Columbia University Press, 2014).

[2] See V. Geetha and S. V. Rajadurai, *Towards a Non-Brahmin Millennium: From Iyothee Thass to Periyar* (Calcutta: Samya, 1998); Samuel Jayakumar, *Dalit Consciousness and Christian Conversion: Historical Resources for a Contemporary Debate* (Oxford: Regnum International, 1999); D. A. Washbrook, "Caste, Class and Dominance in Modern Tamil Nadu: Non-Brahmanism, Dravidianism and Tamil Nationalism," in Francine R. Frankel and M.S.A. Rao, eds., *Dominance and State Power in Modern India: Decline of a Social Order*, vol.1 (New Delhi: Oxford University Press, 1989), pp. 204–264.

[3] See Rosalind O'Hanlon, *Caste, Conflict, and Ideology: Mahatma Jotirao Phule and Low Caste Protest in the Nineteenth Century Western India* (Cambridge: Cambridge University Press, 1985).

Dalit mobilization in both states was aided by recruitment into the colonial army, especially during World War I and II. In the Bombay Presidency, the colonial military recruited from among the Mahars, and in the Madras Presidency, from among the Paraiyars, the largest Dalit subcastes in these states.[4] Military service aided the groups with material as well as organizational resources. Employment with the colonial army entitled soldiers to regular pay and a pension, benefits that are prized and rare even today. It allowed Dalits to experience a taste of life free of caste domination and unequal treatment. On leaving the army, many Dalit soldiers became involved in Dalit movements. Military service facilitated these groups' claims to martial heritage, an important social strategy they adopted to counter the stigma associated with their outcaste status.[5]

Social Mobilization in Tamil Nadu

In the Madras Presidency, untouchable groups began to mobilize as early as the latter half of the nineteenth century. Dalit leaders Rettamalai Srinivasan and his son-in-law Iyothee Thass started the Adi-Dravida Mahajan Sabha, a caste association for Paraiyars, in 1891. In 1898, Thass and a group of his followers converted to Buddhism, rejecting the Hindu traditions that had accorded them such lowly status.[6] Later, under the influence of Dalit leaders such as M. C. Rajah, the caste organization representing Dalits demanded the replacement of traditional caste names, such as Paraiyan and Panchamas, now regarded as derogatory, with the more acceptable Adi-Dravidas in the official census. They also demanded higher and at times fixed membership in governing councils and the state administration.

In the mid-1920s, E. V. Ramasamy Naicker (EVR), or "Periyar," (respected one) as he was more popularly known, launched the self-respect movement

---

[4] See DeWitt C. Ellinwood, "Ethnicity in a Colonial Asian Army: British Policy, War, and the Indian Army, 1914–1918," in DeWitt C. Ellinwood and Cynthia H. Enloe, eds., *Ethnicity and the Military in Asia* (New Brunswick: Transaction, 1981), pp. 89–143; according to Stephen P. Cohen, "The Untouchable Soldier: Caste, Politics, and the Indian Army," *Journal of Asian Studies*, vol. 28, no. 3 (1969), pp. 453–468, Mahars were recruited in much larger numbers than were Paraiyars. The Chamars in the north have also claimed participation in the colonial Bengal army, but recruitment patterns in the north shifted after the mutiny of 1857. The Mazhabi Sikhs from Punjab replaced the lower castes from Uttar Pradesh. A Chamar regiment was very briefly constituted in the final years of World War II and was dissolved after the war. The Mahar and Sikh regiments were retained and continue to date.

[5] See Philip Constable, "The Marginalization of a Dalit Martial Race in Late Nineteenth- and Early Twentieth-Century Western India," *Journal of Asian Studies*, vol. 60, no. 2 (2001), pp. 439–478.

[6] See G. Aloysius, "Rediscovering God: Iyothee Thassar and Emancipatory Buddhism," in Subhadra Mitra Channa and Joan P. Mencher, eds., *Life as a Dalit: Views from the Bottom on Caste in India* (New Delhi: Sage, 2013), pp. 208–224.

that had a lasting impact on politics in the state. He first made his name in the agitation demanding temple entry for untouchables. A self-proclaimed atheist, Periyar spent a substantial part of his life attacking Hindu traditions, rituals, and hierarchy. He argued for social inclusion of Adi-Dravidas, encouraged intercaste marriages, and denounced the practice of untouchability. He also advocated for the removal of income inequality, and identified it as a prerequisite for self-respect and dignity. Already alive to the ideas of self-authorship for the purpose of status uplift, both untouchable and Backward Castes were drawn to the self-respect movement in large numbers.[7] Periyar was not an untouchable. In fact, he was born into a wealthy merchant caste family. Nevertheless, the movement was popular among Dalits because it attacked the caste system and mobilized in the name of dignity. Dalit movements and multiethnic and ethnic parties that emerged in the subsequent decades followed in these footsteps. Periyar, even today, is revered among Dalits.

In the Madras Presidency, the adoption of the demand for social equality meant that Dalits also gained access to other movements. They participated alongside members of other groups in the Tamil nationalist movement and peasant movements to demand more rights for landless workers.[8]

In the Madras Presidency, Dalit assertion against the caste system preceded the anti-Brahmin and Dravidian movements, but once these movements took hold, they slowly absorbed Dalits. The parts of the movement that remained independent were also overshadowed by the Dravidian movement. More recently, a challenge to the Dravidian movement has emerged from among the Dalits. Protesting ongoing atrocities against them and their continued deprivation, Dalit theoreticians now implicate the Dravidian Backward Castes in caste-based oppression, alongside Brahmins. According to this narrative, as outsiders, members of Backward-Caste groups have also collaborated with Brahmins to exploit and oppress the purest Dravidians, the Dalits.[9] The record of the Dravidian parties justifies such censure by Dalits. These parties failed to nurture Dalit leadership or grant Dalits an autonomous voice in the organizations. They also failed to protect Dalits from violent attacks by members of dominant castes. The criticism, however, still amounts to a rejection of hierarchy. It does not entirely reject Dravidian politics or Tamil nationalism but appropriates it for the Dalit cause.

---

[7] See Geetha and Rajadurai, *Towards a Non-Brahmin Millennium*. For the effects of the Dravidian movement among Tamil Dalit migrants in Mumbai, see Owen M. Lynch, "Political Mobilisation and Ethnicity among Adi-Dravidas in a Bombay Slum," *Economic and Political Weekly*, vol. 9, no. 39 (1974), pp. 1657–1668.

[8] See M.S.S. Pandian, *Brahmin and Non-Brahmin: Genealogies of the Tamil Political Present* (New Delhi: Permanent Black, 2007).

[9] See Pandian, *Brahmin and Non-Brahmin*; Ravikumar, *Venomous Touch: Notes on Caste, Culture, and Politics*, trans. R. Azhagarasan (Calcutta: Samya, 2009).

But since this is an already appropriated narrative by most social movements and political parties in the state, claiming it for Dalits alone has proven to be difficult.

Social Mobilization in Maharashtra

Untouchable uplift began in Maharashtra under the leadership of a lower-caste social reformer named Jyotirao Phule in 1848. He was the first Hindu to open a school to educate female children among the untouchables. Phule was not seeking mere accommodation within the caste system; rather, his efforts represented a rejection of the hierarchical social order.[10] Other social reformers in the twentieth century followed in his footsteps. Prominent among them were Shahu Maharaj and Dr. Bhimrao Ramji Ambedkar.[11]

Dr. B. R. Ambedkar emerged as the Dalit face of the movement against caste-based discrimination and exclusion in the Bombay Presidency. His impact on the struggle against untouchability and on Dalit politics is unparalleled and has been felt far beyond Maharashtra. Born in the house of an army soldier, he was given a scholarship by a local prince to study in the United States, where he earned a PhD in Economics at Columbia University. In New York, he came face to face with the African American experience with discrimination and the legacy of slavery.[12]

Dr. B. R. Ambedkar returned to India after passing the bar at Gray's Inn in London and became involved in the struggle for the civil and political rights of Dalits. In addition to representing the untouchable population in the three roundtable conferences in London in the 1930s, he agitated for equal access of untouchables to public spaces, including water tanks and temples. He led protests, ran newspapers, and wrote more than ten books highlighting the exclusionary nature of Hindu society. He was deeply skeptical of Hindu reform movements because, according to him, while working for the inclusion of Dalits, they did not reject the hierarchical differentiation in the social order. His views brought him in direct conflict with Gandhi, who was also devoted to the cause of untouchable uplift, and had made it into a central plank of India's freedom movement. Dr. Ambedkar demanded and was able to convince the colonial

[10] See O'Hanlon, *Caste, Conflict, and Ideology.*

[11] Eleanor Zelliot, "Learning the Use of Political Means: The Mahars of Maharashtra," in Rajni Kothari, ed., *Caste in Indian Politics* (New Delhi: Orient Longman, 1970), pp. 29–69; Gail Omvedt, *Dalit Visions: The Anti-caste Movement and the Construction of an Indian Identity* (New Delhi: Orient Longman, 1995); Gail Omvedt, *Building the Ambedkar Revolution: Sambhaji Tukaram Gaikwad and the Kokan Dalits* (Mumbai: Bhashya Prakashan, 2011); Gail Omvedt, *Cultural Revolt in a Colonial Society: The Non-Brahman Movement in Western India* (New Delhi: Manohar, 2011).

[12] See Eleanor Zelliot, *From Untouchable to Dalit: Essays on the Ambedkar Movement* (New Delhi: Manohar, 1992).

government to provide separate electorates to Dalits. He had to compromise on this demand, however, when Gandhi undertook an indefinite fast against this policy in 1932.[13] In principle, Dr. Ambedkar remained opposed to Gandhi and held him responsible for undermining the Dalit cause.[14] A prolific writer, Dr. B. R. Ambedkar wrote extensively against the caste system and went so far as to burn sacred Hindu texts in public in 1927. Late in his life, he pledged to leave the Hindu faith. He led many hundreds of thousands of untouchables in Maharashtra in a mass conversion to Buddhism in 1956.[15]

Dr. Ambedkar also gave a call to Dalits to leave villages for the anonymity of urban areas. He despised village life, calling villages a cesspool and citing them for their ignorance, narrow-mindedness, and communalism.[16] He gave a call to Dalits to educate, organize, and agitate. In keeping with his commitment to the cause of educating Dalits, Dr. Ambedkar opened a number of colleges for Dalit students. Dr. Ambedkar recognized the coincidence of caste and class. He was therefore interested in building a broader lower-class coalition that included members from other lower castes in addition to Dalits. He went on to form the Independent Labor Party and proposed the creation of the Republican Party of India, which came into existence soon after his death.

Like Mahatma Gandhi, both Periyar and Dr. Ambedkar emerged as leaders with a social as well as a political agenda. Both disagreed with Gandhi in a fundamental way, however. They believed internal reform was not possible within the Hindu social order. The influence of Periyar and Dr. Ambedkar, and the growing popularity of the ideas they represented, forced the issue of caste-based discrimination onto the national agenda. To maintain its legitimacy, the freedom movement led by Congress had to acknowledge the issue of untouchability. Gandhi championed it, making it one of the important tenets of the freedom struggle. In the words of Eleanor Zelliot, "The paths of Gandhi and Ambedkar, while they often diverged, ultimately converged, forcing on the Indian conscience the

---

[13] Today, Indian history textbooks rarely mention Dr. B. R. Ambedkar's capitulation under pressure. But, Dalits see the pact that killed their demand for separate electorates as a great betrayal by Gandhi.

[14] For Dr. B. R. Ambedkar's view on the Pune pact and his view of Gandhi's politics, listen to his interview with the BBC, recorded in 1955 and available at http://www.youtube.com/watch?v=ZJs-BJoSzbo; see Bhimrao Ramji Ambedkar, *What Congress and Gandhi Have Done to the Untouchables* (Bombay: Thacker, 1945).

[15] Although there is a long history of lower-caste conversion to Islam, Sikhism, and Christianity, Dr. B. R. Ambedkar's action turned religious conversion into a political act, an act of civil disobedience. It made religious conversion politically controversial. Conversion became an instrument of protest against social exclusion.

[16] See Zelliot, "Learning the Use of Political Means: The Mahars of Maharashtra," pp. 29–69; Zelliot, *From Untouchable to Dalit* ; Christophe Jaffrelot, *Dr Ambedkar and Untouchability: Analysing and Fighting Caste* (London: Hurst, 2005).

problem of untouchability as an issue of national concern."[17] This convergence ensured that after independence, India's Constitution would have to address the issue of discrimination by formulating a set of laws that protected Dalits and encouraged their social, economic, and political inclusion. Dr. Ambedkar was the chairman of the drafting committee and India's first law minister.

Many of the Dalit movement activities appeared in urban Maharashtra first; however, they gradually percolated into rural areas. Songs, poems, stories, and folk theater became instruments for spreading the message of self-assertion among rural Dalits.[18] In 1971, a prominent Dalit movement arose in western Maharashtra—the Dalit Panthers. Fashioned after the militant Black Panthers in the United States, the Dalit Panthers movement was formed by a younger generation of Dalit leaders who alleged that the Dalit movement in Maharashtra had been captured by middle-class interests, and that the moment had arrived for Dalits to retaliate against their exploitation and violence against them. The Dalit Panthers attracted support from urban, slum-dwelling Dalits. Their activities were not confined to urban areas, though. They responded to atrocities committed against Dalits by members of the dominant castes in the villages. They were far more militant in their approach than the previous movements. The Dalit Panthers failed to develop a coherent program, though, and disintegrated by the mid-1980s because of ideological differences among their leaders. Although it had few tangible gains to report, the movement forced political parties in Maharashtra to become more attentive to Dalit concerns.[19] It established a militant edge to Dalit mobilization, which continues to surface when acts of atrocity and violence against Dalits are reported in the state.

Dalit literature has also contributed to spreading the message of the Dalit movement among members of the community and beyond. Maharashtra is home to the oldest and most vibrant Dalit literary movement. The publications of Dalit authors in the regional language of Marathi are read and celebrated not only among Dalits but across society. Though not as well developed, Dalit writing in the Tamil language has also grown over the decades and is viewed as an important part of Tamil literature.[20] Dalit biographies, novels, and other literary

[17] See Eleanor Zelliot, "Gandhi and Ambedkar: A Study in Leadership," in Michael Mahar, ed., *The Untouchables in Contemporary India* (Tuscan: University of Arizona Press, 1972), p. 91.

[18] Jayant Lele, "Caste, Class, and Dominance: Political Mobilization in Maharashtra," in Francine R. Frankel and M. S. A. Rao, eds., *Dominance and State Power in Modern India: Decline of a Social Order*, vol. 2 (New Delhi: Oxford University Press, 1990), pp. 115–211; Jayashree B. Gokhale, "Evolution of Counter Ideology: Dalit Consciousness in Maharashtra," in Francine R. Frankel and M. S. A. Rao, eds., *Dominance and State Power in Modern India: Decline of a Social Order*, vol. 2 (New Delhi: Oxford University Press, 1990), pp. 212–277.

[19] See Lata Murugkar, *The Dalit Panther Movement in Maharashtra: A Sociological Appraisal* (Mumbai: Popular Prakashan, 1991).

[20] By comparison, the growth of Dalit writing in Hindi is a relatively recent occurrence.

publications remain some of the most important media for spreading the message of the Dalit movement. Rising literacy rates among Dalits have meant that Dalit literature has a wide following among the members of the community in the two states.

Tables 3.1 and 3.2 summarize the historical Dalit organizations and leaders associated with social movements in Tamil Nadu and Maharashtra. The difference in the number of organizations listed in Tables 3.1 and 3.2 is a reflection of the strength as well as independence of the two Dalit movements. The Dalit movement in Maharashtra was stronger than its counterpart in Tamil Nadu. It was also more independent. Since a fledgling Dalit movement was subsumed by the broader anticaste movement, fewer independent Dalit organizations emerged in the Madras Presidency and later in Tamil Nadu. By contrast, in the Bombay Presidency, after Phule, a broader anticaste effort that brought the intermediate castes and Dalits under one umbrella did not materialize, and Dalits mobilized independently.

Table 3.1. **Historical Dalit organizations in Tamil Nadu**

Organization Name	Location	Founded	Activities	Leader(s)
Adi-Dravida Mahajan Sabha	—	1891	Political	MC Rajah, Rettamalai Srinivasan, Iyothee Thass
Sakya Buddhist Society	Madras	1891	Religious	Iyothee Thass, Rettamalai Srinivasan
Dravidar Kazhagam	Madras	1892	Social reform	EV Ramasamy ("Periyar")
Panchama Kalvi Abhivarthi - Abhimana Sangh	—	1917	Political	—
Self-Respect Movement	—	1925	Social reform	EV Ramasamy ("Periyar"), WPA Soundara Pandian, MR Jayakar, RK Shamugam Chettiyar

Table 3.2. **Historical Dalit organizations in Maharashtra**

Organization Name	Location	Founded	Activities	Leader(s)
Satyashodhak Samaj	Pune	1873	Religious	Jyotirao Govindrao Phule, Savitribai Phule, Tarabai Shinde
Anarya Dosh Parihar Mandali	Dapoli	1886	Social reform, religious	Gopalbaba Walangkar
Sanmarg Bodhak Nirashrit Samaj	Nagpur	1903	Social reform	Kisan Fagu Bansod
Mahar Tarun Mandal	Nagpur	1904	Subcaste association	Fathuji Bapuji Shende
Shri Shankar Prasadik Somavanshiya Hitchintak Mitra Samaj	Aurangabad	1904	Social reform, education	Shivaram Janaba Kamble
Depressed Classes Mission	Bombay	1906	Education	Vitthal Ramji Shinde
Antyaj Samaj Committee	Ramtek	1906	Religious	Vithobaji Moon Pande
Depressed India Association	Pune	1917	Social reform, political	Ganesh Akkaji Gawai
Shri Chokhamela Samaj	Nagpur	1920	Social reform, Political, education	Vithoba Mistri, Kisan Fagu Bansod, Umaji Master, Bodi Buwa, Raghunath Shambharkar, Dashrath Laxman Patil, Vishramji Sawaitul, Hemchandra Kandekar, VD Makesar, UG Khandekar, Sambhaji Godghate, Hariprasad Buwa
Central Provinces and Berar Depressed Classes Education Society	Nagpur	1922	Education	GM Thaware, Naslkrao Tirpude

(continued)

Table 3.2. **Continued**

Organization Name	Location	Founded	Activities	Leader(s)
Shri Chokamela Samaj Girls Education Society	Nagpur	1922	Education	Tukaram Borkar, Vithobaji Pantawane, Ramaji Dongre, Vithalrao Sawaitul, Advocate Sukhdeve
Rohidas Dnyanodaya Samaj	Bombay	1923	Social reform, political	RB Chandorkar
Bahishkrit Hitkarini Sabha	Bombay	1924	Social reform	Dr. BR Ambedkar, Jivappa Suba Aydale
Madhya Prant Varhad Bidi Majoor Sangh	Kamathi	1925	Labor union	—
Vidarbha Asprushya Samaj Sudharak Seva Mandal	Akola	1926	Religious, social reform, political, education	Sambhuji Ansuji Khandare
Bharat Sant Samaj	Ramtek	1927	Religious	Patit Pawan Das, Mahant Mangal Tulsiram Gajbhiye, Dasrath Gajbhiye
Samata Sainik Dal	Nagpur	1927	Social reform	Dr. BR Ambedkar, Sitaram Gangaram Gangurle, Sasalekaf, Lalingkar, RR Patil, HL Kosare, Sardar GopalSingh, Bhagwan Das, LR Bali
Bahujan Shikshan Sangh	Ahmednagar	1928	Education	DT Rupvate, RK Gaikwad
Depressed Classes Association	—	1928	Social reform	Rao Bahadur MC Rajah, Ganesh Akhaji Gawai, GM Thaware
Municipal Kamgar Sangh	Bombay	1935	Labor union	Dr. BR Ambedkar, Ganpatbuwa ("Madakebuwa")
Mahanubhav Panthiya Asprushya Samaj	Nagpur	1935	Religious	Raosaheb Thaware

Organization	Location	Year	Type	Key People
Independent Labour Party	Bombay	1936	Political	Dr. BR Ambedkar, MB Samarth, KV Chitre, SA Upashyam
Paschim Khandesh Dalit Shikshan Prasarak Mandal, Dhule	Dhulia	1939	Education	PL Lalingkar, Raosaheb Niley
Sahitya Charcha Mandal	Nagpur	1941	Cultural	—
All India Scheduled Castes Federation	Nagpur	1942	Social reform, political	Dr. BR Ambedkar, Rao Bahadur N Shivaraj, PN Rajbhoj, Pyarelal Kuril Talib, RP Jadhav, JN Mandal, MR Krishna, JH Subbiah, BK Gaikwad, BS More, Babu Haridas Awale, Rajabhau Kho-bragade
Lok Seva Natye Mandal	Akola	1942	Cultural	Deenbandhu Shegaokar
Mahar Dnyati Panchayat Samiti	Bombay	1942	Social reform	Sambhaji Tukaram Gaikwad
Dalit Seva Ashram	Bhandara	1943	Social reform	NR Shende
Mehtar Kamgar Union	Nagpur	1944	Subcaste association	Chouthmal
People's Education Society	Bombay	1945	Education	Dr. BR Ambedkar, SP Gaikwad
Bombay State Inferior Village Servants Association	Bombay	1955	Labor union, political	Dr. BR Ambedkar
Buddhist Society of India	Nagpur	1955	Religious	Dr. BR Ambedkar, Yashwantrao Ambedkar, Meeratai Y Ambedkar

Both in Tamil Nadu and Maharashtra, Dalits came to be influenced by ideas that challenged the social order. However, these ideas gained mass popularity and became politically consequential because of two factors: the pattern of rural-to-urban migration as well as the land tenure system in these two states.

Dependence and Dalit Mobilization in Tamil Nadu and Maharashtra

A cultivator-based land settlement system in large parts of Tamil Nadu and Maharashtra, *ryotwari*, made it possible for the message and influence of the self-respect, Dravidian, and Dalit movements to penetrate the rural parts of the two provinces.[21] Under this system, the state collected taxes directly from the cultivators instead of relying on an intermediary landlord as was the case under the other tenure system, *zamindari*, implemented across large parts of Uttar Pradesh and Bihar, where the large landlords were responsible for collecting taxes for the state. Under this system, the colonial state extracted rents from the cultivators keeping the cultivators poor, and inequality levels low.[22] While Dalits were predominantly poor and landless under this system, and subjected to severe discrimination, a class of large landlords did not exercise overwhelming control over rural life as they did under the zamindari system. In Tamil Nadu and Maharashtra, then, a prominent class of landlords that had much to lose from democratic politics and the mobilization of the marginalized, and therefore, was wary of such mobilization, was absent. Such conditions gave outside agents (political and social activists) more access to Dalits. Most importantly, under the cultivator-based land tenure system rural Dalit localities in Tamil Nadu and Maharashtra were more likely to be autonomous. As local social and political entrepreneurs emerged and began to organize in these localities, parties became attentive to them. Political parties then began to recruit Dalit party activists to mobilize Dalits instead of relying on intermediaries belonging to dominant castes.

Migration and Dalit Mobilization in Tamil Nadu and Maharashtra

During the colonial era, the higher rates of industrialization and accompanying urbanization in the Madras and Bombay Presidencies (located in peninsular

[21] According to Abhijit Banerjee and Lakshmi Iyer, 75% of the cultivated area in Tamil Nadu and 78% of the cultivated area in Maharashtra was under the cultivator-based land tenure system. See Abhijit Banerjee and Lakshmi Iyer, "History, Institutions, and Economic Performance: The Legacy of Colonial Land Tenure Systems in India," *The American Economic Review*, vol. 95, no. 4 (2005), pp. 1190–1213.

[22] See Banerjee and Iyer, "History, Institutions, and Economic Performance," pp. 1190–1213.

India) brought more labor, including Dalits, to the cities. In cities such as Madras and Madurai in Tamil Nadu, and in Bombay, Pune, and Nagpur in Maharashtra, a small Dalit middle class emerged alongside a substantial proletariat class. In cities, Dalits continued to be segregated from others, living in their separate localities, but the shadow of dominance by other castes lifted from their daily lives, allowing them to organize more easily.

Often in small groups, and under the leadership of a more resourceful individual in the localities, Dalits organized themselves, first as a social and only later as a political group. In these new spaces, early claims were for equal treatment by others living around them. Cities placed Dalits proximate to the state. Dalit mobilization, when it occurred, often petitioned the state to intervene on its behalf. The family and kinship networks stretching across the urban-rural divide took these movements and the ideas associated with them to the villages in the two states.

Movements of the marginalized in general are more likely to emerge and grow in urban areas, where there are fewer constraints against collective action.[23] It is noteworthy that in the absence of similar constraints, members of dominant groups are better positioned to mobilize through movements in rural areas and take their voices to the cities. Take, for example, some of the disruptive movements that have arisen in more recent decades: the Jat-dominated protests that arose in western Uttar Pradesh in 1988 and Haryana in 2016, the Vanniyar agitation in northern Tamil Nadu in 1987, and the Gujjar protests in Rajasthan in 2008.[24] In all these cases, a powerful rural caste took its protest to the cities. These groups had the resources to sustain their protests over days, besides enjoying a degree of authority and control to mobilize freely. In sharp contrast, Dalits living in the same villages, as the Jats, Vaniyars, and Gujjars, do not enjoy the same degree of freedom and do not command the resources to take a rural protest to urban centers. Instead, for the marginalized, protest-based interventions often travel in the opposite direction, when the more empowered urban members of the group mobilize and also act on behalf of their co-ethnics based in the

---

[23] See Frances Fox Piven and Richard A. Cloward, *Poor People's Movements: Why They Succeed, How They Fail* (New York: Pantheon, 1977); Robert H. Bates, *States and Markets in Tropical Africa: The Political Basis of Agricultural Policy* (Berkeley: University of California Press, 1981); James C. Scott, *Weapons of the Weak: Everyday Forms of Peasant Resistance* (New Haven: Yale University Press, 1985).

[24] On the protests in western Uttar Pradesh, see Dipankar Gupta, *Rivalry and Brotherhood: Politics in the Life of Farmers in Northern India* (New Delhi: Oxford University Press, 1997); Ashutosh Varshney, *Democracy, Development, and the Countryside: Urban-Rural Struggles in India* (Cambridge: Cambridge University Press, 1998). On the Vanniyar agitation, see Andrew Wyatt, *Party System Change in South India: Political Entrepreneurs, Patterns, and Processes* (Abingdon: Routledge, 2010).

countryside. Protests of rural Dalits against acts of violence and discrimination in Tamil Nadu and Maharashtra are often supported from urban centers.[25]

These movements are instrumental in infusing the ideology of Dalit assertion into rural areas and especially in mobilizing Dalits along this identity. Outside the protest movements, Dalit publications are produced in urban areas and inform ideas and views in rural Tamil Nadu and Maharashtra. Dalit nongovernmental organizations (NGOs) based in cities support self-mobilization of Dalits in rural areas. Some Dalits based in villages also travel to rallies and events in cities and are exposed to the scale of Dalit mobilization in their regions.

The process of urbanization of Dalits continues today. According to the 2011 census figures, 35% of Dalits in Tamil Nadu and 46% of Dalits in Maharashtra reside in towns and cities. In Uttar Pradesh and Bihar, fewer Dalits live in urban areas (22% and 7.9%, respectively). Of the 203 interview subjects in Tamil Nadu and Maharashtra, 76% said that a member of their immediate or extended family was working in an urban area. Among these interview subjects, 68% reported that the city the family member worked in was in the same state.

Dalit movements have a distinct regional character, and they draw from the local cultural, historical, economic, and political contexts. The Dalit movement in Maharashtra, for example, expresses itself in the Marathi language, protests historical Dalit exploitation and oppression in Maharashtrian villages, centers mobilization on local symbols, and relies on folk stories, festivals, and traditional street theater to disseminate its messages.

Despite its regional expression, these are not movements that promote regional Marathi identity. Dalit movements in Tamil Nadu, Maharashtra, and Punjab are not about Tamil, Marathi, or Punjabi subnationalism, respectively. Dalit movement activities and discourse represent counterpublics, parallel discursive arenas, where members of subordinated social groups invent and circulate counterdiscourses, which in turn permit them to formulate oppositional

---

[25] Mobilization constraints faced by Dalits, in this sense, are different from those faced by another marginalized group, the Adivasis (indigenous people). As among the Dalits, poverty is also a source of marginalization among Adivasis, but since their villages are not organized hierarchically in the same way as caste Hindu villages are, they are not dispossessed of authority as Dalits are. Adivasis are not held back by a dominant caste. This makes their mobilization for protest more feasible, even in rural areas. The protest movements of Adivasis and the movements of indigenous groups in Latin America share similarities. For movements of indigenous groups in Latin America, see Deborah J. Yashar, *Contesting Citizenship in Latin America: The Rise of Indigenous Movements and the Postliberal Challenge* (Cambridge: Cambridge University Press, 2005); Donna Lee Van Cott, *From Movements to Parties in Latin America: The Evolution of Ethnic Politics* (Cambridge: Cambridge University Press, 2005); Courtney Jung, *The Moral Force of Indigenous Politics: Critical Liberalism and the Zapatistas* (New York: Cambridge University Press, 2008).

interpretations of their identities, interests, and needs.[26] In these counterpublics, Dalits discover their own agency, and Dalits define their own identity, sometimes in opposition to regional identities. Regional subnationalist movements have tried to subsume Dalit movements, but to conflate the two movements is a serious categorization error because neither in Tamil Nadu, nor in Maharashtra, were Dalits voluntarily invited to sit at the high table of regional nationalism. Dalits' self-assertion enabled them to gatecrash the discourse of regional identities. They brought with them their stories and literature as well as their heroes and heroines. One of my interview subjects who was a correspondent for a Marathi daily put it best. He said, "You can hear the pain of the Dalit in Marathi literature because the voiceless Dalit has spoken. If it was not for our [Dalit] poets and writers, the world would have been deaf to our stories. No one else would have spoken for us." A Tamil Dalit scholar echoed a similar sentiment as he explained the connection of the Dalit movement to the politics of Tamil identity. He said, "The Dravidian movement and parties lost their soul to electoral politics. . . . Dalits are recovering it by adopting Tamil caste free names. The true Tamil identity is casteless, it demands the annihilation of caste." He gave the example of Thol. Thirumavalavan, the President of the Viduthalai Chiruthaigal Katchi, Tamil Nadu's most prominent Dalit party, who began to promote the ancient Tamil practice of using caste-free names. Since the last name of an individual can reveal his or her caste, Dalits are encouraged to drop their last names.

Dalit Social Mobilization in Uttar Pradesh and Bihar

Social Mobilization in Uttar Pradesh

Untouchable mobilization began comparatively later in the state of Uttar Pradesh. It was led by an emergent middle class of Dalits in the small industrial centers of the state in the 1920s and 1930s. Dalits were particularly prominent in the leather industry.

Swami Achhutanand, a Dalit born in a family of army soldiers, launched his Adi-Hindu movement in 1921. He asked Dalits to reject caste hierarchy and urged them to see themselves as the original Hindus.[27] In some respect similar to the ideas being propagated in Bombay and Madras presidencies at that time, the

---

[26] See Nancy Fraser, "Rethinking the Public Sphere: A Contribution to the Critique of Actually Existing Democracy," *Social Text*, vol. 25, no. 6 (1990), pp. 56–80, p. 67.

[27] Om Prakash Singh, "Evolution of Dalit Identity: History of Adi Hindu Movement in United Province (1900–1950)," *Proceedings of the Indian History Congress*, vol. 70 (2009–2010), pp. 574–585.

message was different in one fundamental respect. It did not reject Hinduism or threaten an exit from the faith.[28] Swami Achhutanand organized public meetings, began a monthly newspaper that ran from 1925 to 1942, and critiqued the caste system in his poetry. But the Adi-Hindu movement remained limited in its influence and fell away after his death in 1933.[29]

The Dalit assertion that appeared remained confined to select urban pockets.[30] Most Dalits, however, lived in rural Uttar Pradesh and were landless laborers or marginal farmers[31] Rural penetration of these movements was hindered by the control exercised over Dalits by landlords. In areas of the landlord-based zamindari land settlement system, the landed class exercised substantial control on rural life, and Dalits were mostly dependent on the landlords. Under these conditions sustained mobilization from within the group was not possible in vast parts of rural Uttar Pradesh—not that group mobilization from outside had not been attempted.

During the period of the Indian freedom movement, untouchable uplift was a part of the Congress Party's agenda. In 1920, Gandhi made it a central plank of his mobilization effort.[32] His exaltations sent Congress Party workers into Dalit localities for the first time.[33] In order to replace their derogatory caste names, he gave the untouchables a new name, calling them *Harijans*, meaning "God's children." Nevertheless, Gandhi's efforts and ideas failed to be broadcast into rural Uttar Pradesh. Moreover, the activism directed at including untouchables into

[28] Both Periyar and Dr. B. R. Ambedkar threatened such an exit.

[29] See Kanwal Bharti, ed., *Swami Acchutanand ji "Harihar" Sanchayita* (New Delhi: Swaraj Prakashan, 2011), p. 150.

[30] See Owen M. Lynch, *The Politics of Untouchability: Social Mobility and Social Change in a City of India* (New York: Columbia University Press, 1969); Sudha Pai, "Changing Socioeconomic and Political Profile of Scheduled Castes in Uttar Pradesh," *Journal of the Indian School of Political Economy*, vol. 12, nos. 3–4 (2000), pp. 405–422; Nandini Gooptu, *The Politics of the Urban Poor in Early Twentieth-Century India* (Cambridge: Cambridge University Press, 2001); Nicolas Jaoul, "Learning the Use of Symbolic Means: Dalits, Ambedkar Statues, and the State in Uttar Pradesh," *Contributions to Indian Sociology*, vol. 40, no. 2 (2006), pp. 175–207.

[31] Ram Rawat's and Om Prakash Singh's pathbreaking work that documents Dalit assertion in Uttar Pradesh prior to independence notwithstanding, my considered view is that the Dalit movement in Uttar Pradesh was not as strong as in Maharashtra or Tamil Nadu. See Ramnarayan S. Rawat, *Reconsidering Untouchability: Chamars and Dalit History in North India* (Bloomington: Indiana University Press, 2011); and Singh, "Evolution of Dalit Identity," pp. 574–585.

[32] For Gandhi's statements on untouchability, see several small volumes: *Caste Must Go; All Are Equal in the Eyes of God; None High: None Low; The Bleeding Wound!; My Soul's Agony; My Varnashrama Dharma; The Removal of Untouchability*, and others. These draw chiefly from his two newspapers, *Young India* and *Harijan*.

[33] See Gyanendra Pandey, *The Ascendancy of the Congress in Uttar Pradesh: Class, Community, and Nation in Northern India, 1920–1940* (London: Anthem, 2002).

the national mainstream weakened after Gandhi's assassination in 1948. Over time, the term *Harijan* was popularized by the Congress Party's electoral mobilization of the group; however, Dalits came to view the term as patronizing.

Another attempt at inclusion of Dalits in Uttar Pradesh was made by Hindu reform movements such as the Arya Samaj. With the introduction of census enumeration of caste and religious communities in the early part of the twentieth century, Hindu organizations became conscious of the relative size of their community. Fearful of losing the substantial number of untouchables to the Muslim, Christian, and Sikh communities through conversion, they focused on bringing untouchables more firmly into the Hindu fold. Different reform movements appeared across North India. These movements viewed Dalits as members of the larger Aryan community who had gradually become lost and needed to return home. By reforming themselves, Dalits could return to the Hindu fold as equal members. Arya Samaj opened schools and hostels for Dalits. Dalit groups began giving up "polluting" activities such as leatherwork, consumption of beef and meat products, and engaging in Hindu ritual and religious practices. These efforts were the predecessors of the Hindu nationalist movement. Today Hindu nationalists, encompassed by the Sangh Parivar, work to transform the Hindu identity, which is essentially a religious identity, into a political one. To achieve this aim, they are committed to absorbing Dalits into the existing fold of upper- and Backward-Caste members. The movement has tried to do this through organizations such as Seva Bharati, which runs schools in Dalit localities, holds indoctrination camps, and performs ceremonies of ritual purification, *shuddi*.[34] It has focused its efforts in North and Central India. So far, however, these efforts have met with limited success.

One reason for this outcome has been that the Dalit community was urged to adopt the behavior of the upper castes to attain higher social acceptance generations earlier. This process was known as Sanskritization. Greater cleanliness and abstinence from the consumption of meat and alcohol were commonly encouraged by sants (holy men) and reformers.[35] This, though, put the burden of social inclusion on Dalits. Another reason was that these self-purification measures did not change the social mindset on purity and pollution prevalent in the rest of society. Even after Dalits were ritually included in the Hindu fold, their treatment by other members of Hindu society did not undergo any significant change. For the most part, society in Uttar Pradesh remained segregated.

[34] See Christophe Jaffrelot, *India's Silent Revolution: The Rise of the Lower Castes* (New York: Columbia University Press, 2003).

[35] See Mysore Narasimhachar Srinivas, *Social Change in Modern India* (Berkeley: University of California Press, 1966).

When Uttar Pradesh's peasantry mobilized against the colonial state in the 1920s and 1930s, Dalits participated in these movements.[36] And yet, unlike other castes, Dalits failed to find a home in peasant politics. When the farmers' movement of the 1970s and 1980s swept Uttar Pradesh, it, for the most part, was led by members belonging to Backward Castes. It demanded higher procurement prices, greater fertilizer subsidies, free power, and loan waivers from the state.[37] The economic focus of these demands notwithstanding, ethnicity was deeply implicated in the successful organizing of the farmers.[38] It involved the participation of the Backward Castes, who were the chief beneficiaries of the limited land reforms as they had transformed from tenant farmers to landowners. Yet the farmers' movement did not go beyond making economic demands. It did not attack the principle of social hierarchy or denounce the hegemony of the upper castes. The farmers' movement was also fairly antagonistic to the needs of Dalits. The Backward Castes and Dalits were divided by identity as well as economic interests. Not only are Dalits ranked lower than the Backward Castes, the economic interests of the two castes also differ since more Dalits fall among landless or marginal farmers.[39]

Until the 1980s, Dalit movement politics in Uttar Pradesh was weaker as compared to movement states; it was sporadic and primarily confined to a few pockets in western Uttar Pradesh. Kanshi Ram's mobilization of Dalits in Uttar Pradesh altered this trend. A Dalit Sikh from Punjab, Kanshi Ram was a government employee who founded the All-India Backward and Minority Communities Employees' Federation (BAMCEF) in 1976. This union was created to build an alliance of government workers who belonged to marginalized groups such as Dalits and Adivasis (also known as Tribals or Scheduled Tribes [STs]).[40] Although intended to be national in scope, BAMCEF attracted its core membership in Maharashtra and Delhi. Few Adivasis joined the organization, yet BAMCEF still assisted in the consolidation of a common Dalit identity across different subcastes.[41]

---

[36] See Rawat, *Reconsidering Untouchability.*

[37] See Varshney, *Democracy, Development, and the Countryside.*

[38] See Gupta, *Rivalry and Brotherhood.*

[39] See Paul R. Brass, "The Politicization of the Peasantry in a North Indian State," in Sudipta Kaviraj, ed., *Politics in India* (New York: Oxford University Press, 1997), pp. 200–221.

[40] See Sudha Pai, *Dalit Assertion and the Unfinished Democratic Revolution: The Bahujan Samaj Party in Uttar Pradesh* (New Delhi: Sage, 2002); Sudha Pai, *Dalit Assertion* (New Delhi: Oxford University Press, 2014).

[41] For the life and times of Kanshiram, see Oliver Mendelsohn and Marika Vicziany, *The Untouchables: Subordination, Poverty, and the State in Modern India* (Cambridge: Cambridge University Press, 1998); and Badri Narayan, *Kanshiram: Leader of the Dalits* (New Delhi: Penguin, 2014).

Kanshi Ram created the *Dalit Soshit Samaj Sangharsh Sanghatan* (the organization for the struggle of the oppressed Dalit community; also known as DS4) in 1981 to enter politics. After competing in local elections in a few North Indian states, the organization launched the Bahujan Samaj Party in 1984. The BSP contested its first elections in Uttar Pradesh in 1986. An overwhelming majority of Dalits in Uttar Pradesh live in rural areas and are not employed by the state. They remained untouched by BAMCEF activities. During interviews in Dalit localities in 2004, I asked Dalit subjects about BAMCEF. Only 9% of the subjects had heard of the organization.[42] BAMCEF in this sense did not constitute grassroots-based social mobilization among Dalits. As Chapters 5 and 6 will show, the average Dalit in Uttar Pradesh came to be mobilized fully by the BSP first.

The polity in Uttar Pradesh has undergone a social churn, taking different forms and impacting different groups. However, until the appearance of their ethnic party, the Dalits in Uttar Pradesh experienced limited mass social mobilization. Dalit assertion in Uttar Pradesh arrived a few generations later than Tamil Nadu and Maharashtra. Protests among Uttar Pradesh Dalits appeared sporadically and could not cohere into a statewide anticaste movement on their own. The most prominent among them, the Adi-Hindu movement, remained limited in its influence among urban Dalits. After the death of Swami Achhutanand, no local social leader emerged to ensure its continuity. Leaders of the stature of M. C. Raja, Periyar, and Dr. B. R. Ambedkar did not emerge in Uttar Pradesh during this period. Later, when the BSP searched for Dalit symbols to associate with, it turned to historical personalities outside the state who were known for their opposition to the caste system.

Social Mobilization in Bihar

Bihar's feudal land settlement system and limited industrialization during the late nineteenth and the early twentieth centuries ossified the state's social structure. This deprived Dalits of resources and opportunities to organize. In urban Bihar, a Dalit movement, even a limited one, did not arise. Unlike in Uttar Pradesh, there was little industrial activity to create a demand for labor from rural areas. Untouchables remained confined to rural Bihar, and the emergence of an organizing elite class was delayed. This group appeared only after independence, largely as a consequence of affirmative action policies on the part of the state.

[42] BAMCEF members I interviewed in Uttar Pradesh, Delhi, and Maharashtra confirmed this. In fact, several BAMCEF members expressed their opposition to the BSP and disapproved of Mayawati Kumari (popularly known as Mayawati), who has served several terms as chief minister. So, while it did provide limited assistance in the launching of the Bahujan Samaj Party (BSP) in Uttar Pradesh, the organization had a very limited role to play in its eventual success there.

In rural Bihar, in addition to living in abject poverty, untouchables remained substantially subservient to the will of the dominant landed castes. Without social stirring among the lower orders in Bihar, the principle of hierarchy was not challenged and denounced. In an environment devoid of opportunities and resources for the spread of subaltern movements, the correlation between social and economic hierarchy was very strong.[43]

Even outside efforts for the inclusion of untouchables were for the most part absent. Gandhi's call for the uplift of untouchables failed to motivate the Congress Party to work toward their social inclusion in Bihar. Similarly, the Hindu nationalists' self-cleansing movement among untouchables has been weak. As noted earlier, the land tenure system imposed enormous constraints on the peasantry in Bihar. The whole of Bihar was brought under the zamindari landlord-controlled permanent settlement system as early as 1793.[44] Across the state, the peasantry that was drawn largely from the Backward and untouchable castes occasionally revolted; these protests were swiftly quelled with state assistance. They received very little outside support. During this period, the Congress Party, instead of aligning itself with the peasant movement led by tenant farmers, remained wary of it. The party was eager to avoid a confrontation with the landed classes.[45]

The advent of democracy and the compulsions of electoral politics meant that after independence Bihar was the first state to abolish the zamindari land settlement system. Despite this, actual reform took ten years to implement and was not followed by comprehensive land redistribution. State indifference and reluctance on this count were politically motivated. Many members of the ruling Congress Party and of the administrative machinery either belonged to landowning families or were otherwise connected to them.[46] The collusion between the state administration and landlords was responsible for a weak policy and its deeply flawed implementation. The piecemeal reforms did not disturb the social structure. Given the concentration of power in the hands of a small minority

[43] See Francine R. Frankel, "Caste, Land and Dominance in Bihar: Breakdown of the Brahmanical Social Order," in Francine R. Frankel and M.S.A. Rao, eds., *Dominance and State Power in Modern India: Decline of a Social Order*, vol.1 (New Delhi: Oxford University Press, 1989), pp. 46–132.

[44] In fact, Gandhi's first civil disobedience action occurred in Bihar in 1929, where he began a movement in the district of Champaran against the excessive taxation imposed on the peasantry by the indigo plantation owners, but this protest did little to change either the taxation policies or the feudal control that the well-organized landlords exerted over the impoverished peasants.

[45] See Hetukar Jha, "Promises and Lapses: Understanding the Experience of Scheduled Castes in Bihar in Historical Perspective," *Journal of Indian School of Political Economy*, vol. 12, nos. 3–4 (2000), pp. 423–444.

[46] See Arun Sinha, "Legal Loopholes: To Landlords' Rescue," *Economic and Political Weekly*, vol. 13, no. 42 (1978), pp. 1758–1760; see Frankel, "Caste, Land and Dominance in Bihar," pp. 46–132.

made up mainly of upper-caste landed elite and bureaucrats, political contestation was unavoidable. It arose within and outside the electoral arena.[47]

Class relations centered on land ownership defined a key cleavage in Bihar. The landowners, drawn primarily from the upper castes, were pitted against the tenant farmers, drawn from the Backward Castes and the agricultural workers, a large section of whom are to-date Dalits. The resulting polarization enabled a vertical alliance, albeit an asymmetric one, between the Backward Castes and Dalits.[48] Outside electoral politics, this conflict manifested itself in the mobilization of the *Naxalites*, a Maoist guerrilla movement, which, in spite of state repression and the countermobilization of landlord militias, gradually gained in strength since the 1960s. It drew its members from the Backward Castes and untouchables and was especially strong in central Bihar. The Naxalites have attacked the police, massacred opponents, and enforced boycotts on landlords. In retaliation, the state has captured, tortured, and killed Maoists, and landlords' private armies have massacred peasants seen as being sympathetic to them.[49] Thousands have died in this decades-old conflict. The movement weakened the control of the landed elite in rural Bihar, though, and created an opportunity for Dalit mobilization. The Naxalite violence has subsided sharply in recent years.

The influence of the Naxalite movement on the social and political mobilization of Dalits has remained limited for a number of reasons. For one, it is a violent insurgency movement, not a popular mass movement. This, then, restricts its participant base of insurgents and sympathizers to limited pockets within society. Research on violent and peaceful movements points out that violent insurgencies often fail to draw broad support because they make extraordinary demands on their participants. People have to give up their livelihoods and families and be willing to kill others.[50] The threat of reprisals by security forces and upper-caste militia is particularly pronounced for Dalits, which undercuts the

---

[47] See Frankel, "Caste, Land and Dominance in Bihar," pp. 46–132.

[48] Such an alliance failed to emerge in Uttar Pradesh, where Dalits had acquired enough mobilization resources by the late 1980s to mobilize independently; Dalits are typically socially and economically more deprived than members of Backward Castes.

[49] See Pradhan H. Prasad, "Agrarian Violence in Bihar," *Economic and Political Weekly*, vol. 22, no. 22 (1987), pp. 847–852; B. N. Prasad, *Radicalism & Violence in Agrarian Structure: The Maoist Movement in Bihar* (New Delhi: Manak, 2002); Bela Bhatia, "The Naxalite Movement in Central Bihar," *Economic and Political Weekly*, vol. 40, no. 15 (2005), pp. 1536–1549; Ashwani Kumar, *Community Warriors: State, Peasants, and Caste Armies in Bihar* (New Delhi: Anthem Press, 2008).

[50] Chenoweth and Stephan compare hundreds of violent and nonviolent movements between 1900 and 2006. They rely on this mechanism to explain variation in the success rate of violent and nonviolent movements. See Erica Chenoweth and Maria J. Stephan, *Why Civil Resistance Works: The Strategic Logic of Nonviolent Conflict* (New York: Columbia University Press, 2011).

appeal of the Maoists. Second, the Maoists view their struggle primarily in terms of class conflict. Hence, theirs is not a movement directed at rejecting social hierarchy but merely its class manifestation. The Maoists are less focused on the redressal of the social as well as cultural exclusion of Dalits, an issue that has increasingly become relevant to them as the group of Dalits have been released from their relationship of total dependence on landlords. Third, the leadership of the Naxalite movement is largely drawn from among the Backward Castes, which further restricts the appeal of the movement to Dalits. A section of the Naxalite movement that has renounced violence and competes in electoral politics in Bihar has failed to draw a substantial vote share among the Dalits.[51]

The structural domination of Dalits in Bihar imposed overwhelming constraints against mobilization. Unlike Uttar Pradesh, rural Bihar experienced fewer movements. Mobilization was primarily centered on land relations. However, with a gradual waning of the power of the landed elite and the breakdown of their control over agricultural workers, Dalits have begun to mobilize. This mobilization is primarily restricted to electoral politics, however.

Both rural-urban migration patterns and a land tenure system in Uttar Pradesh and Bihar undermined the prospects for social mobilization of Dalits.

Dependence and Dalit Mobilization in Uttar Pradesh and Bihar

In these states, during the colonial period, rural labor was locked in dependent relations for much longer than in Tamil Nadu and Maharashtra because of the landlord-based land tenure system.[52] Under the zamindari system, the landlords, who were mostly upper caste, were granted substantial sovereignty over the areas under their control by the colonial government, and as a result, the lower orders had little autonomy to mobilize. Over time, such a relationship increased rural inequality, with the landlord class getting wealthier at the expense of the peasantry.[53] The landlords therefore became wary of democratic politics and movements of the marginalized, and remained opposed to the social and electoral mobilization of the lower castes. Political parties and social activists in

---

[51] See Nicolas Jaoul, "Naxalism in Bihar: From Bullet to Ballot," in Christophe Jaffrelot and Laurent Gayer, eds., *Armed Militias of South Asia: Fundamentalists, Maoists and Separatists* (New York: Columbia University Press, 2009), pp. 21–43.

[52] According to Abhijit Banerjee and Lakshmi Iyer, 58% of the cultivated land area in Uttar Pradesh and 100% of the cultivated land area in Bihar fell under the landlord-based land tenure system. See Banerjee and Iyer, "History, Institutions, and Economic Performance," pp. 1190–1213.

[53] See Banerjee and Iyer, "History, Institutions, and Economic Performance," pp. 1190–1213.

these regions, then, had limited access to rural Dalits. After India gained independence in 1947, these conditions changed gradually. The abolition of the land tenure system, increased use of mechanized agricultural technology, remittances from migrant family members, and fragmentation of landholdings weakened the control exercised over Dalits by dominant castes.

Migration and Dalit Mobilization in Uttar Pradesh and Bihar

Even as the dependence of Dalits on the landed elite gradually broke down, Dalits had fewer urban opportunities to escape to in these two states. The industrial sector in Uttar Pradesh gradually stagnated, and even cities such as Agra, Kanpur, and Allahabad, the traditional centers of Dalit movements in the middle of the twentieth century, could not emerge as hubs for statewide Dalit movements in the following decades.

In Bihar, again, cities did not have the economic opportunities that drew the poor in large numbers. The migrating poor, including Dalits, both skilled and unskilled, often headed to cities located far from home. They went to Gujarat, Maharashtra, and Andhra Pradesh in addition to northern states such as Delhi and Punjab. Since the 1980s, as higher economic growth has created more economic opportunities, labor migration has increased. Out of 206 interview subjects in Uttar Pradesh and Bihar, 48% reported that one or more persons in the immediate or extended family had migrated out of the village for work; of these, 43% of the interview subjects reported that the migration was out of the state.

One view on migration out of poor societies suggests that it stunts the prospects of transformational politics since it removes the best and brightest from the society.[54] In Uttar Pradesh and Bihar, outbound migration from the rural areas has had mixed effects. On one hand, it has been beneficial for Dalits. It has undoubtedly accelerated the breakdown of the hold local dominant castes have had on Dalits in the countryside. It has allowed Dalits to break free of dependent relations with them.[55] Remittances, even meager ones from migrant workers, have allowed Dalits to become financially independent. Outside their villages, migrants have begun to live a life free of restrictions and humiliations. When

---

[54] See Paul Collier, "The Political Consequences," in *Exodus: How Migration Is Changing Our World* (New York: Oxford University Press, 2013), pp. 179–194.

[55] Siddharth Dube, *In the Land of Poverty: Memoirs of an Indian Family, 1947–1997* (London: Zed Press, 1998); Dipankar Gupta, "Caste and Politics: Identity over System," *Annual Review of Anthropology*, vol. 34 (2005), pp. 409–427; Devesh Kapur, Chandra Bhan Prasad, Lant Pritchett, and D. Shyam Babu, "Rethinking Inequality: Dalits in Uttar Pradesh in the Market Reform Era," *Economic and Political Weekly*, vol. 45, no. 35 (2010), pp. 39–49.

Table 3.3. **Historical Dalit organizations in Uttar Pradesh**

Organization Name	Location	Founded	Activities	Leader(s)
Jatav Veer Mahasabha	Agra	1917	Subcaste association	Prabhutanand Vyas, Pandit Sundarlal Sagar, Khemchand Bohare
Adi-Dharm Movement	Kanpur	early 1920s	Religious	Swami Achhutanand Harihar
Akhil Bharat Varshiye Nishad Sabha	Lucknow	1920	Subcaste association	Rai Saheb Babu Ramcharanji

they returned to their village, they bring with them the same desire for freedom from domination. Studies corroborate that in some aspects Dalits' treatment by other groups has improved.[56] At the same time, migration failed to create a mobilization infrastructure in these non-movement states. Migrant Dalits from Uttar Pradesh and Bihar did not automatically turn into agents of diffusion. Their participation in Dalit movement-related activities in their new home cities remained limited. For one, they did not share the language and social networks of local Dalit castes that were at the forefront of the Dalit movement. Additionally, they had traveled in search of livelihoods, and often remittance of money back to the village took priority over frequent home travel. Had Dalits migrated to urban centers inside Uttar Pradesh and Bihar, instead of leaving for other states, migration may have been more transformative; the extent of Dalit social mobilization in the two states could have been much greater.

Tables 3.3 and 3.4 summarize the historical Dalit organizations and leaders associated with social movements in Uttar Pradesh and Bihar. Fewer and primarily subcaste-based organizations, by their nature exclusionary, mobilized Dalits in these states.

During the colonial period, at a time when the option of full-fledged electoral politics was not available to Dalits to articulate their demands and grievances, Dalit mobilization took the form of movements. Since the advent of democratic politics took away the rationale for such movements to persist, we would expect them to have disappeared. This, we know, is not true. While multiethnic and ethnic parties both compete to represent Dalits today, Dalits as a historically disadvantaged group have been only so successful in benefiting from the promise of democracy. While Dalits are enthusiastic voters, their continued deprivation

[56] Kapur, Prasad, Pritchett, and Babu, "Rethinking Inequality," pp. 39–49.

Table 3.4. **Historical Dalit organizations in Bihar**

Organization Name	Location	Founded	Activities	Leader(s)
Bharatiya Dusadh Mahasabha	—	1914	Subcaste association	Hari Govindji Bhagat
Khet Mazdoor Sabha	—	1930s	Labor union	Jagjivan Ram
Bihar Rajak Sangh	—	early 1940s	Social reform	Nayantara Das
Musahar Sevak Sangh	Ranchi	1953	Subcaste association	Somar Ram

suggests that routine institutional politics has not responded adequately to their needs.

The institutional structure has been unable to fulfill the promise of representing Dalits' interests and addressing their needs; Dalits therefore, have continued to turn to extra-institutional measures to assert themselves. Dalit protests and organizations have appeared in a competitive party system made up of Dalit and multiethnic parties. Some of these organizations have turned themselves into political parties—the Republican Party of India, which emerged in Maharashtra; the Dalit Soshit Samaj Sangh (DS4), which gave rise to the BSP; the Dalit Panthers of India (DPI), in Tamil Nadu, which turned itself into Viduthalai Chiruthaikal Katchi (VCK), the Liberation Panthers Party—but many other organizations have not taken that route.

Moreover, the threshold for successful collective action is far lower for the social mobilization of Dalits than it is for their electoral mobilization by political parties. This, then, makes sustaining movement activities easier than ensuring party success. Even when movements do not turn into political parties, they end up performing a vital function in politics. Dalit movements have articulated demands for inclusion and social justice, built a Dalit political identity, and produced Dalit leaders. The two forms of mobilization follow different trajectories. When mobilization is conducted primarily through political parties, levels of ethnic mobilization follow the electoral cycle, peaking around elections and subsiding subsequently. When mobilization occurs outside party politics and is motivated by social rather than electoral objectives, it is more continuous. It is important to note that even as demands and the elite are brought into the fold of institutional politics, an infrastructure of mobilization remains and continues to discover new uses for itself. High levels of social mobilization can be sustained even when high-intensity events such as protests do not occur regularly. Movement activity can hum along and continue to perform its most vital purpose—that of socializing individuals and spreading the discourse of the movement.

Dalit mobilization through movements in the Madras and Bombay Presidencies was markedly different in its objectives and strength from the movements that mobilized Dalits in Uttar Pradesh and Bihar. First, Dalit mobilization in the Madras and Bombay Presidencies was stronger; it was more widespread and involved more actors than the non-movement states. Dalit mobilization in Uttar Pradesh remained sporadic and limited to regional pockets. Dalits experienced little social mobilization in Bihar outside peasant movements. Second, after independence, as institutional opportunities expanded with the provision of adult franchise, Dalit social mobilization did not disappear in the movement states. Its limited energy was not all channeled into party mobilization. In fact, new waves of Dalit movements have appeared in Tamil Nadu and Maharashtra, and some of this mobilization has even been critical of the previous generation of movements in these states, pointing to deeper ideological penetration within the group. By contrast, Dalit social mobilization, when it appeared, has often been the launching pad for electoral politics in Uttar Pradesh and Bihar. Third, Dalit social mobilization adopted a decidedly anticaste character in the movement states. Both Periyar and Dr. B. R. Ambedkar openly attacked the Hindu culture for its reliance on the caste system. The anticaste movements influenced social attitudes even among non-Dalits by challenging some of the foundational beliefs on which the caste system rests. In Uttar Pradesh and Bihar, the hierarchical Hindu social order and its accompanying rituals and practices did not get challenged similarly. The few Dalit organizations that emerged in the first half of the twentieth century restricted their activities to promote subcaste interests instead of attacking the caste system. Dalits as well as non-Dalits remained more closely rooted in the notions of social hierarchy. One way to gauge the strength of a historical movement in a society is to measure movement effects. The next chapter presents a variety of evidence on the difference in movement effects across the four states.

4

The Effects of Historical Dalit Social Mobilization

Dalit social mobilization has aimed to empower Dalits and transform Indian society. It has sought to produce a special "consciousness," what is commonly described by Marathi-speaking Dalit activists as *chaitanya*; in Hindi this concept translates as *jagriti* or "awakening." Dalit social mobilization in the movement states of Tamil Nadu and Maharashtra was sustained by anticaste movements as well as Dalit movements. Similar forms of anticaste collective action and Dalit assertion failed to gain strength in Uttar Pradesh and did not emerge in Bihar. Much of this mobilization was aimed at social transformation. Has mobilization actually done this, though? To what extent can we measure the ideological penetration of movements among Dalits? Among non-Dalits? To what extent do we detect any behavioral changes among either group? As it turns out, there is clear variation between movement and non-movement states across multiple survey measures and qualitative indicators. Information, attitudes, and behavior differ strikingly in ways that point to a connection with movement effects.

Familiarity with Dr. B. R. Ambedkar

Dr. Bhimrao Ramji Ambedkar was the premier champion for Dalit rights and arguably the only pan-Indian Dalit hero. He was named "the greatest Indian after Gandhi" in a nationwide poll by a prominent weekly news magazine in 2012[1] and is featured in standardized Indian school curriculum across all Indian states and territories. His birthday, April 14th, is celebrated as an official national holiday. His image, life story, and message of equality are spread through Dalit-themed posters and publications and carried to the illiterate through street

---

[1] Uttam Sengupta, "A Measure of the Man," *Outlook India,* August 20, 2012.

theater, poetry, and songs.[2] Dalit "power" is frequently equated to *"Bhim shakti"* by Dalit social activists and politicians.

Pictures of Gandhi, anointed the father of the nation in independent India because of his leadership of the freedom movement, and sometimes Nehru, India's first and longest-serving prime minister, are omnipresent in the country. Any visitor to government offices will find them gathering dust on the walls. But one seldom finds them in households. The same is not true for Dr. Ambedkar, however. To be sure, his statues can be found in public spaces across the length and breadth of India. But unlike any of his contemporaries, Dr. Ambedkar is revered even in private spaces, in Dalit homes. Treated like a deity by Dalits, his image is cleaned regularly and people keep the area around it spick and span. And unlike other Dalit heroes and heroines whose popularity is confined to the regions and Dalit subcastes to which they belong to, Dr. Ambedkar is revered across regions and subcastes. For this reason, a familiarity with Dr. B. R. Ambedkar serves as a good proxy to assess the initial ideological penetration of Dalit social movements.

In a 2006 nationwide, representative sample survey, the Centre for the Study of Developing Societies collaborated with the television news channel CNN-IBN and the newspaper *Hindustan Times* to assess India's "State of the Nation" ahead of its 57th Republic Day.[3] Among the questions it asked, the survey sought to establish how familiar Indians were with a set of individuals, including states-men, artists, film stars, and athletes. While a strong majority could identify a picture of Mahatma Gandhi (88%) and Jawaharlal Nehru (67%), only half could match the then-current Indian president, A.P.J. Abdul Kalam, with his image. Nationwide, a similar number of Indians (48%) recognized Dr. B. R. Ambedkar.

The survey results are more revealing, however, when considered by Dalit respondents across states. Almost all Dalits in Maharashtra, Dr. Ambedkar's home state and the focus of much of his own Dalit social mobilization, were able to recognize him (98%). In Tamil Nadu in the South, where Periyar eclipses Dr. B. R. Ambedkar among leaders Dalits revere, Dr. Ambedkar still garnered a high level of recognition (78%). The results in Bihar (33%) are not entirely surprising; the state struggles across basic human development indicators related to education and literacy, both of which could increase exposure to Dr. Ambedkar's image over time (see Table 4.1). Uttar Pradesh's middling recognition (53%) among Dalits parallels the national average for all Indians, but is a puzzle in context. At the time the CSDS poll was conducted, Uttar Pradesh had thrice elected Mayawati, a Dalit woman who uses only one name, as its chief minister.

---

[2] Sharmila Rege, "Songsters from the Mudhouse," *Outlook India*, August 20, 2012.

[3] Republic Day is celebrated every January 26th. It marks the date in 1950 when the Indian Constitution came into effect.

Table 4.1. **Percentage of Dalits able to recognize Dr. B. R. Ambedkar's picture**

	States	Dalits	Averages
Movement States	Tamil Nadu	78 ($N = 84$)	88
	Maharashtra	98 ($N = 68$)	
Non-movement States	Uttar Pradesh	52 ($N = 110$)	42.5
	Bihar	33 ($N = 79$)	

Source: CSDS State of the Nation Survey, 2006.

Table 4.2. **Percentage of Dalits able to name an achievement of Dr. B. R. Ambedkar**

	States	Dalits	Averages
Movement States ($N = 203$)	Tamil Nadu	34	44
	Maharashtra	55	
Non-movement States ($N = 206$)	Uttar Pradesh	25	19
	Bihar	14	

N = Number of Dalit Respondents.

Source: Ahuja Locality-level survey, 2004.

At the forefront of Mayawati's agenda in office was the installation of thousands of Dr. Ambedkar statues across the state, the construction of large memorials to Dr. Ambedkar in the state capital Lucknow, and the highly publicized launch of welfare programs targeting Dalits and bearing Ambedkar's name.

There is a distinction to be made between mere recognition and ideological penetration. Recognition is one measure of familiarity, but the ability to give meaning to the symbol of Dr. Ambedkar is a stronger one. In my focus groups, Dr. Ambedkar was frequently discussed with a great deal of reverence. One participant recalled, "He is our greatest leader." Another saw him as "god-like." To probe this familiarity and admiration further, I asked my one-on-one interview subjects to tell me more about Dr. Ambedkar to gauge whether they could associate the man with his achievements. In movement states, 44% of my Dalit informants could do this. In non-movement states, 19% could (see Table 4.2). Most often, respondents said "Ambedkar gave India the Constitution," "Ambedkar fought for our rights," or "Ambedkar protested against our discrimination and exclusion in Hinduism." Across the four case study states, I also spoke with a fair number of Dalit college students immersed in Dalit ideology. The variation that

I observed generally persisted even among them. This suggests it is primarily socialization within the family and locality rather than education and literacy that spreads Dr. Ambedkar's ideas.

Indeed, Dalit activists in the movement and non-movement states have very different relationships with Dr. Ambedkar. For a Dalit businessman in Maharashtra who operates a charity educating low-income children, Dr. Ambedkar is vital: "Today's generation has not witnessed the type of discrimination I saw while growing up. Through Ambedkar, we remind them who is responsible for liberating us and what liberation means." By contrast, a Dalit political party worker in Bihar attached little value to Dr. Ambedkar as a mobilizing symbol: "There is no point campaigning in the name of Ambedkar. Paswan and Lalu they know. They are great leaders of this land. They do not understand Baba Ambedkar. They are untouched by him."[4] A Dalit in Uttar Pradesh, home to tens of thousands of Dr. Ambedkar statues, lamented about their upkeep: "Ambedkar statues are everywhere. Many people do not know about him. When his statues began to be put up in the villages, it started fights. Other communities alleged that we [Dalits] wanted to grab land. So the government started putting them in strange places, they are even in ponds and in jungles. But no one maintains them because people don't know about them and few here [in and around his village] understand the true significance of Ambedkar." These statements give a sense that it is social entrepreneurs who inculcate the spirit of Dr. Ambedkar in others and build Dalit culture over time; politicians and educated Dalits in non-movement states differed in their capacity to do so.

Policing Caste Boundaries

A second strategy for assessing the ideological penetration of social mobilization relates to how strongly Dalits and non-Dalits police their caste boundaries. Dalit social movements have called for the "annihilation," using the language of Dr. B. R. Ambedkar, of caste altogether through two controversial strategies: intercaste marriage and religious conversion.

Since caste is literally reproduced through endogamy, intercaste couples and their progeny represent a group of mixed caste individuals that defy the laws of Hindu ritual purity. Both Dr. Ambedkar and Periyar called for intercaste marriages.[5] In practice, few Indians marry across castes; a recent study found that roughly 5% of rural and urban Indians reported they were in intercaste

---

[4] "Paswan" is Ram Vilas Paswan, the leader of the Lok Janshakti Party. "Lalu" is Lalu Prasad Yadav, the leader of the Rashtriya Janata Dal.

[5] Dr. B. R. Ambedkar (a Dalit) married Dr. Sharada Kabir, a Saraswat Brahmin, in 1948. Periyar (a BC) married Manniammai Ammaiyar of the Mudaliar forward-caste community also in 1948.

marriages.[6] General attitudes toward the practice, however, allow us to measure the levels of in-group and out-group boundary policing of caste identity in Indian society.

Religious conversion removes Dalits from the Hindu purview and, in principle, affords them social and spiritual equality among a new community of believers. Dr. Ambedkar encouraged conversion, and in 1956, with hundreds of thousands of followers, converted to Buddhism. Periyar attacked Hinduism as superstitious and exploitative and promoted a kind of rational atheist philosophy as an alternative. These actions and the legacy of Dalit social mobilization have politicized the issue of religious conversion and made it communally sensitive. Various state governments, often compelled by leaders connected to the Hindu nationalist Bharatiya Janata Party, have pushed for bans on religious conversion and limited the activities of missionaries as a result.[7] A sizable majority of Indians, 79.8%, were counted as Hindu in the 2011 census; while Dalits have converted to Buddhism, Islam, Sikhism, and Christianity in numbers as a form of protest, the populations of all religious communities have tended to vary along differential fertility rates rather than continuous mass conversion.

In the 2004 Indian National Election Study, a nationwide and representative instrument, two questions on attitudes toward policing caste boundaries were asked. The results are reported in Tables 4.3, 4.4, 4.5 and 4.6 for both Dalits and non-Dalits.

Attitudes toward intercaste marriage and religious conversion are more relaxed for Dalits and non-Dalits in the movement states of Tamil Nadu and Maharashtra. Asked whether they agreed with the proposition: "Intercaste marriage should be banned," only 40.5% of Dalits and 43.25% of non-Dalits in movement states agreed (this contrasts with 62.1% of Dalits and 57.95% of non-Dalits in the non-movement states of Uttar Pradesh and Bihar who supported a ban). A comfortable majority of society in movement states is open

---

[6] Srinivas Goli Jr., Deepti Singh Jr., and T. V. Sekher, "Exploring the Myth of Mixed Marriages in India: Evidence from a Nationwide Survey," *Journal of Comparative Family Studies,* vol. 44, no. 2 (2013), pp. 193–206.

[7] Article 25 of the Indian Constitution guarantees the "free profession, practice and propagation of religion." Still, a number of states (Arunachal Pradesh, Chhattisgarh, Gujarat, Himachal Pradesh, Madhya Pradesh, Odisha, and Tamil Nadu) have laws restricting "forced" conversions while others have proposed them (Jharkhand and Uttarakhand). These laws frequently include advance notice of an intent to convert and a waiting period in order to change one's religious identity in official documents. For a detailed review of laws and court decisions related to religious conversion in India, see Laura Dudley Jenkins, "Legal Limits on Religious Conversion in India," *Law and Contemporary Problems,* vol. 71, no. 2 (2008), pp. 109–128. In December 2014, Parliamentary Affairs Minister M. Venkaiah Naidu announced the central government's support for additional national and state-level laws regulating conversion.

Table 4.3. **Percentage of Dalits who agreed with the proposition: "Intercaste marriage should be banned."**

	States	Dalits	Averages
Movement States	Tamil Nadu	35.5 ($N = 166$)	40.5
	Maharashtra	45.5 ($N = 215$)	
Non-movement States	Uttar Pradesh	64.5 ($N = 404$)	62.1
	Bihar	59.6 ($N = 222$)	

N = Number of Dalit Respondents.

Source: CSDS Indian National Election Study, 2004.

Table 4.4. **Percentage of non-Dalits who agreed with the proposition: "Intercaste marriage should be banned."**

	States	Non-Dalits	Non-Dalit Averages
Movement States	Tamil Nadu	44 ($N = 666$)	43.3
	Maharashtra	42.5 ($N = 1120$)	
Non-movement States	Uttar Pradesh	63.5 ($N = 1337$)	58
	Bihar	52.4 ($N = 934$)	

N = Number of Non-Dalit Respondents.

Source: CSDS Indian National Election Study, 2004.

Table 4.5. **Percentage of Dalits who agreed with the proposition: "Religious conversions should be banned."**

	States	Dalits	Averages
Movement States	Tamil Nadu	41 ($N = 166$)	43.3
	Maharashtra	45.5 ($N = 215$)	
Non-movement States	Uttar Pradesh	52 ($N = 404$)	52.2
	Bihar	52.3 ($N = 222$)	

N = Number of Dalit Respondents.

Source: CSDS Indian National Election Study, 2004.

Table 4.6. **Percentage of non-Dalits who agreed with the proposition: "Religious conversions should be banned."**

	States	*Non-Dalits*	*Averages*
Movement States	Tamil Nadu	49.2 ($N = 666$)	47.8
	Maharashtra	46.3 ($N = 1120$)	
Non-movement States	Uttar Pradesh	60.6 ($N = 1337$)	60.9
	Bihar	61.2 ($N = 934$)	

N = Number of Non-Dalit Respondents.

Source: CSDS Indian National Election Study, 2004.

to marriage across subcastes and sometimes between upper and lower castes, Dalits included. Boundary policing around marriage is markedly higher in non-movement states for both Dalits and non-Dalits. Dalits in non-movement states may reject intercaste marriage in even greater numbers than non-Dalits because their community is more often than not the target of violence when there is opposition to such unions.

Asked whether they agreed with the proposition: "Religious conversion should be banned," 43.3% of Dalits and 47.8% of non-Dalits in movement states agreed (this contrasts with 52.2% of Dalits and 60.9% of non-Dalits in non-movement states who supported a ban). While the survey results indicate religious conversion is a slightly more contentious issue than intercaste marriage, for a majority of Dalits and non-Dalits in movement states, it is an acceptable choice and a path out of untouchability. Again, attitudes on boundary policing on the issue of religious conversion are more relaxed in movement states for both Dalits and non-Dalits than in non-movement states.

The Practice of Untouchability

Dalit social movements are aimed not at just influencing attitudes, but changing the behavior of non-Dalits around ritual pollution; this is a strong test of the success of movements. In the public sphere, laws have provided Dalits with the right to attend schools, use public water sources, and travel freely. Private behavior cannot be similarly compelled. In 2011, the Indian Human Development Survey, a joint effort between the Indian National Center for Applied Economics Research and the University of Maryland, provided the first nationally representative baseline data on the practice of untouchability in contemporary India. As part of its survey instrument, two questions were included. First, survey

Table 4.7. **Percentage of non-Dalits who practice untouchability**

	States	Non-Dalits
Movement States	Tamil Nadu	28.91 (*N* = 1431)
	Maharashtra	4 (*N* = 2780)
Non-movement States	Uttar Pradesh	53.44 (*N* = 2997)
	Bihar	56.68 (*N* = 1229)

N = Number of Non-Dalit Respondents.

Source: India Human Development Survey-II (IHDS-II), 2011–12.

Table 4.8. **Percentage of Dalit respondents who experienced untouchability in the last 5 years**

	States	Dalits	Averages
Movement States	Tamil Nadu	11.6 (*N* = 516)	15.1
	Maharashtra	18.6 (*N* = 441)	
Non-movement States	Uttar Pradesh	26.6 (*N* = 796)	27.7
	Bihar	28.8 (*N* = 260)	

N = Number of Dalit Respondents.

Source: India Human Development Survey-II (IHDS-II), 2011–2012.

respondents were asked if anyone in their home practiced untouchability. For those who answered no, a second question was asked: "Would it be okay for someone from the low caste community to enter your kitchen or use your cooking utensils?" The second question probes comfort with interdining, a practice that violates traditional ritual purity. By these measures, 27% of all Indians were found to practice untouchability; the figures were 30% for rural Indians and 20% for urban Indians. The survey administrators acknowledge the issue of untouchability is sensitive and that their results may underreport the actual practice. Still, this data is valuable for allowing us to again assess variation between movement and non-movement states.

At the turn of the twentieth century, caste relations very clearly defined social relations in India. Dalits were outcastes, untouchability was a norm, and practices guarding ritual purity were sometimes stricter in Tamil Nadu and other culturally Brahmin-dominated societies in South India than in the North. In Tamil Nadu, even the shadow of the untouchables was regarded as polluting. In the northern states, including Uttar Pradesh and Bihar, the touch was perceived as polluting. At the turn of the twenty-first century, however, the practice of untouchability has anecdotally declined, and substantial state-level variation can be documented. In Tamil Nadu (28.91%) and Maharashtra (4%) non-Dalits report practicing untouchability. By contrast in Uttar Pradesh (53.44%) and Bihar (56.68%) non-Dalits report practicing untouchability (see Table 4.7). The survey also inquired about the experience of untouchability among Dalits. The pattern of responses remained the same. In Tamil Nadu (11.6%) and in Maharashtra (18.6%) Dalits reported that someone in the household had experienced untouchability. By contrast, in Uttar Pradesh (26.6%) and in Bihar (28.8%) Dalits report the same (see Table 4.8).

Dalit Assertion

The effect of Dalit social mobilization is seen in how members of the group respond to caste-based discrimination and violence. Because of their marginalized social and economic status, Dalits remain vulnerable to those situated above them in the caste hierarchy. In my focus groups and one-on-one interviews, Dalits discussed the specific challenges they faced and their reactions to them. Within each state, I found caste-based discrimination and the threat of violence was greatest in villages where Dalits were heavily outnumbered by other groups. Overall, it was less pronounced in Tamil Nadu and Maharashtra and more pronounced in Uttar Pradesh and Bihar.

Dalits in Tamil Nadu and Maharashtra were not resigned to their social and economic subjugation; they often expressed anger at their poor treatment by others and a desire to retaliate. In a district known for caste-based tensions in Tamil Nadu, a group of young Dalit farmers said: "If we are attacked, we will hit back. We will not turn to the law, instead [we will] pay back in kind." A group of Dalit villagers in Maharashtra recounted that they used to be regularly harassed and intimidated by a locally dominant caste. They noted, "But once we started fighting back, things changed. Now when there is a dispute, there is tension. They know that we don't wear bangles [and they also know] we can retaliate."[8]

By contrast, Dalits in Uttar Pradesh and Bihar seemed more acutely aware of their socioeconomic position and the vulnerability that accompanies it; they were more likely to state this cognizance directly limited their assertion. A woman agricultural laborer in Bihar lamented: "Without outside help, how does a poor family take on the dominant caste? Everyone and anyone can control our lives in this village. We are like cattle—[we] will work for food and never protest." In such a context, Dalits tended to view the state as a mirror of society and not

---

[8] Since women wear bangles, the idiom of wearing bangles in this context refers to emasculation of Dalit men.

a source of assistance. A focus group participant in Azamgarh, Uttar Pradesh, explained: "We have to be careful; the authorities are often with them [the dominant caste]." A brick kiln worker in Bihar put it in starker terms: "Raising one's voice here is futile. If one does, one either picks up a gun and becomes a rebel or one leaves the village. I have a family to support—I cannot do this." In all four states, as the upward mobility of Dalits gradually increases, the threat of violence against them will also increase. A large majority of Dalits are below the age of thirty-five years, and they are more likely to resist this threat.

Over the last century, Dalits mobilized in Tamil Nadu and Maharashtra to oppose the caste system and claim their basic human rights. In Uttar Pradesh and Bihar, until recently, Dalit communities were largely untouched by similar levels of mobilization. In this chapter, I have traced the effects of Dalit social mobilization through variation in the information, attitudes, and behavior of Dalits and non-Dalits in these states. Taken together, this evidence points to a movement-driven transformation in society. Such shifts in attitudes are gradual and cannot be explained by levels of economic development and urbanization alone. We must account for the agents as well as the discourse of such a transformation. The anticaste movements that Dalits led and joined are the transformative agents. This transformation is consequential for how political parties mobilize voters. Ethnic and multiethnic political parties each face different challenges and do not mobilize Dalit or non-Dalit publics in a vacuum. Political parties sometimes shape social contexts, but, as is more often the case, their behavior is shaped by them.

5

Dalit Party Performance and Bloc Voting

Dalit political parties became competitive in India's democratic politics following the decline of the Indian National Congress and the fragmentation of India's political party system beginning in the late 1980s. Their electoral performance and ability to attract blocs of Dalit voters have varied across movement and non-movement states, though. In the movement states of Tamil Nadu and Maharashtra, where Dalit social mobilization has produced measurable social change, Dalit collective action has failed to transfer into the electoral arena for Dalit political parties. The Republican Party of India (RPI), the Bahujan Samaj Party (BSP), and the Viduthalai Chiruthaigal Katchi (VCK) have been unable to consolidate enough votes to emerge as major state-level parties or significant coalition partners in pre-poll alliances in movement states. In the non-movement states of Uttar Pradesh and Bihar, outcomes have been quite different. The BSP has formed governments four times in Uttar Pradesh and used its success there to project itself as a national party. In Bihar, the Lok Janshakti Party (LJP) has leveraged its electoral performance to control key ministries in coalition governments at the state and national levels. Non-movement states largely untouched by Dalit collective action in the social sphere have paradoxically proved fruitful environments for Dalit political parties. This chapter illustrates the variation in Dalit party success and failure by examining election results, Dalit and other party vote shares, and variation in Dalit attitudes toward bloc voting across movement and non-movement states.

Tamil Nadu, Maharashtra, Uttar Pradesh, and Bihar are among the largest and most politically important states in India. They elect 40% of the *Lok Sabha*, the lower house of India's parliament, and contain 43% of the total Indian Dalit population. Each state has a *Vidhan Sabha*, a state legislative assembly, with hundreds of seats. Both the Lok Sabha and Vidhan Sabhas include general seats and reserved seats for Scheduled Castes (SCs) and Scheduled Tribes (STs). All political parties, including Dalit parties, are eligible to compete for general and

Table 5.1. **Number of Lok Sabha (lower house of parliament) seats per state**

State	General Seats	SC (Dalit) Reserved Seats	Total Seats
Maharashtra	39	5	48
Tamil Nadu	32	7	39
Uttar Pradesh	63	17	80
Bihar	34	6	40

Note: ST reserved seats are not included. Numbers reflect the Delimitation of Parliamentary and Assembly Constituencies Order, 2008.

Table 5.2. **Number of Vidhan Sabha (state legislative assembly) seats per state**

State	General Seats	SC (Dalit) Reserved Seats	Total Seats
Maharashtra	234	29	288
Tamil Nadu	188	44	234
Uttar Pradesh	318	85	403
Bihar	203	38	243

Note: ST reserved seats are not included. Numbers reflect the Delimitation of Parliamentary and Assembly Constituencies Order, 2008.

reserved seats.[1] Tables 5.1 and 5.2 provide information on the number of Lok Sabha and Vidhan Sabha seats for each state.

This chapter is organized into two major sections of content. In the first, I trace the electoral performance of Dalit political parties in movement and non-movement states. In the second, I examine how ethnic bloc voting has varied across movement and non-movement states.

[1] Across all four states, reserved districts may act as incubators for Dalit candidates; see Francesca R. Jensenius, *Social Justice through Inclusion* (New York: Oxford University Press, 2017). But, they are unable to sustain Dalit party success. This is because while they have a higher proportion of Dalit voters, they are not safe seats for Dalit parties.

Dalit Party Performance

Dalit political parties are ethnic parties; by their very nature they make appeals based on the marginalized status of the Dalit community and primarily rely on blocs of Dalit voters for their electoral success. In a fragmented political party system, Dalit parties need only gain a plurality of total votes in an election to become competitive and to be included in electoral alliances. To do this in the first-past-the-post (FPTP) electoral system, though, Dalit parties have to garner substantial numbers of Dalit votes across electoral districts. If a Dalit party can capture a bloc of Dalit voters in a state and either emerge as a swing player in an alliance, or win elections outright, it has four key advantages: (1) It can convince fence sitters and strategic voters that it is a viable competitor. These voters may then defect from stronger political parties and expand the initial electoral opportunity created by party system fragmentation. (2) It can attract stronger non-Dalit candidates with name recognition, muscle power, and finances. This draws in voters tied to specific candidates and provides vulnerable Dalit voters protection during and after elections. (3) It creates a stronger bargaining position for the party in pre-poll alliances among political parties. Even if Dalit parties cannot win seats on their own, if they control a substantial Dalit vote share, they send a strong signal to potential alliance partners. Dalit parties can push for additional seat assignments in electoral districts they are more likely to win. (4) It appears as a powerful strategic partner to other ethnic voting blocs. Dalit parties may leverage initial electoral success to ally with other ethnic groups across elections. These factors support the long-term endurance and success of Dalit political parties.

Like most Indian political parties today, Dalit parties first become viable at the state-level. For this reason, much of the analysis of Dalit party performance that follows focuses on state-level electoral outcomes. Few Indian parties are truly national. In 2014, the Election Commission recognized 6 parties as national parties and 51 parties as state parties out of a total of 1,766 parties registered with it.[2] The BSP has been the only "national" Dalit party in India's electoral history. In Bihar, the LJP is officially registered as a "state" party.[3] This status has

---

[2] The six national political parties in India are the Congress Party, the Bharatiya Janata Party (BJP), the Communist Party of India (CPI), the Communist Party of India—Marxist (CPI(M)), the Bahujan Samaj Party (BSP), and the Nationalist Congress Party (NCP). A political party must meet one of three criteria be recognized as a "national" party: (1) It has to win a minimum of 2% of the seats (currently eleven seats) in the Lok Sabha from at least three different states; (2) In general elections, the party must win 6% of the votes and at least four Lok Sabha seats; (3) The party should be recognized as a "state level party" in at least four states.

[3] A political party must meet one of four criteria to be recognized as a "state" party: (1) The party has to win at least three seats or 3% of the seats in the state legislative assembly; (2) In the most recent Lok Sabha elections, the party should have won at least one seat for every twenty-five allotted

so far eluded other Dalit parties in Tamil Nadu and Maharashtra, which remain "registered unrecognized parties." Being recognized as a national or state party carries with it certain benefits, among them exclusive use of the party's symbol. Voters, many of whom are illiterate, rely on symbols to link candidates with parties on their ballots. Parties include symbols on their election materials and frequently reference them in campaign slogans. Securing a pan-Indian symbol or one whose use is reserved for a particular recognized party alone assists parties with their outreach to prospective voters over time. Nascent parties that lack an electoral record to gain registered status frequently slate candidates on an independent basis.

Electoral Mobilization of Dalits in Tamil Nadu

As was the case in other parts of India, the Congress Party in the Madras Presidency was dominated by Brahmin notables.[4] The Congress made its claim as the party of the freedom movement and the harbinger of Indian nationalism. Nevertheless, the party in the state faced a strong challenge from the Dravidian movement, with Periyar staunchly opposing Mahatma Gandhi and setting his own approach to the caste system. While Gandhi had opposed the social exclusion of untouchables, he was unwilling to denounce the theological underpinnings of the caste system. Periyar, by contrast, had publicly committed himself to the destruction of the caste system. Faced with this ideological challenge from the Dravidian movement and the movements of the lower castes and electoral challenge from the Dravidian party, the Congress Party appointed Kumaraswami Kamaraj as its party president in 1946 and as chief minister in 1954. Kamaraj belonged to the Nadar caste, a Backward Caste group ranked only slightly above Dalits. With the introduction of universal franchise, the Congress Party had to turn to the support of lower-caste voters. The hold of the Congress Party on state politics lasted until 1967. During the 1960s, the central government's decision to make the use of Hindi mandatory triggered strong opposition in the Tamil-speaking state, paving the way for the victory of the *Dravida Munnetra Kazhagam* ("Dravidian Progress Federation"; DMK) in the 1967 election.[5] In

---

to the state; (3) In the general elections, the party should have polled a minimum of 6% of votes in a state and should have won one Lok Sabha seat or two state legislative assembly seats; or (4) The party wins at least 8% of the total votes cast in the state but fails to win either a Lok Sabha or state legislative assembly seat.

[4] See Lloyd I. Rudolph and Susanne Hoeber Rudolph, *The Modernity of Tradition: Political Development in India* (Chicago: University of Chicago Press, 1967); Christophe Jaffrelot, *India's Silent Revolution: The Rise of the Lower Castes* (New York: Columbia University Press, 2003).

[5] Hindi and Tamil come from different language families and use different scripts.

1972, the DMK split in two, and the *All India Anna Dravida Munnetra Kazhagam* ("All India Anna Dravidian Progress Federation"; AIADMK) was founded. Both Dravidian parties consistently emphasized issues of social as well as economic justice in their campaigns and discourse.[6]

The Dravidian parties mobilized voters on the basis of Tamil nationalism. The Dravidian or Tamil nationalist movement had been more inclusive of the lower castes and attracted a significant number of Dalits.[7] The existence of Dalit movements and the influence of egalitarian ideas popularized by Periyar meant that Dalits were drawn into the Tamil nationalist movement in search of equality. Through it, they had access to an identity that, at least in principle, situated them on par with everyone else. Moreover, the leaders of the major parties in the state were not viewed as icons for a particular caste group. Voters were encouraged to embrace party ideology and develop a deep loyalty for party leaders. The two Dravidian parties, the DMK and the AIADMK, used the medium of cinema to propagate their ideology and encouraged the development of fan clubs for film-star politicians. These fan clubs acted as a means of recruiting party workers across the state.[8] The attachment that parties were able to develop with voters has meant that political parties other than caste-based parties have come to acquire salience in the electoral arena. Indeed, populist politics directed at mobilizing the lower orders formed the foundation of Tamil politics.[9] This Dravidian populist politics followed two models. The model of patriarchal populism was centered on the benevolent leader who was the protector and caretaker of the poor and downtrodden. The politics of the AIADMK, under the leadership of M. G. Ramachandran and, later, Jayalalitha, fit this model. The model of assertive populism was based on the idea of claims made by the mobilized excluded groups. The DMK under Karunanidhi was an example of this model.[10]

The electoral opportunity that saw the emergence of multiple caste-based and multicaste parties in Tamil Nadu appeared because of the decline in the vote

[6] See Narendra Subramanian, *Ethnicity and Populist Mobilization: Political Parties, Citizens, and Democracy in South India* (New Delhi: Oxford University Press, 1999).

[7] See M.S.S. Pandian, *Brahmin and Non-Brahmin: Genealogies of the Tamil Political Present* (New Delhi: Permanent Black, 2007).

[8] See M.S.S. Pandian, *The Image Trap: M.G. Ramachandran in Film and Politics* (New Delhi: Sage, 1992).

[9] See Subramanian, *Ethnicity and Populist Mobilization*.

[10] Scholars have argued that often the pro-poor rhetoric has remained unmatched by policies. See D. A. Washbrook, "Caste, Class and Dominance in Modern Tamil Nadu: Non-Brahmanism, Dravidianism, and Tamil Nationalism," in Francine R. Frankel and M.S.A. Rao, eds., *Dominance and State Power in Modern India: Decline of a Social Order*, vol. 1 (New Delhi: Oxford University Press, 1989), pp. 204–264; Pandian, *The Image Trap*; Atul Kohli, *Democracy and Discontent: India's Growing Crisis of Governability* (Cambridge: Cambridge University Press, 1990).

Table 5.3. **Dravidian party vote shares in Tamil Nadu state assembly elections**

Year	DMK	AIADMK	Total
1967	40.69%	—	40.69%
1971	48.58%	—	48.58%
1977	24.89%	30.36%	55.25%
1980	22.10%	38.75%	60.85%
1984	29.34%	37.03%	66.37%
1989	33.18%	21.15% (JL) 9.19% (JR)	63.52%
1991	22.46%	44.39%	66.85%
1996	42.07%	21.47%	63.54%
2001	30.92%	31.44%	62.36%
2006	26.46%	32.64%	59.1%
2011	22.39%	38.40%	60.79%
2016	31.64%	40.77%	72.41%

Note: In 1989, the AIADMK was temporarily split into two factions led by Jayalalitha (JL) and Janaki Ramachandran (JR). Both women claimed authority to lead the party after the death of its longtime leader M. G. Ramachandran. Jayalalitha's faction prevailed in the elections and the dispute.

Source: Election Commission of India.

share of the two strong regional parties, the DMK and AIADMK, in the 1990s.[11] For decades, Tamil politics had revolved around these two parties. The total vote share of the rival Dravidian parties in the assembly elections stood at 67% in 1991, declined to 59.1% in 2006, and stood at 60.8% in 2011 (see Table 5.3). A similar decline also occurred in the combined parliamentary vote share of these rival Dravidian parties.[12] Party system fragmentation gathered pace at both the state and national levels, creating opportunities for smaller parties to succeed. Ethnic and multiethnic parties appeared during this phase, yet their success varied. Dalits have not turned to their ethnic parties in substantial numbers, and those Dalits who have turned away from the Dravidian parties have supported multiethnic parties in larger numbers than they have a Dalit ethnic party.

[11] See Andrew Wyatt, *Party System Change in South India: Political Entrepreneurs, Patterns, and Processes* (Abingdon: Routledge, 2010).

[12] As the Dravidian parties' vote share declined, they began to contest elections in alliances. This, then, makes it difficult to assess their actual vote share in the state. And it could very well be that the vote shares of the parties overestimate their popularity.

Table 5.4. **VCK performance in Tamil Nadu parliamentary elections**

Election	Seats Won/ Seats Contested	Vote Share	Alliance Details
2009	1/3	1.58%	In the national United Progressive Alliance (UPA) with the DMK. Thirumavalavan wins the Chidambaram (SC reserved) constituency.
2014	0/2	1.51%	Partnered with DMK in alliance with PT.

Source: Election Commission of India.

Table 5.5. **VCK performance in Tamil Nadu state assembly elections**

Election	Seats Won/ Seats Contested	Vote Share	Vote Share in Seats Contested	Alliance Details
2006	2/9	1.29%	36.09%	Partnered with AIADMK; given 8 SC-reserved seats and 1 general seat; wins 2 SC-reserved seats in Kattumannarkoil and Mangalore.
2011	0/10	1.51%	34.10%	Partnered with DMK; given 8 SC-reserved seats and 2 general seats.
2016	0/25	0.77%	6.98%	Partnered with the People's Welfare Alliance, a collection of 6 small parties.

Source: Election Commission of India.

The Emergence of VCK: The *Viduthalai Chiruthaigal Katchi* ("Liberation Panthers Party"; VCK), began to compete in elections in Tamil Nadu in 1999 under the leadership of the firebrand party chief Thol. Thirumavalavan. The VCK has been able to win an election to the national parliament only once, in 2009 (see Table 5.4). In the 2006 state assembly elections, it recorded its highest success when it won two electoral districts of the nine it contested as part of an electoral alliance with AIADMK (see Table 5.5). In 2011, it contested ten electoral districts as part of the DMK alliance and did not win a single seat. It also lost the two seats it contested in the 2014 parliamentary election. In the 2016 state assembly elections, the VCK, instead of joining one of the two Dravidian parties in an alliance, joined the People's Welfare Alliance, the third, weaker alliance of six small parties, in which it was allotted twenty-five seats. It failed to win a single seat and registered its lowest vote share. According to survey evidence gathered by the Center for the Study of Developing Societies after the different rounds of assembly and parliamentary elections, the percentage of Dalits who identify themselves as traditional supporters of the VCK has never been more than 5%.

A majority of the VCK's supporters come from among the numerically strong Paraiyars or Adi-Dravidas. The party and its workers, however, go to great lengths to refute the idea that they are a Paraiyar party. They view themselves as advocates for all Tamil Dalits. In Dalit localities, VCK party workers compete with workers from other political parties. Dravidian parties draw on Tamil identity-related issues to mobilize voters. To remain competitive and broaden his appeal beyond Dalits, Thol. Thirumavalavan also projects himself as a true champion of Tamils.[13] He has aligned himself with a variety of causes including the defense of Tamil culture and protection of the Tamil minority in Sri Lanka. In a crowded field of "Tamil political leaders," these efforts have had limited success.

The VCK's inability to mobilize Dalits in sufficiently large numbers hurts the party in pre-poll alliances.[14] The party has failed to claim a greater share of seats from its alliance partners. The VCK was given three seats in 2009 and two in the 2014 parliamentary elections as part of the DMK-led alliance. In the assembly elections, it was offered eight seats by DMK in 2001, nine seats in its alliance with AIADMK in 2006, and ten seats by the DMK alliance in 2011. The VCK had to turn to a much weaker alliance in 2016 to get an allotment of twenty-five seats. Alliance politics practiced by the VCK is sometimes viewed as a compromise on the ideals of Dalit assertion. But, in an FPTP system, there are few other ways for an emergent caste-based party to remain viable.[15]

A noteworthy fact is that even as the Dalit party has failed to attract the group to its fold, the *Desiya Murpokku Dravida Kazhagam* ("National Progressive Dravidian Party"; DMDK), a new multiethnic party that was launched as recently as the 2006 state assembly elections, has attained more popularity among Dalit voters. It garnered an 8.6% vote share among Dalits in the 2006 assembly elections and a 12% share in the 2009 parliamentary elections.[16] As an

[13] To improve his profile among Dalit voters, Thirumavalavan acted in two Tamil films, following in the footsteps of other film-star politicians. He also undertook a fundraising drive by soliciting donations of gold to the party. But these have not improved the electoral performance of the VCK.

[14] It is difficult to accurately assess the strength of a political party when it competes in elections as a part of an alliance. In such cases, the allotment of the number of electoral districts in the pre-election arrangement with the alliance partners, and the number of cabinet positions, can be used to assess the strength of the political party.

[15] Thirumavalavan himself acknowledged the constraints of alliance politics calling it a necessary evil when I interviewed him in 2006.

[16] DMDK did not contest the 2014 parliamentary elections.

emergent multiethnic party, it obtained a more favorable seat-sharing arrangement in a pre-poll alliance with the AIDMK in 2011; it contested forty-two electoral districts in that election.

Two other Dalit parties also compete in Tamil Nadu. These are the *Puthiya Tamilagam* ("New Tamil Society"; PT) and the BSP. Their vote shares have remained negligible, however (see Tables 5.6 and 5.7). The aggregate vote share of all the Dalit parties is less than 3% (see Table 5.8). A large majority of the Dalit vote share, including the Adi-Dravida vote share, has remained with the two

Table 5.6. **PT performance in Tamil Nadu state assembly elections**

Election	Seats Won/ Seats Contested	Vote Share	Vote Share in Seats Contested	Alliance Details
2001	0/10	1.27%	33.75%	Partnered with DMK; given 2 general seats and 8 SC-reserved seats.
2006	—	—	—	PT candidates compete under BSP symbol.
2011	2/2	0.4%	54.42%	Partnered with AIADMK; wins 2 SC-reserved seats in Nilakkottai and Ottapidaram.
2016	0/4	0.51%	33.00%	Joined the DMK alliance.

Source: Election Commission of India.

Table 5.7. **BSP performance in Tamil Nadu state assembly elections**

Election	Seats Won/ Seats Contested	Vote Share	Vote Share in Seats Contested
1991	0/11	0.01%	0.29%
1996	0/9	0.05%	1.38%
2001	0/17	0.07%	1.01%
2006	0/164	0.79%	1.14%
2011	0/193	0.54%	0.65%
2016	0/158	0.23%	0.34%

Note: The BSP has not allied with other parties at the state-level outside of Uttar Pradesh.

Source: Election Commission of India.

Table 5.8. **Dalit party vote shares in Tamil Nadu state assembly elections**

Year	VCK	PT	BSP	Total
1991	—	—	0.01%	0.01%
1996	—	—	0.05%	0.01%
2001	—	1.27%	0.07%	1.34%
2006	1.29%	—	0.79%	2.08%
2011	1.51%	0.40%	0.54%	2.45%
2016	0.77%	0.51%	0.23%	1.51%

Source: Election Commission of India.

Dravidian parties. According to the CSDS national and state assembly election studies, the combined vote share of DMK and AIDMK among Dalits has never gone below 60% in the parliamentary and state assembly elections between 1991 and 2016.

Electoral Mobilization of Dalits in Maharashtra

Maharashtra is home to India's oldest Dalit party, the Republican Party of India (RPI), formed in 1957, soon after the death of Dr. B. R. Ambedkar. Dr. Ambedkar created the Scheduled Caste Federation (SCF), which competed in the state assembly and parliamentary elections in 1952, and later developed into the RPI. After early success, the RPI's vote share declined. Still, RPI in the 1950s and 1960s counts as Maharashtra's most successful Dalit party.

The success of both SCF and the RPI drew on a strong Dalit movement. Mobilized Dalits, and Mahars (Maharashtra's largest Dalit subcaste) especially, voted in substantial numbers for these parties. In the 1951 state assembly elections, the SCF received 3.1% of the total vote share. Between 1957 and 1972, RPI's vote share went from 6.23% in 1957, to 5.38% in 1962, to 6.66% in 1967, and to 5.11% in 1972 (see Table 5.9).[17] The early success of SCF and RPI is attributable to two distinct factors. To begin with, franchise, in elections in the colonial period, was restricted on the basis of socioeconomic status across all provinces. Only 20% of India's colonial subjects enjoyed franchise in the

---

[17] The figures for RPI's vote share among Dalits are not available; however, their vote share of the total votes suggests that from 1957 onward the RPI received substantial support among Dalits.

provincial elections of 1937.[18] Prior to independence, then, political parties had few incentives for the electoral mobilization of the poor, including Dalits. The Congress, therefore, had a limited presence in Dalit localities.

A longer period of Congress dominance in Maharashtra was the second, more consequential reason. In Tamil Nadu, the DMK emerged as an early competitor to the Congress Party and compelled the Congress to make Dalit recruitment a priority. In Maharashtra, the Congress did not face similar pressures until later. As a result, when the SCF (and later the RPI) emerged from the Dalit movement, it was successful at mobilizing Dalits as an electoral bloc. With the commencement of electoral politics after independence in 1952, the dominant Congress Party was alerted to the strength of the RPI. The Congress, then, recruited among Dalits and appropriated their symbols and issues. Later, it allied with the RPI. Gradually, the Dalits shifted to the Congress. In the absence of electoral opportunity during the 1950s and 1960s, RPI's road to political office was blocked. This, then, made it difficult for the party to hold on to its Dalit vote share. Even as the Congress Party's dominance has declined, it has been able to retain a significant vote share among Dalits. Historically, Dalits have voted for the Congress Party, but with increasing fragmentation of the party system, other parties began to build a support base within the group (see Table 5.10).

After Dr. B. R. Ambedkar's death in 1956, the Dalit movement in Maharashtra was pulled in different directions. One faction was interested in promoting Buddhism while another was eager to take up the cause of the landless Dalits in the villages while cooperating with the Left and various Communist parties. Later, a divide appeared between a part of the movement that was focused on making demands related to better implementation of affirmative action policies, regarded as a middle-class interest, and a more militant, urban, slum-dwelling faction that wanted to protest and retaliate against atrocities suffered by Dalits. These ideological divisions appeared within the RPI as well and produced multiple factions. By 1989, there were as many as fifteen RPI factions all making a claim on Dr. B. R. Ambedkar's legacy. Divided, the RPI leaders became even more dependent on the Congress, which made their support easier to co-opt. But the Congress did not rely on the RPI alone to mobilize Dalits.

Since Dalits were organized, the Congress was compelled to recognize them to gain their support. It mobilized Dalits through direct recruitment in their localities and honoring their symbols rather than through intermediaries. It was attentive to issues of social as well as economic deprivation. Given the growing acceptance of the principle of social equality, the party has been able to mobilize

---

[18] Ornit Shani, "Making India's Democracy: Rewriting the Bureaucratic Colonial Imagination in the Preparation of the First Elections," *Comparative Studies of South Asia, Africa and the Middle East,* vol. 36, no. 1 (2016), pp. 83–101.

Table 5.9. **RPI performance in Maharashtra state assembly elections**

Election	Seats Won/ Seats Contested	Vote Share	Vote Share in Seats Contested
1962	3/66	5.38%	22.06%
1967	5/79	6.66%	22.15%
1972	2/118 (RPI)	3.77%	8.34%
	0/56 (RPK)	1.34%	6.03%
1978	2/25 (RPI)	1.06%	13.08%
	2/23 (RPK)	1.41%	17.96%
1980	0/36 (RPI)	0.76%	6.20%
	1/42 (RPK)	1.36%	9.18%
1985	0/54 (RPI)	1.00%	5.30%
	0/16 (RPK)	0.52%	8.56%
1990	0/21 (RPI)	0.70%	9.29%
	1/18 (RPK)	0.50%	7.89%
	0/1 (RPI (B))	0.00%	0.62%
	0/1 (RPPI)	0.00%	0.06%
1995	0/61 (RPI)	0.15%	0.66%
	0/13 (RPI(K))	0.17%	3.40%
	0/129 (BBMS)	3.03%	6.67%
1999	1/10 (RPI)	0.69%	19.82%
	0/1 (RPI(KH))	0.00%	1.01%
	3/34 (BBM)	1.85%	15.39%
2004	0/4 (RPI)	0.15%	11.03%
	1/20 (RPI(A))	0.49%	6.84%
	0/18 (RPI(D))	0.03%	0.41%
	0/2 (RPI(KM))	0.00%	0.22%
	1/83 (BBM)	1.23%	3.99%
2009	0/6 (RPI)	0.10%	4.73%
	0/79 (RPI(A))	0.85%	3.20%
	0/15 (RPI(D))	0.02%	0.48%
	0/5 (RPI(KH))	0.00%	0.14%
	0/1 (RPIE)	0.02%	6.09%
	1/103 (BBM)	0.83%	2.34%

Table 5.9. **Continued**

Election	Seats Won/ Seats Contested	Vote Share	Vote Share in Seats Contested
2014	0/39 (RPI)	0.12%	0.88%
	0/5 (RPI(A)	0.19%	11.65%
	0/5 (RPIE)	0.00%	0.24%
	0/3 (RPI (KH))	0.00%	0.08%
	0/2 (RPI(KM))	0.00%	0.18%
	1/70 (BBM)	.89%	3.64%

RPK/RPI(K)/RPI(KH) is the Republican Party of India (Khobragade) faction.
BBMS/BBM is the Bharipa Bahujan Mahasangha led by Prakash Ambedkar.
RPI(A) is the Republican Party of India (Athawale) faction.
RPI(D) is the Republican Party of India (Democratic) faction.
RPI(KM) is the Republican Party of India (Kamble) faction.
RPIE is the Republican Party of India Ektawadi faction.
It is not possible to trace RPI factions where the candidates have stood as independents.

Source: Election Commission of India.

Table 5.10. **Major party vote shares in Maharashtra state assembly elections**

Year	INC	NCP	BJP	Shiv Sena	Total
1962	51.22%	—	—	—	51.22%
1967	47.03%	—	—	—	47.03%
1972	56.36%	—	—	1.84%	58.20%
1978	18.34%	—	—	1.82%	20.16%
1980	44.50%	—	9.38%	—	53.88%
1985	43.41%	—	7.25%	—	50.66%
1990	38.17%	—	10.71%	15.94%	64.82%
1995	31.00%	—	12.80%	16.39%	60.19%
1999	27.20%	22.60%	14.54%	17.33%	81.67%
2004	21.06%	18.75%	13.67%	19.97%	73.45%
2009	21.0%	16.37%	14.02%	16.26%	67.65%
2014	17.95%	17.24%	27.81%	19.35%	82.35%

Source: Election Commission of India.

voters by using a mixture of caste-based and economic appeals. Other parties have also been following, gradually, in the same direction.

A large share of Dalit voters support the Congress Party and its allies, but with the fragmentation of the party system in the 1990s, other parties also recruit Dalit party workers in the state. In Maharashtra, the Congress Party's decline has been slower than in other states. The Congress Party's total vote share in 1951 was 51.1%. By 1996, it had fallen to 34.7%. It fell further to 23.6% in 2004. The party's vote share among Dalits fell from 77.3% in 1971 to 33% in 1996. In 2004, it stood at 38% and had fallen to 20% by 2009. Part of this vote share has gone to its alliance partner, the Nationalist Congress Party (NCP) that emerged from the Congress Party in 1998. Part of it has also shifted to the Hindu nationalist parties, the Shiv Sena and the Bharatiya Janata Party ("Indian People's Party"; BJP). The vote share of the Shiv Sena among Dalits increased from 9.8% in the 1996 parliamentary elections to 14% in 2014. During the same time, the vote share of the BJP also increased from 9.6% to 19%. In recent elections, the majority of the Dalit vote share got divided between the Congress Party–NCP alliance, on the one hand, and the alliance between the BJP and the Shiv Sena, on the other. For example, in the 2009 parliamentary election, the Congress Party–NCP alliance received 38% of the Dalit vote, whereas the Shiv Sena–BJP alliance received 19% of the Dalit vote. In the 2014 parliamentary elections, the Congress Party–NCP alliance received 42.9% of the Dalit vote, whereas the Shiv Sena–BJP alliance received 35.4% of the Dalit vote. In the 2014 state assembly election, the two alliances broke down, and, competing independently, the four parties received 78% of the Dalit vote share; the Congress 27.1%, the NCP 15.5%, the BJP 20.9%, and the Shiv Sena 12.4%.

The Emergence of BSP: The BSP, which entered electoral politics in Maharashtra during this period of opportunity, began contesting elections in 1999. The party contests elections across all the parliamentary and state assembly constituencies and has never been a part of a pre-poll alliance. Even though it has mobilized a Dalit electorate possessing high caste consciousness and immersed in Dalit ideology, the party has failed to gain a substantial share of the Dalit vote.

It is important to note that even in urban electoral districts where Dalit concentrations are high, the BSP has been unable to win a single parliamentary or state assembly district (see Tables 5.11 and 5.12). In 2004, the BSP received 11% of the Dalit vote share. The party's performance among Dalits peaked in the 2009 parliamentary election. The BSP's vote share jumped to 4.8% and it received 23% of the total Dalit votes while contesting across all 48 parliamentary districts. This surge in BSP support among Dalits occurred because the BSP, anticipating a divided verdict at the national level, projected Mayawati, the party president and the chief minister of Uttar Pradesh, as a possible prime ministerial candidate. When this did not come to pass, the party's vote share among Dalits fell back to 8% in the state assembly elections held later in the year. The BSP eschewed electoral alliances with the Congress Party–NCP and the Shiv Sena–BJP alliances. But since its vote share

Table 5.11. **BSP performance in Maharashtra parliamentary elections**

Election	Seats Won/ Seats Contested	Vote Share
1989	0/30	0.66%
1991	0/30	0.48%
1996	0/6	0.29%
1998	0/27	0.75%
1999	0/16	0.32%
2004	0/46	3.05%
2009	0/47	4.80%
2014	0/48	2.61%

Source: Election Commission of India.

Table 5.12. **BSP performance in Maharashtra state assembly elections**

Election	Seats Won/ Seats Contested	Vote Share	Vote Share in Seats Contested
1990	0/122	0.42%	0.98%
1995	0/145	1.49%	2.82%
1999	0/83	0.39%	1.24%
2004	0/272	4.00%	4.18%
2009	0/281	2.35%	2.42%
2014	0/280	2.25%	2.33%

Source: Election Commission of India.

among Dalits has remained limited, it has also failed to attract and retain strong Dalit and non-Dalit rebel leaders from other parties into its fold.

For a number of reasons, the BSP's performance has been a setback for the party, according to its officeholders. The party's founder, Kanshi Ram, had begun his activism in Maharashtra and had close connections with the Dalit movement in the state. Today, Mayawati is viewed as an icon in the Dalit community in the state. And, most important, the state is the land of Dr. B. R. Ambedkar, whose mantle the BSP claims to represent. A strong foothold in Maharashtra should have seriously legitimized the claim of the party to be the true heir of Dr. Ambedkar's legacy. This has not happened, though.

Dalits form 13% of Maharashtra's population. So, even if a majority of Dalits in the state support their ethnic party, such a party cannot come to power on its own.

Still, since the Mahars form a majority among Dalits, their consolidation into an electoral bloc holds the key to the rise of a Dalit party in the state. If the BSP was able to reproduce the early success of the RPI, and its vote share among Dalits in general and among Mahars in particular had risen to 50% or higher, it could have turned into a formidable political force in the state. In a fragmenting party system, it would have been able to attract more powerful candidates, and entered into beneficial social and electoral alliances. As it turned out, BSP's highest Dalit vote share touched 23% in the 2009 parliamentary elections, and fell away after that.

By the time the electoral opportunity arrived with the decline of the Congress during the 1990s and the accompanying fragmentation of the party system, the RPI was in no position to take advantage of the electoral opportunity that presented itself. With the passage of time, Congress's co-optation and factionalization within the party had depleted the RPI as a political force. The few relevant factions such as the one led by Ramdas Athawale, a leader associated with the Dalit Panther movement, and another renamed as Bharipa Bahujan Mahasangh (BBM) led by Prakash Ambedkar, the grandson of Dr. B. R. Ambedkar, contest elections in alliances with major and minor parties. But with the Dalit votes fragmented between multiple parties, their influence, as is visible in the number of seats contested, remains limited (see Table 5.13).

Table 5.13. **Dalit party vote shares in Maharashtra state assembly elections**

Year	All recognized RPI Factions	BSP	Total
1962	5.38%	—	5.38%
1967	6.66%	—	6.66%
1972	5.11%	—	5.11%
1978	2.47%	—	2.47%
1980	2.12%	—	2.12%
1985	1.52%	—	1.52%
1990	1.20%	0.42%	1.62%
1995	3.35%	1.49%	4.84%
1999	2.54%	0.39%	2.93%
2004	1.90%	4.00%	5.90%
2009	1.80%	2.35%	4.15%
2014	1.20%	2.25%	3.45%

Source: Election Commission of India.

Although social mobilization among Dalits is more pronounced in Tamil Nadu and Maharashtra than in Uttar Pradesh and Bihar, it does not automatically translate into electoral success for the VCK and the BSP, the emergent Dalit parties.

The Electoral Mobilization of Dalits in Uttar Pradesh and Bihar

The rise of Dalit parties in the states of Uttar Pradesh and Bihar was enabled by the appearance of the electoral opportunity created by the decline of the Congress Party and a fragmenting party system. It was also enabled by the weakening of mobilization constraints for Dalits, most of whom continue to live in rural areas, where such constraints are far more severe than in urban areas. The weakening of two mobilization constraints has aided the electoral mobilization of Dalits in Uttar Pradesh and Bihar in the past three decades.

First, by the early 1990s, upper-caste control of rural life was in serious decline in Uttar Pradesh and Bihar. Through the late 1960s and 1970s, the rise of intermediate-caste leaders, such as Charan Singh in Uttar Pradesh and Karpoori Thakur in Bihar, began to deny the upper castes ready access to state power for the first time. The sharp increase in agricultural productivity economically empowered landed members of the intermediate castes, who were at the forefront of challenging the upper-caste hegemony that the Congress had come to represent.[19] Further, in these states, the mechanization of agriculture and the fragmentation of landholdings altered the relationship between the predominantly landowning upper castes and the landless peasantry. The relationship of dependence between the landowners and their agricultural workers broke down. At the same time, outbound migration from rural to urban areas also made many rural Dalit families financially independent from dominant castes.[20] Second,

---

[19] Aditya Dasgupta, "Technological Change and Political Turnover: The Democratizing Effects of the Green Revolution in India," *American Political Science Review*, vol. 112, no. 4 (2018), pp. 918–938.

[20] My interviews in rural Uttar Pradesh and Bihar have also found this to be the case. It must be emphasized here, however, that financial independence does not necessarily mean prosperity. See also Dipankar Gupta, "Caste and Politics: Identity over System," *Annual Review of Anthropology*, vol. 34 (2005), pp. 409–427; Devesh Kapur, Chandra Bhan Prasad, Lant Pritchett, and D. Shyam Babu, "Rethinking Inequality: Dalits in Uttar Pradesh in the Market Reform Era," *Economic and Political Weekly*, vol. 45, no. 35 (2010), pp. 39–49.

although affirmative action policies have been imperfectly implemented, by the 1990s they had produced a fledgling Dalit middle class to support political entrepreneurs. The appearance of parties representing marginalized groups and Dalit leaders is an outcome of this process. Most of this mobilization still occurs around elections, however.

As already noted, mobilization in Uttar Pradesh and Bihar was affected by the zamindari landlord-based land settlement systems prevalent in the two states. Almost the entire Dalit population in these states lived in rural areas and was subservient to the authority of the landed castes. In the rural areas, Dalit mobilization remained constrained. In the first few decades after Indian independence in 1947, the landed elite enjoyed significant influence in local and state-level politics. The Congress Party relied on them to deliver the Dalit vote, and it did not have to mobilize Dalit voters directly in large parts of these two states.

Later, in 1969, under the leadership of Indira Gandhi, the Congress Party experienced an internal split that resulted in the temporary exit of the landed elite.[21] The Congress Party then tried to reach out to Dalits directly. Since Indira Gandhi no longer commanded the machine that had delivered the support of the subordinate groups, the party appealed to Dalits and highlighted its pro-poor programs. It took steps to make voting more secure for the marginalized. In order to reduce voter intimidation, the counting of votes was moved from polling booths to district headquarters, to ensure the anonymity of group voting.[22]

During the period of its dominance, the Congress Party adopted the strategy of mobilizing a coalition of caste groups. Each group was mobilized separately. Leaders were promoted from within the group, and different groups were brought together in an electoral coalition. In this asymmetric alliance, the Congress Party's leaders did not derive their importance from the numerical strength of their respective caste groups; instead, this leverage depended on whether the groups were well organized. In this arrangement, Dalits were doubly disadvantaged. Dalits were at the bottom of the social hierarchy, and despite their numerical strength, since they were the least organized, their leaders possessed the least leverage. But the separate mobilization of caste groups, including Dalits, as vote blocs, laid the foundation

---

[21] Their exit was temporary: after Indira Gandhi tightened her control over the party and political power, the landed elite thought better of resisting, and they returned to the party.

[22] While the secret ballot protects an individual voter's anonymity, figures taken from polling booths can reveal the parties for which particular groups are voting. Because politicians generally know the demographic breakdown that will be reflected in the figures coming from a particular polling booth, the practice of taking figures from polling booths is one that compromises a group's anonymity. For an illustration, see Harry W. Blair, "Ethnicity and Democratic Politics in India: Caste as a Differential Mobilizer in Bihar," *Comparative Politics,* vol. 5, no. 1 (1972), pp. 107–127.

for strong ethnic solidarity in voting and entrenched the practice of mobilization of vote blocs, which continues to be followed even today by the parties that have emerged in the wake of the Congress's decline.

In Uttar Pradesh and Bihar, the Congress Party, during the dominant phase that lasted until 1989, relied on a handful of Dalit leaders within the party to mobilize the Dalit vote. Even the prominent among these, such as Jagjivan Ram and B. P. Maurya, did not use their positions to denounce caste hierarchy or encourage the social mobilization of Dalits. As an organization, the Congress Party remained conservative. It did not include Dalits at the grass-roots level by spreading its network in their localities. The Congress Party worker was often from the dominant caste in the village and lived in a non-Dalit locality. Occasionally the Congress turned to the Dalit notables in the district to campaign in Dalit localities. Despite having come to rely heavily on Dalit support by the 1980s, the Congress Party's leadership could not promote a Dalit chief minister in either state.[23]

After driving out her political rivals and challengers from the Congress Party in 1969, Indira Gandhi centralized the party. This meant that chief ministers of states did not reflect popular choices but instead were appointed at her whim, and that, above all, Indira Gandhi was at the center of the mobilization. When she was assassinated in 1984, a wave of sympathy brought the Congress Party to power with the largest vote share in its history. But her death also took away the focal point around which the party had been organized in these two northern states. The significance of Indira Gandhi to Congress's mobilization can be gauged from the following slogans that were in use in 2004, twenty years after her death.

Jaat par na paat par, Indira-ji ki baat par, mohar lagegi haath par
Our vote will not be guided by caste or creed, but will go to Indira-ji on the hand symbol.[24]
Sonia nahi ye andhi hai, dusri Indira Gandhi hai
Sonia is a storm, a second coming of Indira Gandhi.[25]

---

[23] Of the four states, Maharashtra has the smallest Dalit population. Nevertheless, it is one of the very few states where the Congress Party has had a Dalit chief minister: Sushil Kumar Shinde, who went on to become home minister in the federal government. Although Shinde is a prominent Congress Party leader in the state, chief ministerial positions are decided by the national leadership. The decision to appoint Shinde was a strategic one, made in response to the BSP's entry into electoral politics in the state, and was noteworthy for this reason. While the Congress Party was able to appoint a Dalit chief minister in Maharashtra, it was not able to do so in Uttar Pradesh and Bihar, where the party relied on a much larger base of Dalit supporters.

[24] An open palm is the Congress's electoral symbol.

[25] Current Congress Party president, the widow of Rajiv Gandhi, and the daughter-in-law of Indira Gandhi.

During the 1991 parliamentary election campaign, Rajiv Gandhi, her son, was also assassinated. In the ensuing political vacuum, the social coalition that had defined Congress's electoral politics unraveled fairly swiftly, creating the opportunity for the emergence of caste-based parties. A period of fragmentation in the party system then set in. During this time, Dalits began to shift their votes to other parties in the two states. Between the 1960s and 1980s, the first stage of the Congress Party's decline in Uttar Pradesh and Bihar was gradual. Then the sudden loss of Indira Gandhi in 1984, and of her son Rajiv Gandhi in 1991, dealt a severe blow to the electoral fortunes of the party in both states, and triggered the second stage of decline, which was far more rapid. As a result, despite being the largest national party, it was unable to respond to the twin challenges of lower-caste as well as religious mobilization that swept Uttar Pradesh and Bihar during this period.[26]

The Rise of the BSP in Uttar Pradesh

The vote share of the Congress Party in parliamentary and state assembly elections in Uttar Pradesh fell sharply in the 1990s (see Table 5.14). The expanding political opportunity enabled the rise of a number of political parties, including the BSP. The BSP was not the first Dalit party to appear in Uttar Pradesh. The RPI competed in some parts of the state during the 1960s and 1970s; however, its influence remained limited outside a few semi-urban districts especially in western Uttar Pradesh. Agra, Aligarh, and Meerut emerged as important centers for RPI's assertion.[27] It recorded its best electoral performance in 1962 when its vote share touched 12.32% in state assembly elections. Just as in Maharashtra, under the shadow of the Congress Party's dominance, and in the absence of political opportunity, the party disappeared, with its key leaders such as B. P. Maurya joining the Congress Party.[28] The BSP made an appearance in the state

---

[26] Had the Congress Party not lost Indira and Rajiv Gandhi in quick succession, it is likely that it would have survived the twin challenges of Hindu nationalist and lower-caste mobilization, instead of suffering a dramatic fall in its vote share. The Backward-Caste mobilization demanded quotas in government jobs and educational institutions. The upper-caste-led Hindu nationalist mobilization demanded the construction of a temple for Lord Ram in the town of Ayodhya, at the site of a sixteenth-century mosque. The Hindu nationalists alleged that the mosque was built by destroying a Ram temple, and launched a countrywide movement for the restoration of the temple.

[27] See Owen M. Lynch, *The Politics of Untouchability: Social Mobility and Social Change in a City of India* (New York City: Columbia University Press, 1969); Paul. R. Brass, *Caste, Faction and Party in Indian Politics* (New Delhi: Chanakya, 1985); Jagpal Singh, *Capitalism and Dependence: Agrarian Politics in Western Uttar Pradesh, 1951–91* (New Delhi: Manohar, 1992).

[28] See Ghanshyam Shah, ed., *Caste and Democratic Politics in India* (Dehli: Anthem Press, 2004); Jaffrelot, *India's Silent Revolution*.

Table 5.14. **Major party vote shares in Uttar Pradesh state assembly elections**

Year	Congress	BJP	BSP	SP
1951	47.93%	—	—	—
1957	42.42%	—	—	—
1962	36.33%	—	—	—
1967	32.20%	—	—	—
1969	33.69%	—	—	—
1974	32.29%	—	—	—
1977	31.94%	—	—	—
1980	37.65%	10.76%	0.00%	—
1985	39.25%	9.83%	0.00%	—
1989	27.90%	11.61%	9.41%	—
1991	17.32%	31.45%	9.44%	—
1993	15.08%	33.30%	11.12%	17.94%
1996	8.35%	32.52%	19.64%	21.80%
2002	8.96%	20.08%	23.06%	25.37%
2007	8.61%	16.97%	30.43%	25.43%
2012	11.65%	15.00%	25.91%	29.13%
2017	6.25%	39.67%	22.23%	21.82%

Source: Election Commission of India.

in 1986 and subsequently emerged as India's most successful and prominent Dalit party.

The BSP's electoral performance improved steadily from 1986 on, and its vote share expanded among Dalits. In 2007, the party became the first Dalit party to form a government on its own in any state in India. The BSP held the chief ministerial position on four occasions. Three of these governments were in coalition with other parties that collapsed because of internal differences.[29] In the 2007 state assembly elections, the BSP was able to win a majority in the state assembly.

Consider the electoral performance of the BSP since 1984, the year it first contested elections in Uttar Pradesh. Its tally of electoral victories in the national

---

[29] The BSP held this position not on its own strength, but as part of a ruling coalition, which collapsed each time before the expiration of the tenure of the state assembly. Mayawati, the president of the BSP, herself a Dalit, held the chief minister's position.

Table 5.15. **BSP performance in Uttar Pradesh parliamentary elections**

Election	Seats Won/ Seats Contested	Vote Share
1989	2/75	9.93%
1991	1/67	8.70%
1996	6/85	20.61%
1998	4/85	20.90%
1999	14/85	22.08%
2004	19/80	24.67%
2009	20/80	27.42%
2014	0/80	19.77%

Source: Election Commission of India.

Table 5.16. **BSP performance in Uttar Pradesh state assembly elections**

Election	Seats Won/ Seats Contested	Vote Share	Vote Share in Seats Contested	Alliance Details
1989	13/372	9.41%	10.72%	—
1991	12/386	9.44%	10.26%	—
1993	67/164	11.12%	28.53%	BSP-SP coalition government.
1996	67/296	19.64%	27.73%	BSP-BJP coalition government; Mayawati is chief minister.
2002	98/401	23.06%	23.19%	—
2007	206/403	30.43%	30.43%	—
2012	80/403	25.91%	25.95%	—
2017	19/403	22.23%	22.23%	—

Note: Before 1989, BSP candidates stood as independents in elections in Uttar Pradesh.
Source: Election Commission of India.

elections went from one in 1991, to six in 1996, to fourteen in 1999, to nineteen in 2004, and to twenty in 2009 (see Table 5.15). In 2014, despite a vote share of 19%, it did not win a single seat in the parliamentary elections. In the state assembly elections, its tally increased from 13 in 1989, to 67 in 1993, to 98 in 2002, and to 206 in 2007. It fell to 80 in 2012 and to 19 in 2017 (see Table 5.16). Although the BSP's vote share among other communities gradually increased, its electoral success was built largely on the support that the BSP has been able to garner from the Dalit community in general and the Chamar or Jatav community in particular. Jatavs form 55% of the Dalit population in Uttar Pradesh, and Mayawati, the BSP president, belongs to this caste. Its electoral strength and the shared stigma of untouchability have also drawn other prominent Dalit castes such as Valmikis and Pasis to the BSP. The party received plurality support among these groups. For example, in the 2012 state assembly election in which the BSP government was voted out of power, 42% of the Valmiki and 57% of the Pasi vote was cast for the BSP.

According to survey data gathered by CSDS after the 1996 and the 2004 parliamentary elections, 63.8% and 68% of Dalits, respectively, voted for the BSP. This share jumped to 78% by 2009 and fell to 56.2% in the 2014 elections. But in the 2014 parliamentary elections, 70% of the Jatavs still voted for the BSP. A similar pattern of Dalit support for the BSP was visible in the state assembly elections. High levels of support within the caste allowed the BSP to enter into advantageous pre-election alliances during the state assembly elections in 1993 and 1996 and to establish itself as a major party in the state.[30] The BSP's hold over the Dalit vote, especially that of the Jatavs, also made it attractive to political entrepreneurs belonging to other caste groups—a prerequisite for electoral success. These have varied in strength and duration. Although the BSP's electoral fortunes have changed, the majority of Dalits have continued to vote for the party.

For emergent Dalit parties, capturing a substantial part of the group's vote allows them to attract electable candidates from outside the caste group. Such candidates bring with them additional vote share as well as resources. These resources take two forms—financial resources and, occasionally, the ability to provide protection from threatening dominant castes. A dominant-caste candidate ensures that Dalits enjoy protection through the duration of campaigning as well as on polling day. Given their support base, Dalit parties usually lack these resources. A BSP official summed up this challenge for me pithily: "To succeed,

---

[30] In 1993, the BSP was in an alliance with the Samajwadi Party (SP), the ethnic party of the Backward Castes. In 1996, the BSP was in alliance with the Congress Party, the only other party with significant Dalit support. In both instances, the BSP improved on its previous vote share, establishing itself as a major political party in the state.

any party needs the support of the three M's—money, media, and mafia. We are without the three Ms. That is why we pick candidates who can contribute to the party and who can take on the strongmen of other parties." Explaining the significance of security in the mobilization process, a BSP district president said, "*Jagriti* [awareness] is important for people to seek self-respect, but *suraksha* [security] is equally important. Once voting became free in this area, the rest happened on its own." The *bahubalis*—strongmen with a criminal background who have entered politics in substantial numbers—rarely come from among the Dalits.[31] Given the direct and indirect role of such individuals in electoral politics, every party turns to them. Dalit parties that have the most vulnerable voters rely on them for the ability to campaign in dominant-caste strongholds, to mobilize Dalit voters, and to guarantee safety to their voters after the elections.

A high vote share also enables a Dalit party to enter into favorable seat-sharing arrangements with larger parties. The larger the vote share that a Dalit party is projected to control, the more substantial its bargaining power in the negotiation over electoral districts. A strong base of dedicated voters has enabled the BSP to form strategic alliances with other parties that possess a favorable seat distribution; however, the party discarded this strategy after the 1996 election and will return to it in the 2019 parliamentary elections to revive its electoral fortunes. To counter the rising vote share of the BJP, the BSP has allied with its former rival, the SP, for the 2019 parliamentary elections. The BSP has also experimented with the strategy of building group-based alliances.[32] It has forged strategic group alliances between Dalits and Other Backward Castes (OBCs), Dalits and Brahmins, and Dalits and Muslims. These have varied in strength and duration. In fact, the 2007 state assembly election saw a complete reversal of the BSP's early position of being an anti-upper-caste party. It ran a campaign as a Dalit-Brahmin alliance. Two things are noteworthy about the BSP's strategy of widening its base of support. First, the party has mimicked the Congress Party's strategy of bringing caste and religious blocs together to build an electoral coalition. Whether it is a Dalit-Brahmin alliance or a Dalit-Muslim alliance, it assumes the existence of these caste and religious blocs. It therefore relies on making group-based appeals rather than cross-group appeals during the electoral campaign. Second, the party enjoys enough loyalty among its core supporters to practice complete ideological reversals. It has insulted the upper castes during an electoral campaign and also allied with them.

[31] See Milan Vaishnav, *When Crime Pays: Money and Muscle in Indian Politics* (New Haven: Yale University Press, 2017).

[32] According to functionaries in a party alliance, while Dalits transfer their votes to other parties, supporters of the ally do not transfer their votes to the BSP.

As support for the Congress Party declined among Dalits, it was the BSP that benefited, not another multiethnic party. The electoral rise of the Hindu nationalist BJP in Uttar Pradesh corresponds with the Congress Party's decline. In 1989, the BJP's vote share in Uttar Pradesh was 7.6%; by 1996 it had increased to 33.4%, but it fell to 22.1% in 2004 before rising to 44.4% in the 2014 parliamentary elections. The BJP, as it expanded its vote share in the 1990s, broadened its caste base, and to this end, made inroads into the intermediate or Backward Castes.[33] Among Dalits, however, the BJP's influence remained limited in rural areas, where most Dalits live. Interviews showed that for the BJP local leaders in rural areas, the primary focus of recruitment was on Backward-Caste members. Members of these castes, as compared to Dalits, were less vulnerable to intimidation and disrespect from other groups. The BJP's attempt to recruit Dalits met with less success. "We recruited Dalit boys and even put them in a position of authority," a BJP district president said during an interview in 2004, "but the party workers from higher castes did not accept their authority, so after a point the Dalit boys would leave our party." I also heard this view repeatedly during my conversations with Dalit party workers.

The rise of the BSP in Uttar Pradesh has produced two changes. First, it has increased self-awareness and a sense of security among Dalit political aspirants, especially at the local level. The BSP's electoral success has mainstreamed Dalit politics in the state and has begun to normalize the presence of Dalits in positions of authority. An upper-caste member of the Uttar Pradesh legislative assembly who was previously with the Congress and had subsequently joined the BJP, noted the change in 2015, "The new generation of Dalits is far more confident and fearless. The upper caste resent this change, but the ground has shifted, the days of domination are ending." "When people from the upper caste have to turn to Jatav leaders and officials to get work done," he explained, "then they cannot continue to look down on them. There is no jati or caste greater than the state." Second, BSP[34] has also popularized Dalit symbols. The BJP has benefited from these changes. The BJP has gradually begun deploying Dalit symbols, increasing recruitment among Dalits, and expanding its support among the community. To break the hold of the BSP on the Dalit vote, the BJP has especially targeted smaller non-Jatav Dalit subcastes in search of Dalit electoral blocs instead of using cross-caste appeals to mobilize Dalits. In this sense, it is following in the footsteps of the Congress and the BSP. The party has few Dalit faces internally, and has recruited emergent Dalit leaders such as Udit Raj to promote its image

---

[33] See Jaffrelot, *India's Silent Revolution*.

[34] He meant that Dalits who are state officials or in elected office, because of their association with the state, command respect from everyone, including members of higher castes.

Table 5.17. **Congress Party vote shares in Bihar state assembly elections**

Year	Congress
1951	41.38%
1957	42.09%
1962	41.35%
1967	33.09%
1969	30.46%
1972	33.12%
1977	23.58%
1980	34.20%
1985	39.30%
1990	24.78%
1995	16.27%
2000	11.06%
February 2005	5.00%
October 2005	6.09%
2010	8.37%
2015	6.66%

Source: Election Commission of India.

within the group.[35] According to the NES, BJP's vote share among Dalits in Uttar Pradesh had reached 25% in 2014.

The Rise of the LJP in Bihar

The decline of the Congress Party in Bihar was swift. The vote share of the party in the state assembly elections slipped from 41.38% in 1951, to 34.20% in 1980, and then to 24.78% in 1990 (see Table 5.17). The pattern of Congress decline was replicated in the parliamentary elections. According to CSDS, its vote share among Dalits fell from 70% in 1971, to 19.6% in 1996, and then to 4.1% in 2004. The Congress Party's collapse in Bihar did not result in the immediate emergence of a Dalit party as it did in Uttar Pradesh. In response to this

---

[35] Udit Raj is a former senior government official who set up the Indian Justice Party. He belongs to the Valmiki subcaste among Dalits.

period of opportunity in the political system, parties dominated by intermediate castes came to control state politics. The *Janata Dal* ("People's Group"; JD) came to power in 1990. The JD had among its ranks two leaders who embodied lower-caste aspirations—Lalu Prasad Yadav and Ram Vilas Paswan, one from a Backward Caste and the other a Dalit, but both originally from poor families. These two leaders emerged as a symbol of resistance to upper-caste dominance, which in Bihar was more pronounced than in Uttar Pradesh. In sharp contrast to the pliant lower-caste and Dalit leadership of the Congress, they were assertive in their public pronouncements and openly disdainful of the caste hierarchy. Both had been mentored by Karpoori Thakur, one of Bihar's most prominent lower-caste leaders during the phase of Congress dominance. Under the banner of the JD, Lalu Prasad Yadav was able to develop a broad coalition of the Backward Castes, Dalits, and Muslims, against the upper castes. The JD mobilized Dalits on the basis of an anti-upper-caste alliance constructed against the backdrop of the struggle over land rights in the state. The emergence of this party also coincided with the intensification of the violence between dominant-castes-backed landlord armies and the Maoist guerrillas fighting in the name of the landless peasants during the 1980s and 1990s.

During the tenure of Lalu Prasad Yadav's government, economic development in the state began to stall quite severely between 1990 and 1995. In 1996, though, the JD split. Lalu Yadav formed his own party, the *Rashtriya Janta Dal* ("National People's Group"; RJD) (see Table 5.18). Lalu Yadav's coalition had shrunk to the Yadavs, a sizable Backward Caste group, along with Dalits and Muslims. After a series of scandals related to the laundering of public money, and with a worsening situation in Bihar with respect to the economy and as

Table 5.18. **Lower-caste party vote shares in Bihar state assembly elections**

Year	JD/JD(U)	RJD	LJP	BSP	Total
1990	25.61%	—	—	0.73%	26.34%
1995	27.98%	—	—	1.34%	29.32%
2000	6.47%	28.34%	—	1.89%	36.70%
February 2005	14.55%	25.07%	12.62%	4.41%	56.65%
October 2005	20.46%	23.45%	11.10%	4.17%	59.18%
2010	22.58%	18.84%	6.74%	3.21%	51.37%
2015	16.83%	18.35%	4.83%	2.07%	42.08%

Source: Election Commission of India.

well as to law and order, the RJD began to lose its vote share as different groups drifted away from the party. This development then created another opening for small parties. In 2000, the *Lok Janshakti Party* ("People's Power Party"; LJP) was launched by Bihar's most prominent Dalit leader, Ram Vilas Paswan.

Since the social structure in the state had not been challenged by a movement opposing social hierarchy, caste group separation remained strong. The Congress Party therefore mobilized each group separately and unequally. Initially, Dalits were not mobilized. Later, as the Congress Party began to mobilize them directly, even though Dalits derived minimal benefits from group-based electoral coalitions, repeated group-based mobilization reinforced their caste identity and created bonds of solidarity in the electoral arena. The JD, and later the RJD and LJP, all took advantage of it. For example, while the RJD's appeal transcended different groups, its mobilization strategy was similar to that of the Congress Party, with groups mobilized separately. In this sense, the RJD was also a group alliance, albeit a lower-caste-led one. Electoral mobilization in both Uttar Pradesh and Bihar continues to follow the long-standing pattern of the aggregation of caste blocs.

Despite a political opportunity structure favoring the rise of an ethnic party since the early 1990s, the emergence of a local Dalit party was delayed for a number of reasons. For Ram Vilas Paswan, to launch an independent Dalit party was a risky step. His own caste, the Dusadhs, are not the largest Dalit subcaste in Bihar. Additionally, in Bihar, the Backward Caste and Dalit leadership took the same path to electoral politics and were mentored by the same leaders. This enabled the rise of leaders such as Nitish Kumar, Lalu Prasad Yadav, and Ram Vilas Paswan as political allies. Gradually, as allies turned political rivals, they launched their separate ethnic parties.

In state assembly and parliamentary elections the LJP's electoral performance has varied; however, it has been superior to the performance of the VCK in Tamil Nadu and the BSP in Maharashtra. In the parliamentary elections, the LJP's seat tally went from 4 in 2004, to 0 in 2009, and to 6 in 2014 (see Table 5.19). The LJP's seat tally in state assembly elections fluctuated from 10 in 2005, to 3 in 2010, and to 2 in 2015 (see Table 5.20). As is the case with the other small parties that contest elections as part of pre-poll alliances, because the LJP has been contesting elections in a limited number of electoral districts, it is difficult to judge its statewide popularity among Dalits. In the 2005 state assembly election, when the LJP contested alone, it received 31% of the Dalit vote, a plurality. Its total vote share was 12.6%. It won 29 seats in that election.[36] Expectedly,

---

[36] When parties, especially the RJD and LJP, could not agree on a coalition arrangement, Bihar went to elections again in the same year to elect a new government. Ram Vilas Paswan was blamed for his intransigence in coalition talks, the non-Dalit leaders and their supporters deserted, and LJP won only ten seats the second time around. The party's total vote share fell to 11.1 percent.

Table 5.19. **LJP performance in Bihar parliamentary elections**

Election	Seats Won/ Seats Contested	Vote Share	Alliance Details
2004	4/8	—	In alliance with RJD and Congress.
2009	0/12	6.55%	In alliance with RJD.
2014	6/7	6.50%	In alliance with BJP as part of National Democratic Alliance (NDA).

Source: Election Commission of India.

Table 5.20. **LJP performance in Bihar state assembly elections**

Election	Seats Won/ Seats Contested	Vote Share	Vote Share in Seats Contested
February 2005	29/178	12.62%	17.33%
October 2005	10/203	11.10%	13.22%
2010	3/75	6.74%	21.78%
2015	2/42	4.83%	28.79%

Source: Election Commission of India.

the LJP's popularity is particularly high among Dusadhs. According to CSDS, when the LJP contested the 2005 state assembly election on its own, 65 percent Dusadhs supported the party. Since then a majority has voted for the pre-poll alliance LJP has joined before the state assembly elections, including the 2015 election in which 51 percent of Dusadhs voted for the National Democratic Alliance. In the 2009 parliamentary elections, 55% of the Dusadhs voted for the LJP-RJD alliance, and in the 2014 parliamentary elections, 50% of the Dusadhs voted for the LJP-BJP alliance.[37]

The LJP's support among Dalits has allowed it to attract prominent non-Dalit candidates to its fold. The LJP has also entered into favorable pre-poll alliances with larger parties. In parliamentary elections, the RJD and the Congress Party offered the LJP eight out of forty electoral districts in 2004, the party contested

---

[37] In the 2015 state assembly election, the LJP–BJP alliance received 50 percent of the Dusadh vote share.

twelve districts in alliance with RJD in 2009, and seven electoral districts in alliance with BJP in 2014.

As compared to Dalit parties in movement states, the LJP won more seats in the parliamentary and state assembly elections, successfully bargained for better seat sharing arrangements, and most important, mobilized more Dalits in its support. At the same time, the LJP's electoral success has been limited as compared to the BSP's in Uttar Pradesh because of the overall size of the Dalit population as well as the relative size of the subcaste the party relies upon for its core support. As compared to Dalits in Uttar Pradesh who are 21% of the state's population, Dalits form 16% of the population of Bihar. Moreover, while Jatavs are 56% of the Dalit population in Uttar Pradesh, Dusadhs form only 31% of the Dalit population of Bihar.

The LJP has been unable to distinguish itself in the eyes of Dalit voters to the same extent as the BSP in Uttar Pradesh because the RJD and the JD(U) already represent issues of lower-caste dignity. Lalu Yadav and Nitish Kumar are not Dalits, they are OBC leaders, and still, during my interviews I found that they were held in high regard among Dalits in Bihar. Their popularity among Dalit voters also undercuts the electoral prospects of the LJP. Mulayam Yadav, the most prominent OBC leader in Uttar Pradesh, and his son Akhilesh Yadav, the state's chief minister between 2012 and 2017, by contrast, were not viewed similarly by Dalits in their state. Mayawati was the tallest leader for Dalits in Uttar Pradesh. And yet, unlike the BSP, the LJP, without being in power at the state level in Bihar, has retained its significance in state-level as well as national politics. Ram Vilas Paswan has emerged as the premier Dalit icon in the state.

The BSP also contests elections in Bihar, but its performance has been limited so far. Its best performance in the state was recorded in the 2005 state assembly elections when its vote share among Dalits was 10%, and it won four electoral districts in the state assembly (see Tables 5.21 and 5.22).[38]

Although much of the support for the LJP comes from among the Dusadhs, other Dalits also support the party. Nitish Kumar, who has been Bihar's chief minister since 2005, has tried to draw Dalits away from the LJP and the RJD by creating a new category of *Mahadalits* or "the most disadvantaged Dalit castes." Again this effort of fragmenting Dalit identity has aimed to mobilize Dalit subcastes as a voting bloc through the use of ethnic appeals.

---

[38] The BSP's success in Bihar has been relatively limited because Chamars, the caste from which the BSP draws the majority of its support, are poorer and therefore lack a mobilizing class similar to either the Dusadhs in Bihar or fellow Chamars in Uttar Pradesh.

Table 5.21. **BSP performance in Bihar state assembly elections**

Election	Seats Won/ Seats Contested	Vote Share	Vote Share in Seats Contested
1990	0/164	0.73%	1.41%
1995	0/161	1.34%	2.66%
2000	5/249	1.89%	2.47%
February 2005	2/238	4.41%	4.50%
October 2005	4/212	4.17%	4.75%
2010	0/239	3.21%	3.27%
2015	0/228	2.07%	2.21%

Source: Election Commission of India.

Table 5.22. **BSP performance in Bihar parliamentary elections**

Election	Seats Won/ Seats Contested	Vote Share
1989	0/6	0.10%
1991	0/24	0.14%
1996	0/33	0.63%
1998	0/3	0.53%
1999	0/30	0.95%
2004	0/40	3.58%
2009	0/39	4.61%
2014	0/40	2.17%

Source: Election Commission of India.

During the period of electoral opportunity, how well an ethnic party of the marginalized group performs depends on the level of ethnic solidarity among ethnic voters. Why were the BSP and the LJP far more successful in organizing Dalits into electoral blocs? Since voters are supposed to vote their caste in India, why were similar Dalit electoral blocs not available to the VCK in Tamil Nadu and to the BSP in Maharashtra? Next, I show that the difference in Dalit vote shares of Dalit parties across movement and non-movement states reflects a divergence in group attitudes toward caste-based bloc voting.

Ethnic Bloc Voting in Movement and
Non-movement States

On their own, vote shares are an insufficient indicator of caste-based bloc voting. After all, voters from a particular caste group could support the same party not just out of a sense of group solidarity, but for a number of other reasons. Consider the following hypothetical case: If 60% of an ethnic group votes for its ethnic party, it cannot automatically be assumed that each one of these voters is driven by a sense of ethnic solidarity, and that the majority support represents a case of ethnic bloc voting. Because, for example, 15% of the voters could have supported the ethnic party simply because they thought it was going to be the winning party, while 10% may have turned to the ethnic party to signal their dissatisfaction to another party that they traditionally supported. Yet another 20% group of voters could have voted for the ethnic party because they found the party leader to be charismatic or the candidate to be sincere, not their ethnicity. Taken together, out of the 60% vote share of the ethnic party within the group, 45% of the voters then may not be voting their ethnicity. To establish the existence of ethnic bloc voting with some degree of certainty then, vote shares must be further corroborated by voter testimony. I turn to the data from the Indian National Election Study and my focus group discussions and interviews to confirm divergent dispositions to ethnic bloc voting among Dalits in the movement and non-movement states.

In the 2004 Indian National Election Study, voters were presented with the following proposition: "It is important to vote the same way as members of one's caste or community." In Tamil Nadu and Maharashtra, 38% of Dalits agreed with the proposition, whereas in Uttar Pradesh and Bihar, 54% agreed with it.[39] The same proposition had been put to Dalit respondents in the 1971 Indian National Election Study. At that time, 40.51% of Dalits in movement states and 59.5% of Dalits in the non-movement states agreed with it.

A linear regression of 827 Dalits' attitudes toward voting with caste members across Tamil Nadu and Maharashtra as well as across Uttar Pradesh and Bihar (Table 5.23) shows that when other variables (education, age, location, socioeconomic status, and gender) of voters are controlled for, the variable called *state type* (referring to movement versus non-movement states) is statistically significant. The Dalit respondent's attitude towards caste-based voting is

---

[39] I asked the same question on a survey in 2016 to Dalits in Tamil Nadu and Uttar Pradesh. While in Tamil Nadu, 43.8% Dalits agreed with the proposition, in Uttar Pradesh, 57.2% Dalits expressed agreement. The survey interviewed 584 Dalits in Uttar Pradesh and 458 Dalits in Tamil Nadu. The survey was a part of an ongoing study that explores the relationship between skin color and caste in the two states.

Table 5.23. **Linear regression of Dalit attitudes toward bloc voting**

Independent Variable	t	Standard Error
State type (movement or non-movement)	0.929***	0.160
Education	−0.417***	0.080
Age	−0.067	0.057
Location (rural or urban)	−0.13	0.234
Socioeconomic status	−0.089	0.062
Gender	0.386**	0.162

n = 827 respondents.
*p < 0.1; **p < 0.05; ***p < 0.01

the dependent variable. The location of the Dalit respondent, in a movement or a non-movement state, is the key independent variable. The finding suggests a distinct difference between movement and non-movement states with respect to attitudes toward bloc voting.

Dalits in Uttar Pradesh and Bihar were more likely to agree with the proposition of voting with caste members than were Dalits in Tamil Nadu and Maharashtra. Testimonies of focus group participants and interview subjects reflected this difference. In Tamil Nadu, during a focus group discussion, Dalits pointed out that caste discrimination was only one of the many challenges they faced. Often it was common needs in their area, and not caste, that motivated their support for political parties. One participant said, "Our community is treated badly, but there are other problems, too. We face the same difficulties as other castes living in our area." In addition, voters did not identify parties with particular castes. As one voter in Maharashtra put it, "If a party will look into the welfare of the poor, then why should we look at caste?"

In Uttar Pradesh and Bihar, the testimonies were qualitatively different. The focus group discussions shed light on how Dalits viewed collective voting. "During the elections, the *samaj* [the Dalit community in the locality] decides, and then most follow the *samaj*," explained one participant. The same sentiment was echoed in another discussion: "Most people in the village vote their caste. Our community does the same." When asked whether it was important to vote with members of one's caste community, a discussion participant in Bihar asked, "Who else will one vote with?" "Elections are about caste. Like everyone I will vote with my caste members," said one participant in a focus group in Uttar Pradesh.

When Dalits discussed their interest in bloc voting, they were rarely motivated by the caste of the candidate. For the most part, they were drawn to the party or its leadership. Dalits also interpreted their caste identity as their subcaste identity. So for example, when Jatavs in Uttar Pradesh said that it was important for them to vote with their fellow caste members, they meant fellow Jatavs, and not other Dalit subcastes. The same was true for Dusadhs in Bihar, Adi-Dravidas or Paraiyars in Tamil Nadu, and Mahars in Maharashtra.

The difference in attitudes toward bloc voting is not a reflection of ethnic parties' success in some states and their relative failure in others. It predates the 1990s fragmentation of the party system and the rise of ethnic parties. The Indian National Election Study data help us trace the variation as far back as 1971. Further, a strong preference for bloc voting is also expressed in Madhya Pradesh and Rajasthan, two states where fragmentation of the party system has not occurred and where the success of Dalit ethnic parties has been limited, which suggests that caste-based bloc voting attitudes exist independent of ethnic party success.[40]

Dalits in movement states do not vote in blocs, and instead divide their votes among different parties. Dalit support for political parties has continued to fragment along with the fragmentation of the party system since the 1990s. Voter testimonies in Tamil Nadu and Maharashtra point out that this fragmentation of support extends to the locality level; of 203 Dalit interview subjects, 47.2% said that members of their community in the locality supported different parties, and 23.6% of the subjects reported that members of their community in the locality voted for the same party.

When asked which parties had a stronghold in the locality, a focus group participant in Tamil Nadu said, "It is like the films. People like different stars. Similarly, people like different parties in our locality."[41] During an interview, a subject explained how support for party choice had shifted among the new generation in her locality. She said, "The older generation in our locality supports the AIDMK and sometimes the DMK, but young people support the DMDK or the VCK." The testimonies in Maharashtra pointed to a similar outcome. A teacher in the village school said during the interview, "It is difficult to tell how people in our locality vote. In our community, there are supporters and activists of different parties. In this village alone, there is a group that supports the

---

[40] According to the 2004 Indian National Election Survey, 61 percent of Dalits in Rajasthan and 59 percent of Dalits in Madhya Pradesh agreed with the proposition that it is important to vote with fellow caste members; see Center for the Study of Developing Societies, *Indian National Election Study, 2004* (New Delhi: Center for the Study of Developing Societies, 2004). In both states, fragmentation of the party system has been limited.

[41] A number of prominent Tamil politicians—including M. G. Ramachandran (former chief minister of Tamil Nadu), Vijaykanth (Vijayaraj Alagarswami Naidu, current opposition leader in Tamil Nadu's legislative assembly), and Jayalalitha (Jayalalitha Jayaram)—have used a successful film career as a springboard to a career in politics.

RPI and another that votes for the Congress Party." In a focus group in an urban Dalit locality, a participant said, "In my house, my wife and I support different parties. She voted for the NCP and I voted for the BSP. No one party has a hold on our community." Andre Beteille reminds us, "To the extent that a caste does not identify itself persistently with any particular party but tends to divide and subdivide and to enter into multifarious alliances across its boundaries, its very contours ultimately become blurred."[42]

With Dalits less amenable to bloc voting, sometimes even at the locality level, elections in movement states are not zero sum competitions between caste groups. Dalits there are less likely to view political parties through the caste lens alone. Dalit voters were asked to name the factors that were important in their selection of parties. In Tamil Nadu and Maharashtra, in 40% of forty focus group discussions, and in 32% follow-up interviews with 203 subjects, caste was identified as one of the factors.[43]

By contrast, the habit of banding together during elections has continued among Dalit voters in Uttar Pradesh and Bihar. This has made Dalit support more likely for a single party rather than for multiple parties. In one-on-one interviews, 22.3% of the Dalit subjects said that members of their community voted for different parties, and 55.8% of the subjects said that members of their community voted for the same party. Explaining his support for the Dalit party, an interview subject in Uttar Pradesh said, "Only someone who is from our group and understands our plight will care for us. Other parties will only care for their own." Another subject said, "Earlier we voted for the Congress Party in this locality—men, women, old and young—everyone. Today, people vote for the BSP. Parties have changed [from the Congress to the BSP], but the community has voted together." Bloc voting turns elections into an all-or-nothing contest for Dalit voters, and they view political parties predominantly through their caste interests. Dalits in 75% of forty discussions, and in 54% of the 206 interviews in Uttar Pradesh and Bihar identified caste as one of the factors in their selection of parties.[44]

Lower interest in bloc voting in movement states suggests that these blocs were unavailable not only to ethnic, but also to multiethnic parties. Multiethnic parties in Tamil Nadu and Maharashtra, as a result, were incentivized to rely more on cross-group appeals than ethnic appeals to mobilize Dalits. By contrast,

[42] Andre Beteille, *Society and Politics in India: Essays in a Comparative Perspective* (London: Anthlone Press, 1991), p. 119.

[43] This question was dropped after the 1971 Indian National Election Study, but I included it in my interview questionnaire in order to make a longitudinal comparison of attitudes.

[44] On a survey in 2016, we asked voters in Tamil Nadu and Uttar Pradesh to consider the proposition: "It is important to think about one's caste interest when deciding on which political party to support." In Tamil Nadu, only 36.7% Dalits agreed with the proposition, whereas in Uttar Pradesh,

in non-movement states stronger interest in bloc voting among Dalits incentivized even multiethnic parties to use ethnic appeals more than cross-group appeals to mobilize Dalit voters.

Dalits voted for Dalit ethnic parties in much larger numbers in Uttar Pradesh and Bihar as compared to Tamil Nadu and Maharashtra. The vote shares of the four Dalit parties reflect the relative strength of Dalits' preference for bloc voting. The strength of these attitudes influences the ability of an emergent party, including a Dalit party, to aggregate Dalit votes along the caste cleavage, and, therefore, is consequential for the electoral performance of these parties. Dalit voters in Uttar Pradesh and Bihar have been more amenable to bloc voting than Dalit voters in Tamil Nadu and Maharashtra. Both the BSP and the LJP have used this support to improve their electoral performance. They have drawn other Dalit and non-Dalit castes into their fold. They have attracted popular non-Dalit candidates. They have received favorable terms in pre-poll seat-sharing arrangements with larger parties. The availability of electoral blocs has allowed Mayawati and Ram Vilas Paswan to emerge as Dalit leaders of national stature. By contrast, despite making similar ethnic appeals, the VCK in Tamil Nadu and the BSP in Maharashtra have failed to mobilize Dalits in similar proportions. And Dalit leaders in these states have been unable to develop a national profile.

Why, then, do these attitudes toward bloc voting vary among Dalits across movement and non-movement states? The following chapter closely examines how mobilization at the level of the locality has produced bloc voting among Dalits in Uttar Pradesh and Bihar, whereas the same outcome has not materialized in Tamil Nadu and Maharashtra.

53.6% Dalits expressed agreement. We also asked voters to consider the proposition: "The caste of the candidate should be taken into consideration when deciding whether or not to vote for them." Again, in Tamil Nadu only 34.5% Dalits agreed with the proposition, whereas in Uttar Pradesh 43% were in agreement. The survey interviewed 584 Dalits in Uttar Pradesh and 458 Dalits in Tamil Nadu. The survey was a part of an ongoing study that explores the relationship between skin color and caste in the two states.

6

Dalit Social Mobilization and Bloc Voting

The large Dalit population in Uttar Pradesh, and among that population the sub-stantial percentage of the Jatav or Chamar subcaste, are said to explain the remark-able success of the Bahujan Samaj Party (BSP). While the number of Jatavs does matter, it is noteworthy that if the Viduthalai Chiruthaikal Katchi (VCK) had been able to mobilize the support of even 50% of the Adi-Dravidas, the largest Dalit subcaste in Tamil Nadu, it would have emerged as a serious force in state politics there. Similarly, today neither the Republican Party of India (RPI) nor the Bahujan Samaj Party is able to mobilize a significant majority from among the Mahars, the most powerful group among Maharashtra's Dalits. Adi-Dravidas and Mahars, respectively, constitute a majority of the Dalit population in Tamil Nadu and Maharashtra. At the same time, even though the numerical strength of the Dusadh subcaste in Bihar is not as high as that of the Jatavs in Uttar Pradesh, the majority of Dusadhs support the Lok Janshakti Party (LJP), and so the party has remained a significant actor in Bihar's politics. In this chapter, I explain why these outcomes related to voting blocs vary across movement and non-movement states.

The availability of ethnic blocs is a prerequisite for the success of an ethnic party. The existence of an ethnic group does not automatically imply the suc-cessful mobilization of an ethnic electoral bloc, however. We know that Dalit attitudes on bloc voting vary across Tamil Nadu and Maharashtra, on one hand, and Uttar Pradesh and Bihar, on the other hand. In fact, this difference in attitude predates the fragmentation of the party system. In this chapter, I show that social mobilization of Dalits undermined their electoral mobilization as ethnic blocs. Dalit social mobilization produced mobilization entrepreneurs as well as sym-bolic resources. Prior social mobilization in movement states introduced these into the party system. Consequently, multiethnic parties became more inclusive. These parties widened their base by recruiting Dalits and began to honor Dalit symbols. Since parties could no longer use caste appeals to differentiate them-selves from each other, this process undermined the salience of caste in electoral politics. In a fragmenting, competitive multiparty system, it prevented the emergence of a Dalit electoral bloc. Non-movement states were denied these electoral effects of Dalit social mobilization and hence the possibility of bloc voting was preserved there. (see Figure 6.1.)

The electoral mobilization of Dalits, when it became a possibility, marked a departure from their routine treatment. In the past, authority, whether exercised by state or social actors even in its most benevolent form, had not accorded Dalits a political voice. With the onset of full-scale democratic politics, those who had been denied the choice to escape their stigmatized identity were suddenly being given the ability to choose governments. Those who were considered socially unequal every day were politically equal to others on election day. By being contacted and asked for their votes, the once outcast and still socially undesired were being recognized and acknowledged as never before. And yet how Dalits came to experience electoral mobilization by political parties has varied across states; their electoral mobilization has been predicated on their social mobilization.

Social mobilization facilitates the electoral mobilization of Dalits by political parties in a variety of ways. Social mobilization signals the organization of Dalits to political actors. Parties are alerted to the need for direct mobilization of Dalits. Social mobilization provides parties access to prominent local Dalit faces. It enables parties to adopt and identify with Dalit symbols, and it solves the collective action problem for parties at the neighborhood and locality levels.

Most of the Dalit social mobilization activity takes place at the household and neighborhood level, which is why I study the process of mobilization at this level. Neighborhoods and localities are suitable places in which to situate an inquiry, given their variety of political activities, which may include acts of violence, peace-building efforts, distribution of public goods, and mobilization on the basis of caste, religion, and civic concerns.[1] In the realm of everyday politics, neighborhoods and localities are legitimate units in the eyes of residents and outsiders alike. Neighborhoods and localities are also where citizens share their needs and interests, celebrate festivals, seek assistance in times of need, find opportunities for political discussion, and engage in competitive politics. Scholars are already beginning to gain fresh insights by studying variations in outcomes across neighborhoods and localities—or, as this book does, by using activity at the local level to construct larger, state-level explanations.[2]

---

[1] I defined a Dalit neighborhood as follows: In villages, I categorized the section of the village where Dalits were resident as a neighborhood. In cities and towns, I regarded the lanes and streets containing Dalit households in a large slum or a locality as a neighborhood.

[2] See Saumitra Jha, Vijayendra Rao, and Michael Woolcock, "Governance in the Gullies: Democratic Responsiveness and Leadership in Delhi's Slums," *World Development*, vol. 35, no. 2 (2007), pp. 230–246; Ward Berenschot, *Riot Politics: Hindu-Muslim Violence and the Indian State* (New York: Columbia University Press, 2011).

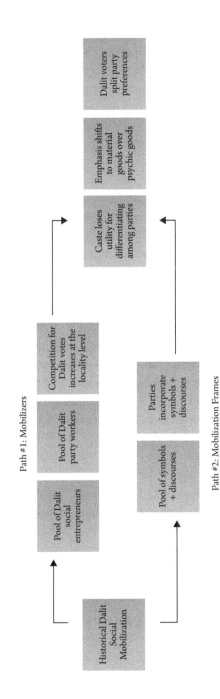

Figure 6.1 How Dalits' prior social mobilization weakens bloc voting

Dalit movements that marked the self-awareness of the group and its gradual struggle against social exclusion are populated by a set of key actors. Individually, they have played and continue to play a small part in the process of mobilization; collectively, however, they are responsible for shaping the trajectory of Dalit mobilization. Let us turn our attention now to the role of these actors, their motivations, and their relationship with political parties.

Social Mobilization Entrepreneurs

Social Mobilizers: The First Movers

In the interviews, it emerged that early mobilizers were often Dalit individuals with some educational and material resources. They could read and write, and they had connections to the urban areas. Their authority rested on their relative independence from the locally dominant castes and on their exposure to the outside world. The first generation of mobilization entrepreneurs belonged to families that were able to acquire enough land to allow them not to seek work elsewhere in the village and that had found employment in the urban industrial sector or with the state, including in the military. The next generation had benefited from reservation policies in public schools and universities as well as government departments and public sector undertakings. Since the mid-1980s, India's average annual economic growth rate of 6% has created more opportunities for Dalits to climb the income ladder, contributing to their independence from the dominant castes in the process.[3] Among the new generation of Dalit social entrepreneurs, a substantial number were employed by the state, but some were also employed in the private sector.

Across the four states, the eighty mobilization entrepreneurs who were interviewed belonged to a diverse set of professions. They were ex-soldiers, contractors, small businesses owners and shopkeepers, lawyers, teachers, NGO activists, state officials, farmers, journalists, and occasionally local strongmen. These individuals shared the caste identity with their localities. At the same time, they shared a socioeconomic identity with members of other castes living in adjoining areas. In fact, even when some of them had moved to urban, middle-class, predominantly higher-caste neighborhoods, they continued to maintain homes in their original Dalit localities to remain involved in those areas' activities.

---

[3] India's post-liberalization economic growth has benefited other groups more than Dalits, but there is no denying that it has reduced poverty among them; see Arun Kumar, *Dalits and Economic Reforms* (Jaipur: Rawat, 2010).

Community Builders

The resources at their command and their relatively higher social status among the Dalit community allowed these individuals to emerge as mobilization entrepreneurs. At the local level, they organized caste members to make social and, at times, political claims. In rural areas, they provided help for community activities during religious festivals, sometimes settled disputes within communities, and defused tensions with members of the dominant group in their areas. In urban areas, they helped by organizing services like medical camps, food distribution, and coaching classes for school students. They supported cultural activities such as production of Dalit street plays, readings of Dalit literature and poetry, commemoration of Dalit icons, and critical lectures on the caste system. In and around the localities and neighborhoods they lived in, these entrepreneurs were respected as community leaders.[4] Their accomplishments were well known around their localities, and they were held in high regard. While these mobilization entrepreneurs were almost always of higher socioeconomic status, not all Dalits of higher socioeconomic status became mobilization entrepreneurs.[5]

It is worth emphasizing that these individuals were not mere fixers or intermediaries between the citizen and the state.[6] They were community builders, and their social stature and worth were connected to the strength of the Dalit

---

[4] The role of community leaders, who are different from traditional political patrons, is not unique to Dalit mobilization. My own research and that of Pradeep Chhibber has found that politicians in Muslim communities turn to religious leaders during electoral campaigns in order to mobilize Muslim voters. These Muslim religious leaders will endorse candidates and parties but rarely join them or stand for election themselves, and for the same reasons as those given by the Dalit entrepreneurs. The same can also be said about the role played by church leaders in Northeastern states such as Mizoram and by the head of the Sikh deras in Punjab. Essentially, these faith leaders become significant for political parties because of the mobilization structures of the followers over whom they exercise influence. It is important to understand, however, that these religious leaders are not controlled by political parties. They keep their distance from political parties for the sake of their own credibility and legitimacy, and they are able to do so not only because they have followers of their own in their communities but also because their livelihoods are not dependent on political parties.

[5] See Nicolas Jaoul, "Political and 'Non-political' Means in the Dalit Movement," in Sudha Pai, ed., *Political Process in Uttar Pradesh: Identity, Economic Reforms and Governance* (New Delhi: Pearson/Longman, 2007) pp. 191–220 for a thoughtful essay that outlines the activities of a social mobilization entrepreneur through the experience of Dhaniram Panther, a Dalit Panther leader in Kanpur, Uttar Pradesh. Most of the mobilization entrepreneurs I encountered during my fieldwork were of higher socioeconomic status than Dhaniram.

[6] See Kanchan Chandra, *Why Ethnic Parties Succeed: Patronage and Ethnic Head Counts in India* (Cambridge: Cambridge University Press, 2004); Anirudh Krishna, "Politics in the Middle: Mediating Relationships between Citizens and the State in Rural North India," in Herbert Kitschelt and Steven Wilkinson, eds., *Patrons, Clients, and Policies: Patterns of Democratic Accountability and Political Competition* (Cambridge: Cambridge University Press, 2007), pp. 141–159.

community in their neighborhoods or localities.[7] During the interviews, it emerged that they had been influenced by different strands of Dalit ideology and were aware of key leaders and events of Dalit history, not only within their own states but also across India. Their focus was on social uplift of the Dalit community so as to strengthen its identity. They supported local and statewide Dalit campaigns. They were involved in the building and maintenance of monuments to Dalit leaders. These community leaders seldom created formal organizations in their localities; even when they did, these were not membership-based associations. Therefore, their power was not located within a formal mobilization structure but instead within informal familial and caste networks in their localities and surrounding areas, networks built through their own work. At the same time, their work within their communities and their appeal to Dalit ideology established their stature within their communities.

Boundary Crossers

Like other middle- and upper-middle-class Dalits, social mobilization entrepreneurs came in contact with middle-class members of higher-caste communities, not as their subordinates but as their equals. They also came in contact with higher-caste individuals of lower socioeconomic status. Together, these distinct interactions reinforced the entrepreneurs' aspirations to be accepted as equals in middle-class localities and neighborhoods. Their middle-class status also enabled them to better identify people from outside the Dalit community who could be relied on as allies. These allies were instrumental in drawing the attention of the local press, the larger public, and state officials to the Dalit community and its concerns. The Dalit mobilization entrepreneurs invested in their community, since they derived their authority on the basis of the respect they enjoyed among fellow community members. Higher socioeconomic status, coupled with education, left Dalit mobilization entrepreneurs better equipped to argue in front of government officials on behalf of the residents of their localities. In fact, this was why educated and employed Dalits were held in high regard, especially in rural localities.

---

[7] For a glimpse into the lives and aspirations of movement activists, and for details about how much more they do than simply serve as "fixers" offering a connection to the state, see Hugo Gorringe, "Taming the Dalit Panthers: Dalit Politics in Tamil Nadu," *Journal of South Asian Development*, vol. 2, no. 1 (2007), pp. 51–73. See also Nicolas Jaoul, "Learning the Use of Symbolic Means: Dalits, Ambedkar Statues and the State in Uttar Pradesh," *Contributions to Indian Sociology*, vol. 40, no. 2 (2006), pp. 175–207; Jaoul, "Political and 'Non-political' Means in the Dalit Movement," pp. 191–220; Nicolas Jaoul, "The 'Righteous Anger' of the Powerless: Investigating Dalit Outrage over Caste Violence," *South Asia Multidisciplinary Academic Journal*, vol. 2 (2008), pp. 2–28.

What Motivates Social Mobilization Entrepreneurs?

During the interviews, multiple motivations for community building work surfaced. A majority of the mobilization entrepreneurs were socialized into these activities as within their family, at work, and during their education they had come into contact with the ideas of community building and assertion against the caste system. In some instances, individuals were driven by a sense of responsibility toward their community. "If I or others like me do not help, then who else does my community have?" asked a mobilization entrepreneur in Tamil Nadu who worked as a clerk in the railways. Such individuals wanted their relative success to be more meaningful. Involvement with fellow Dalits cemented their social status, and brought them respect and veneration from within the community. "People respect someone only if that person can guide them and introduce them to new ideas. That is what is my life's mission," said a retired lawyer in Maharashtra.

One reason this respect was valued among mobilization entrepreneurs was because they felt that members of other communities denied them similar recognition and overlooked their achievements. Another reason was that respect could be converted into influence, especially in moments of mobilization for protests and voting. "It is give and take," explained a school teacher who was connected to the BSP. "If you do good things for your community, then the community will do good things for you."

Social Mobilization Entrepreneurs and Political Parties

The emergence of social entrepreneurs signals the political autonomy of Dalits. Parties are, therefore, compelled to mobilize the group directly, using members of the Dalit community. The one-on-one interviews and my observation of the social mobilization entrepreneurs revealed that they often worked independently with respect to political parties. While they were open to working with parties and aligning with them during election periods, they were seldom under the direct control of a particular party. These social mobilization entrepreneurs were able to enjoy this degree of autonomy because of the influence they exercised in their areas and because political parties needed them. When their emergence had not been engineered by political parties, and when they were either financially independent from political parties or not reliant on a single particular party, they were not party loyalists. They regularly shifted their support from one party to another across elections. It is noteworthy that political parties in India generally have weak grassroots-level organizations.[8] Mobilization activities

---

[8] See Pradeep Chhibber, *Democracy without Associations: Transformation of Party Systems and Social Cleavages in India* (Ann Arbor: University of Michigan Press, 1999).

usually occur at the time of election campaigns. Typically, parties get two weeks for campaigning, which gives them little time for setting up organizational capacity at the neighborhood and locality level. The Dalit entrepreneurs, by contrast, were involved in neighborhood- or locality-level activities throughout the year. Despite its autonomy, Dalit social mobilization cannot remain apolitical. It seeks a connection with the political party urgently for one important reason. Most Dalits belong to the lower income strata, and therefore rely more on state services than those placed in the higher income category.[9] Political parties offer access to state services.

Where more than one social mobilization entrepreneur is present around a locality, they can ally with the same party or with different political parties at the time of an election. During my visits to Dalit localities, I found that some of these entrepreneurs joined political parties while others maintained a limited relationship with them that surfaced only during election periods. By choosing to back candidates and parties, social mobilization entrepreneurs often improved their political leverage and social status in their localities. Party workers, belonging to different parties, competed to have the entrepreneurs in their camps. In the meantime, competing mobilization entrepreneurs often joined rival parties. A member of the legislative assembly (MLA) belonging to the Congress Party who had risen from the position of municipal ward leader explained how Dalit candidates were recruited in Dalit localities: "When an area has more than one leader," he said, "a second party will enter the area. Every party looks for a leader. Those leaders who cannot get an affiliation with the number one party will then go to the number two party or the number three party or stand as independent candidates in local elections." This remark suggests that a higher number of mobilization entrepreneurs in a neighborhood increases the possibility that multiple parties will find a presence there. These entrepreneurs were also aware that even if they did not hold any elected office at the local level, their endorsements of parties and candidates were valued, and this gave them some leverage in a competitive party system. The head of a social organization that worked with Dalit villagers in rural Tamil Nadu said, "Everyone wants us to join their party. We will not. This is a time of coalitions. I don't have to be in a party to be taken seriously." Therefore, even though the incentives that motivate entrepreneurs are not rooted entirely in electoral politics, the more respect and credibility they enjoy within their communities, the more important they are to the political brokers who come calling during election periods. Historically, the strength of social mobilization has varied significantly across movement and

---

[9] Members of higher income strata are better placed to procure services from the market: private healthcare, schooling, drinking water, transportation, security, etc.

non-movement states. This difference reflects itself in the influence of social mobilization entrepreneurs on the electoral mobilization of Dalits by multiethnic and ethnic parties.

Mobilization Entrepreneurs and Electoral Mobilization

In Tamil Nadu and Maharashtra, the early appearance of mobilization entrepreneurs in urban Dalit localities alerted political parties to the organization of the group. Political parties were drawn to these individuals. Instead of relying only on intermediaries (notables belonging to locally dominant castes) to gain Dalit support in elections, parties needed workers within Dalit localities to connect with the voters. When a party had a prominent Dalit worker in the area, other parties interested in mobilizing Dalits had to find one, too. This process spread from cities to towns to rural areas, and Dalits began to organize in the countryside. In Uttar Pradesh and Bihar, by contrast, when Dalit social mobilization arose, it remained localized in a few urban pockets. In large swaths of rural parts of the two states, Dalit organization was weak. Substantially dependent on the landed elite, Dalits were less likely to turn to political parties on their own. Often their participation in the electoral process was externally influenced. As landless laborers or marginal farmers they came in contact with political parties either through higher caste intermediaries or middle-class Dalit notables.

In the movement states of Tamil Nadu and Maharashtra, I was able to identify a total of fifty-four social mobilization entrepreneurs across forty large urban and rural localities; twenty-three in Tamil Nadu and thirty-one in Maharashtra. This number for Uttar Pradesh and Bihar stood at only twenty-six; fifteen in Uttar Pradesh, and eleven in Bihar. The 2004 survey of party workers found that parties were better represented across large Dalit localities in the movement states.[10] The median number of parties in the forty surveyed localities in Tamil Nadu was two; in Maharashtra, it was the same. By contrast, the median number of parties represented through party workers in localities within both Uttar Pradesh and

---

[10] Mobilization entrepreneurs also take on the role of party workers during election campaigns; however, the party worker profiles had a broad range. Party workers and activists in Dalit localities were driven by a variety of motivations. In some instances, they were notables in their localities, people with more resources than the average resident; they hoped that by becoming party representatives they could preserve or enhance their local influence. In other cases, they were ambitious young individuals looking to advance through their links with political parties. A third kind of party worker was a diehard loyalist devoted to the party's cause regardless of circumstances.

Table 6.1. **Number of parties with party workers in Dalit and non-Dalit localities across states**

		2004 Mean	2004 Median	2009 Mean	2009 Median
Movement States	Tamil Nadu				
	Dalits	2.18	2	2.40	2
	Non-Dalits	—	—	2.28	2
	Maharashtra				
	Dalits	2.05	2	2.11	2
	Non-Dalits	—	—	2.24	2
Non-movement States	Uttar Pradesh				
	Dalits	1.47	1	1.50	1
	Non-Dalits	—	—	2.38	2
	Bihar				
	Dalits	1.10	1	1.43	1
	Non-Dalits	—	—	2.04	2

Source: Ahuja locality-level surveys 2004 and 2009. In 2004, 160 Dalit localities were surveyed across the four states. In 2009, 66 Dalit and 72 non-Dalit localities were surveyed across the four states.

Bihar was one.[11] (See Table 6.1.) Across the two non-movement states, as many as 64% of localities or neighborhoods had a party worker or activist from just one party.[12]

The 2009 locality-level campaign survey conducted across sixty-six Dalit and seventy-two non-Dalit localities in the four states found a similar pattern. More parties were represented through their party workers in Dalit localities in movement states than non-movement states. The survey also found that the competition for Dalit votes is higher in movement states than non-movement states. During the campaign period, more parties campaigned in Dalit localities in Tamil Nadu and Maharashtra than Uttar Pradesh and Bihar. (See Table 6.2.)

[11] In each state a large number of Dalit localities were identified as potential sites for focus group discussions and follow-up interviews. In addition to the 20 localities where focus groups were conducted, we randomly selected another 20 localities from our list to ascertain the number of parties represented through their workers in those sites. Overall, then, we surveyed 160 (40 in each state) localities and neighborhoods.

[12] In 22% of the localities, party workers from more than one party were present; in 14% of the localities, no party worker or activist could be identified.

Table 6.2. **Average number of parties that campaigned in Dalit and non-Dalit localities across states in the 2009 Lok Sabha election**

		Dalits	*Non-Dalits*
Movement States	Tamil Nadu	3.5	3.2
	Maharashtra	3	2.5
Non-movement States	Uttar Pradesh	2.2	3.1
	Bihar	2.5	3.06

Source: Ahuja locality-level survey 2009. Sixty-six Dalit and 72 non-Dalit localities were surveyed across the four states.

In Tamil Nadu, established and emergent regional parties—the DMK, the AIDMK, and the DMDK, along with such national parties as the Congress Party and the BJP as well as Dalit parties such as the VCK and the BSP—compete for Dalit votes. In Maharashtra—between the Congress Party and its ally, the NCP, and such Dalit parties as the RPI and the BSP, not to mention BJP and Shiv Sena—many parties compete for Dalit votes.[13] In Uttar Pradesh, outside the BSP, the other competitors for the Dalit vote were Congress and BJP. In Bihar, outside the LJP, other lower-caste ethnic parties, the RJD and Janata Dal (United) [JD(U)], competed for the Dalit vote.[14] In Uttar Pradesh and Bihar in 2009, multiethnic party workers often complained about the Jatavs and Dusadhs voting as a bloc for their ethnic party; they saw little point in campaigning in the localities of these groups.

The campaign survey also found that the competition for Dalit and non-Dalit voters is similar in movement states; however, in non-movement states competition for Dalit voters is lower than for non-Dalit voters. In Tamil Nadu and Maharashtra the number of parties that campaigned in Dalit and non-Dalit localities was similar, whereas, in Uttar Pradesh and Bihar fewer parties campaigned in Dalit localities than non-Dalit localities.

Why do more political parties visit non-Dalit localities than Dalit localities in the two states of Uttar Pradesh and Bihar? In these two states, the members of the upper and Backward Castes have experienced a much greater degree of self-mobilization than Dalits. The localities of these groups have more mobilization entrepreneurs and party workers. More parties are represented through party workers in non-Dalit localities. In Uttar Pradesh, the average number of parties represented through party workers in the Dalit localities was 1.5, and for

---

[13] In both states, many parties contested the elections in alliance with other parties. That is what explains the lower than expected campaign figures in Table 6.2.

[14] Although in 2009, the JD(U) did not target Paswan localities with campaign visits.

non-Dalit localities this number stood at 2.38. In Bihar, the average number of parties represented through party workers in Dalit localities in 2009 was 1.43, whereas for non-Dalit localities the average number was 2.04.

Dalit electoral mobilization in Tamil Nadu and Maharashtra differed sharply from Uttar Pradesh and Bihar. As compared to Dalit localities in non-movement states, Dalit localities in the movement states had a larger number of mobilization entrepreneurs, more parties were represented through their party workers, and more parties campaigned in Dalit localities. In addition to more competition for votes, there is also a qualitative difference in how Dalits are mobilized across movement and non-movement states.

Symbolic Resources and Electoral Mobilization

"This is a bad week for the interview with the MLA. He is busy with all these events this week. It is Babasaheb's birth anniversary," a somewhat irritated personal assistant of a Congress MLA told me in Nagpur in the western state of Maharashtra in April 2003. I was surprised because I had not anticipated this response. Just that morning, I had arrived from Uttar Pradesh in the north, where such frantic activity around Dr. B. R. Ambedkar's birth anniversary was absent. In fact, in an interview a day before, a prominent functionary of the same Congress Party in Uttar Pradesh had taken a very different view toward Dalits. Once the backbone of the powerful Congress Party's support base in Uttar Pradesh, India's most populous and, hence, most politically consequential state, the Dalit vote had shifted to BSP, its caste party. I had asked the functionary: What was Congress doing to regain Dalit support in the state? "The Harijan vote has left us. They will come back. In our culture, when the daughter-in-law leaves home, we do not call her back. Soon, when her good sense returns, she comes back on her own," he had said. The status of a daughter-in-law in a traditional patriarchal North Indian household is the lowest among the family members. By equating her status to that of Dalits, the Congress leader was only highlighting the paternalistic attitude that had contributed to the loss of the Dalit support for the party in his state. His response was especially startling because Dalits make up over 20% of voters in Uttar Pradesh, whereas in Maharashtra where the Congress MLA was running around to attend Babasaheb Ambedkar's birth anniversary events, the percentage of Dalits is only 13%. The two encounters highlight the chasm between how the same Congress Party had come to mobilize Dalits so differently across two Indian states.

We know that historical Dalit social mobilization has created and popularized a repertoire of community symbols and events. Why is symbolic politics meaningful to the marginalized? The public sphere traditionally does not acknowledge marginalized groups. Symbols of the marginalized constitute a correction to this historical wrong by claiming space for them in the public sphere. The recognition and adoption of group symbols affirms the presence of the marginalized as equal members of society. As such, symbols do not directly aid in material advancement; instead their appeal is emotional in nature. They are valuable because they hold meaning for the community and dignify its presence. They are pure public goods for a group—their consumption is indivisible and all group members benefit from them.

The recruitment of Dalit social mobilization entrepreneurs and party workers puts pressure on the multiethnic party to recognize Dalit symbols and mark prominent Dalit events. The party workers and mobilization entrepreneurs demand the usage of such symbols for the sake of their own credibility and popularity with Dalit voters in their localities and neighborhoods. For political parties, the adoption of Dalit symbols offers them an inexpensive tactic to mobilize an ethnic group. By honoring and recognizing Dalit symbols, political parties are able to establish legitimacy with socially mobilized Dalit voters. For example, party workers are present at events such as celebrations of the birth and death anniversaries of Dr. B. R. Ambedkar and other Dalit leaders. Closer to elections, parties fund such events. These symbols are used during election campaigns because they resonate with Dalit voters. "I may belong to any party, but if the voters think I do not respect the Ambedkari ideology, I will lose the Dalit vote in this constituency," declared a Congress MLA in Maharashtra. "A leader must go to the social and cultural functions. That is how a leader builds a relationship with the public," explained a Dalit party worker in Tamil Nadu. He had recently invite his party's MLA to an event marking Dr. B. R. Ambedkar's birth anniversary.

In a competitive multiparty system, the adoption of symbols by one party forces rival parties to do the same. In addition to producing a repertoire of symbols, Dalit movements also enable a discursive change in the public sphere by highlighting the group's demand for recognition and mainstreaming their symbols. This then makes it easier for political parties to adopt these symbols.

Dalit movements in Tamil Nadu and Maharashtra produced a larger repertoire of symbols that had state and nationwide resonance. Without a doubt, the most prominent among these are the two leaders most closely associated with the demand for the abolition of the caste system: Dr. B. R. Ambedkar and Periyar. Besides these nationally known symbols, there are others that are popular at the state level. In Tamil Nadu, Dalits revere historical figures associated with their assertion, including Iyothee Thass, M. C. Rajah, Rettamalai

Srinivasan, and Emmanuel Sekaran. The pantheon of social reformers that Maharashtrian Dalits revere includes Chokhamela, Shahu Maharaj, and Jyotirao and Savitribhai Phule.

In Tamil Nadu and Maharashtra, where parties competed for Dalit votes, Dalit symbols and Dalits' demands for recognition came to the fore much earlier. The use of Dr. Ambedkar as a symbol is a case in point. The celebration of his birthday is a political occasion. In these movement states, workers from rival parties compete to organize the celebrations. The 2009 locality-level campaign survey found that in Tamil Nadu and Maharashtra, in twenty-two (71%) out of the thirty-one large Dalit localities surveyed, Dr. Ambedkar's birthday was observed on April 14 as a community activity. State officials and leaders belonging to different political parties honor Dr. Ambedkar in these movement states. Further, these activities were not restricted to state capitals but were also occurring across different towns and cities.

In movement states, the multiparty support for Dalit symbols is not limited to Dr. B. R. Ambedkar. For example, to commemorate Rettamalai Srinivasan, a Tamil Dalit icon, the AIADMK during its tenure in government in 2005 issued a postage stamp and laid the foundation for his memorial. DMK, the other Dravidian party, inaugurated this memorial during its rule in 2009. The Communist Party in Tamil Nadu also works for Dalit rights and often joins Dalit temple entry protests. Ideologically, the party views all forms of the struggle of the marginalized groups as a form of class struggle; however, in Tamil Nadu, it recognizes caste-based disadvantage and has formed a Dalit union. It builds and maintains memorials for Dalit victims of caste violence. Meanwhile, the Dravidar Kazagam, the parent body of the Dravidian parties that is today mostly independent of them, continues to organize intercaste self-respect marriages.

Some of the other symbolic activities of significance organized by parties include holding conferences around Dalits' concerns, raising demands for the extension of reservation policies for Dalits to the private sector, running campaigns for the reduction of landlessness among Dalits, naming public utilities such as state transportation companies after Dalit movement leaders, and honoring such leaders on their birth and death anniversaries. The Congress Party in Maharashtra celebrated Dr. Ambedkar as a state icon, honored other Dalit movement leaders, promoted Dalit literature, and co-opted the Dalit political elite. Other parties, such as the Nationalist Congress Party (NCP), Shiv Sena, and the Bharatiya Janata Party (BJP), follow similar strategies and also honor Dalit symbols.

The use of Dalit symbols by political parties is not motivated by instrumentalist reasons alone; it also reflects the diffusion of ideas and the discourse of dignity and social justice that the Dalit movement has introduced to the public sphere. Non-Dalit members of multiethnic parties have become more accepting of Dalit symbols and the significance of honoring them. In an interview, a

Dalit MLA from the Congress Party was frank about the generational change in attitudes: "The Congress Party was very allergic to Ambedkar and his ideology earlier. I was told that if I used '*Jai Bhim*' as a greeting, they would not make me a cabinet minister.[15] But now attitudes have changed. The Congress Party has learned that it is not possible to suppress us. The Shiv Sena will also learn this lesson. Everyone wants to win elections."

In Maharashtra, the BJP and Shiv Sena, as elements of the Hindu nationalist movement, historically have had an antagonist relationship with Dalits. The Shiv Sena, for example, opposed the renaming of Marathwada University as Dr. B. R. Ambedkar University in the late 1970s and the early 1980s, and had been at the center of organizing the social backlash against Dalit mobilization. The BJP, on different occasions, has expressed its opposition to reservations (quotas) for Dalits. Both parties have gradually distanced themselves from these positions. To expand their vote shares, they have tried to mobilize Dalit voters by recruiting Dalit party activists across Dalit localities. During interviews, Shiv Sena and BJP district presidents acknowledged their anti-Dalit image: "Because of our ideology, there is a stigma attached to our party. Dalits fear that if we come to power, we will remove the reservation policies. But that is not true. It is only propaganda against us," a senior Shiv Sena leader insisted. A BJP leader went to great lengths to explain that the party was against the caste system and that Dalits are Hindus, like everyone else: "We view Ambedkar as a great Indian leader. Like Savarkar, he has awakened a people." A Shiv Sena leader said, "Dalits know that the Congress Party and the NCP are fooling them. We understand Dalits' power and pride. They are Maharashtrians, after all. In our party we believe that Marathas and Dalits are one blood. Shivaji [a seventeenth-century warrior general and ruler who is the Shiv Sena's icon] and Babasaheb are the two great souls our land has produced. Which is why our leadership has called upon Dalits to join hands with us." BJP and Shiv Sena party functionaries pointed to prominent Dalits who had joined their parties. They explained that even though there are sometimes caste-based tensions among their supporters on the ground, they have to include all castes: "We contest elections at the local, state assembly, and parliamentary levels, and for that we need everyone." The presence of Dalit mobilization entrepreneurs and the availability of Dalit symbols should not guarantee their inclusion by multiethnic parties. After all, a competitive party system does not necessitate the mobilization of a stigmatized group; the African Americans, for example, have been mobilized in recent decades only by one party in a two-party system.[16]

---

[15] Bhimrao (Bhim) is Dr. B. R. Ambedkar's first name, and so "Jai Bhim" means "Hail to Ambedkar."

[16] Since the 1970s, the Democratic Party has been the predominant mobilizer of the African American vote. The Republican Party has either ignored or been hostile to the group. As a result, the

Why, then, do multiethnic parties mobilize Dalits? Why do they recruit Dalit workers and honor Dalit symbols? Party system fragmentation in movement states produced a multiparty system that was far more competitive than the two-party system that African Americans navigate in the United States. When multiple parties compete for the Dalit vote, inclusion emerges as a bidding strategy to attract new Dalit voters and hold on to the current supporters. Additionally, once Dalits have mobilized as a group, parties can ill afford to be anti-Dalit, because of the existence of reserved electoral districts. In the Indian parliament, 84 out of the 543 seats are reserved for Dalits. Across state assemblies, 590 out of 4,020 electoral districts are reserved for Dalits. This, then, means that political parties have to recruit Dalit candidates and seek some degree of Dalit support across all these districts.[17] In this context, open hostility toward Dalits or expressing of support for caste hierarchy, in the face of mobilization and heightened competition, could potentially put the offending party out of the running in reserved electoral districts. The party would very likely be unable to recruit a popular Dalit candidate, in addition to losing support among potential Dalit voters. But this process of inclusion is contingent on Dalit social mobilization.

Symbols of Dalit emancipation and self-assertion, originally produced by movements, have been gradually appropriated by a number of political parties in Maharashtra and Tamil Nadu. In comparison, in Uttar Pradesh and Bihar fewer Dalit social reformers confronted the caste system directly. Still, Dalits have discovered their historical heroes and heroines. Among those who are revered, their popularity has been limited to a few districts. For example, figures such as Jhalkari Bai, Bijli Pasi, and Swami Achhutanand are not known across the entire state in Uttar Pradesh. Although Ravidas and Kabir enjoy wide popularity, they do so more as religious rather than social or political icons across Uttar Pradesh and Bihar. Badri Narayan's groundbreaking work points to Dalit symbols of resistance that appeared in pockets of rural Uttar Pradesh.[18] For symbols and appeals to be truly powerful, however, they must be universal in their appeal; they must be widely recognized and should enjoy mass popularity. In Uttar Pradesh, the resonance of these symbols had remained, at most, localized at the district level. Parties and movements act as transmitting mechanisms for these symbols. In

---

African American voters have been denied the benefits of the two-party system and its underlying promise of competition and choice. See Paul Frymer, "Race, Parties, and Democratic Inclusion," in Christina Wolbrecht, Rodney E. Hero, Peri E. Arnold, and Alvin B. Tillery, eds. *Politics of Democratic Inclusion* (Philadelphia: Temple University Press, 2005), pp. 122–142.

[17] Reserved districts have sizable Dalit populations; still, the majority of voters in these districts are non-Dalits.

[18] Badri Narayan, *The Making of the Dalit Public in North India: Uttar Pradesh, 1950–Present* (New Delhi: Oxford University Press, 2011).

Uttar Pradesh, it is only under the BSP's patronage that local symbols were discovered and popularized. In Uttar Pradesh and Bihar, only fourteen (43%) of the thirty-five large Dalit localities surveyed in the 2009 locality survey observed Dr. B. R. Ambedkar's birthday as a community activity. Moreover, across these states, the marking of this occasion at the neighborhood level has been a recent phenomenon and has coincided with the rise of Dalit political parties. Unlike movement states, competitive adoption of Dalit symbols did not exist in Uttar Pradesh and Bihar. There, only workers from Dalit parties were involved in the commemoration of anniversaries of major Dalit figures.[19] Large public events to honor Dr. B. R. Ambedkar, when they occurred, were sponsored by the BSP or the LJP, while the other parties mostly stayed away. Since 2014, the BJP has begun to incorporate Dalit symbols and commemorate Dalit icons in Uttar Pradesh and Bihar to increase its vote share among the members of the group.

In the non-movement states, a self-authored Dalit agenda did not take hold before the 1980s, nor did a discourse of social equality like that in Tamil Nadu or Maharashtra underpin Dalit mobilization by political parties. To mobilize Dalits, the Congress relied only on direct caste-based appeals by appointing pliable Dalit leaders to national and state government cabinets.[20] Moreover, the Congress Party governments in Uttar Pradesh and Bihar did not promote or honor Dalit symbols; in both states, these were absent from the public sphere. The Congress Party did not borrow symbols from outside the states either. The party may have had few popular in-state Dalit symbols to draw on, but it also failed to draw lessons from its policies in Maharashtra. It even neglected its own prominent Dalit leaders. After their deaths, the Congress could have turned to Babu Jagjivan Ram and B. P. Maurya, the party's two most prominent Dalit leaders in North India, as Dalit icons. But it did not. The only icons that the Congress used to mobilize Dalits were the members of the Nehru-Gandhi family. Dalits were acknowledged only as Harijans, a name that Gandhi had given the group that they felt did nothing to uplift their status and, instead, acquired its own pejorative burden over time. After a focus group discussion, I asked a participant what he thought of being called *Harijan* (one of God's children), a name Gandhi had given the group. He said, "Hum Harijan hain, to baki log ka kuttajan hain kya?" ("If we are God's children, then are other people dogs' children?") His caustic response pointed to a clear rejection of the name Congress had used for them for decades.

---

[19] The interviews in Dalit localities as well as the locality-level survey found that the birthdays of other leaders—M. G. Ramachandran and Periyar in Tamil Nadu, Kanshi Ram in Uttar Pradesh, and Phule in Maharashtra—are also celebrated in Dalit localities.

[20] These leaders came to be ridiculed by the BSP as *chamcha*, or lackeys of the Congress Party.

Dalit and lower-caste parties, when they emerged in the 1980s and 1990s, through their campaigns represented a statewide challenge to the sensibility of upper-caste dominance. They openly confronted upper-caste hegemony by using inflammatory slogans. One slogan announced a desire for becoming rulers. "Vote se lenge PM/CM, arakshan se lenge SP/DM." With votes we will get our chief minister and prime minister. Through reservations or quotas we will get our district magistrate and superintendent of police (The two senior most administrative positions at the district level.) Another slogan used in the early campaigns of BSP in Uttar Pradesh was "Vote hamara, raj tumhara, nahin chalega" ("We vote, you rule, this will not continue"). Epithets reached a high point during the 1993 Uttar Pradesh assembly election campaign, the most notorious being "Tilak, Tarazu, Talwar. Maaro unko joote char." This slogan, with its insistent rhythm in Hindi, advocates that Brahmins, Banias, and Rajputs, each identified with a slighting term, be beaten four times with a shoe—a traditionally demeaning form of punishment because of the ritual impurity of leather. In Bihar, the Janata Dal (JD) went so far as to use the slogan "Vikaas nahin, sammaan chahiye," meaning we need dignity, not development. RJD also used the slogan, "Vote ka Raj, chot ka raj," meaning the rule of the vote is the rule of the (socially) wounded. Another slogan, "Bhurabal hatao," meaning "Wipe out the upper castes [from politics]," was also common.[21]

The slogans may sound provocative; however, used by a subordinate group, they represent an empty threat. They empower the subordinate group more than frighten the dominant groups that they are used against. By contrast, when members of a dominant group threaten members of a subordinate group through slogans, the menace is made real by the dominant group's capacity to carry out the threat, intimidating the targeted group.

During an interview in Delhi in 2003, I asked Kanshi Ram, the BSP founder and president, about anti-upper-caste sloganeering at BSP political rallies during the 1990s. At those gatherings there were large crowds, often in the thousands, that shouted abusive slogans against the upper castes. Kanshi Ram justified the sloganeering in the name of Dalit dignity. Most of the people who attended those rallies, he said, were not able to oppose the upper castes in their own villages and localities. "They would have been thrashed," he said. "In a group, they were free. For centuries, they have been taking abuse. Our caste is used as an insult among the upper castes. Shouting those slogans was a release for them. They became human beings!" I heard similar justifications for the sloganeering at rallies of the Rashtriya Janata Dal (RJD) and the LJP in Bihar.

---

[21] "Bhurabal" is a Hindi-language acronym for the four upper-caste groups in Bihar: Bhumihars, Rajputs, Brahmins, and Lals (Kayasths). All three slogans were used under the leadership of Lalu Yadav.

The slogans were also responding to a need—the rejection of hierarchy—that made them effective with Dalit voters. The Dalit and lower-caste parties success-fully projected themselves as symbols of empowerment. Unlike the Congress Party, which had been reluctant to go beyond recognition of their impoverish-ment while mobilizing the untouchables, the BSP turned itself into a symbol of self-respect. It was not mobilizing Dalits merely along caste cleavages but acknowledging the fundamental deprivation of dignity related to their identity. In this way, the BSP harvested the defining attribute of the Dalit identity—its invisibility.

Leaders such as Mayawati, Ram Vilas Paswan, and Lalu Yadav, who were in many ways historic firsts, mobilize new segments of voters situated at the periph-ery of mainstream politics. Their visibility raised the salience of caste identity and historic grievances that were shared between these leaders and members of the marginalized group.[22] Mayawati, Ram Vilas Paswan, and Lalu Prasad Yadav each emphasized their caste during election rallies, and Lalu Prasad Yadav went a step further by highlighting his rustic mannerisms.[23] When Mayawati and Lalu Prasad Yadav became chief ministers of their respective states, their public repri-mands of upper-caste bureaucrats, their visits to Dalit localities, not to mention Mayawati's elaborate birthday parties, marked a significant shift in the status quo as far as the formerly excluded and invisible were concerned in Uttar Pradesh and Bihar. These reprimands and celebrations embodied empowerment because they were perceived and valued as new freedoms among lower-caste groups.

In Uttar Pradesh, since the 1980s, the creation of Dalit symbols and the prop-agation of those symbols has been a project undertaken by the BSP. While in government, the BSP has disseminated party publications; renamed districts, public avenues, and buildings; created public parks, schools, colleges, welfare programs, and monuments and named them after Dalit icons including Kanshi Ram; and celebrated Dalit festivals.[24] Most of these icons have been borrowed from movement states: Dr. B. R. Ambedkar, Shahu Maharaj, and Phule from Maharashtra; Narayana Guru from Kerala; and Periyar from Tamil Nadu. Bihar, however, has not experienced such an upsurge in the use of Dalit sym-bols. In Uttar Pradesh and Bihar, Dalit and lower caste parties, through their leaders, campaigns, and promotion of icons of anticaste movements, emerged

---

[22] Drawing on examples from American politics, Evelyn Simien explains how leaders like Barack Obama, Hillary Clinton, and others, who are historic firsts, symbolically empower hitherto excluded groups. See Evelyn M. Simien, *Historic Firsts: How Symbolic Empowerment Changes U.S. Politics* (New York: Oxford University Press, 2015).

[23] Mayawati reminded her Dalit voters that she was a "*Dalit ki beti*" ("Dalit's daughter"). She also told them, "Chamari hun, or Tumahari hun" ("I am a *Chamar*, and I am yours").

[24] See Narayan, *The Making of the Dalit Public in North India*. See also Badri Narayan, *Kanshiram: Leader of the Dalits* (New Delhi: Penguin, 2014).

as symbols of empowerment for Dalits in a political landscape devoid of such representations.

Prior Dalit social movements in Tamil Nadu and Maharashtra diffused prominent Dalit symbols into the party system. These were used by multiethnic and ethnic parties to mobilize Dalits. In Uttar Pradesh and Bihar, by contrast, until the rise of the BSP, JD, and LJP, Dalits remained largely invisible, and, despite electoral participation, their need for recognition was not met.

Mobilization and Bloc Voting

In rural and urban India, in matters of life (dining, residence, marriage)—and death (funerals)—Dalits remain segregated from others.[25] This separation traps them in their caste identity. Their separation should therefore aid bloc voting in electoral politics. But Chapter 5 has already illustrated that bloc voting among Dalits and the salience of caste in their selection of parties vary across states.

As discussed previously, social mobilization had two distinct effects in the movement states. In Tamil Nadu and Maharashtra, social mobilization resulted in the recruitment of Dalits in multiethnic parties and widened the base of these parties. Social mobilization also introduced Dalit symbols and demand for recognition to the process of electoral mobilization.

Bloc Voting in Movement States

In Tamil Nadu and Maharashtra, the presence of workers from multiple parties points to support for different parties in the same neighborhood and locality. Interview subjects reported campaign visits of multiple parties, and they were more likely to say that fellow Dalits in the neighborhood supported different parties.[26] Additionally, Dalits in these localities also expressed a greater willingness to vote for different parties across elections. "When the DMK forgets the people," said a focus group participant in Tamil Nadu, "the people will forget the party and vote for another party." "In this village, people used to vote for the RPI," remembered an elderly villager during an interview in Maharashtra, "Gradually many voters shifted to the Congress. But today we even have some Shiv Sena supporters." Focus group participants and interview subjects reported voting for different parties when they were dissatisfied with government responsiveness.

---

[25] Dalit streets, localities, and house clusters are separate from others. In their daily lives, Dalits continue to face social exclusion.

[26] See Center for the Study of Developing Societies, *Indian National Election Study, 1971* (New Delhi: Center for the Study of Developing Societies, 1971).

During the focus group discussions and follow-up interviews, voters were also asked to list their reasons for supporting political parties. In Tamil Nadu and Maharashtra, the responses revealed that voters did not turn to caste as frequently as voters did in non-movement states. And, in the instances when they selected a party for caste-based reasons, voters did not turn to the same multi-ethnic or ethnic party. Discussion participants and interview subjects cited government programs for schooling, the building of water tanks, and access to loans, development programs, and flood relief as well as populist policies advanced by parties. Others were drawn to party leaders or to particular candidates. In both Tamil Nadu and Maharashtra, Dalits supported multiple parties. A distinguishing feature of Dalits' responses to the questions was that access to government programs was reported as often being linked to political parties rather than to caste. To get access to government programs or obtain assistance from a state official, party affiliation and ties to a party worker or a party official mattered more than caste solidarity. In movement states, Dalits consistently report lower interest in bloc voting, are less likely to vote as a bloc behind a single party at the locality level, and are less likely to rely on ethnicity to choose political parties. The presence of social mobilization entrepreneurs and party workers from multiple parties produces these outcomes.

On the one hand, mobilization entrepreneurs and party workers support activities related to caste identity; on the other hand, they connect these localities to political parties. For voters in these localities, different political parties have a Dalit face, which makes it more difficult for voters to rely on caste identity to choose a party. This lowers the salience of caste in the selection of parties at the locality level.[27]

In movement states, to attract Dalit voters competing parties had to move beyond just caste-based appeals. Beyond a point parties could not distinguish themselves on the bases of such appeals. Dalit voters, despite sharing a caste identity in Tamil Nadu and Maharashtra, were divided in their preferences for political parties and party leaders, their engagement with electoral promises, and their interests. Dalit and non-Dalit party workers belonging to multiethnic parties corroborated these views. These party workers did not perceive Adi-Dravidas in Tamil Nadu and Mahars in Maharashtra as supporters of a single party, and they thought it beneficial to compete for these votes. This is why more parties visit Dalit localities and neighborhoods in these two states.

Besides party competition for Dalit votes, the recognition Dalits enjoyed in the party system also has a bearing on the attitudes toward bloc voting. Symbols

---

[27] The interviews showed that a Dalit voter did not always vote for the same party across elections—indeed, 28% of the subjects reported that their party loyalties often shifted from one election to another—but at the level of the locality, Dalits were not voting as a bloc.

of Dalit emancipation and self-assertion, originally produced by movements, have been gradually appropriated by a number of political parties. Together, these factors deny Dalit parties the use of potent ethnic appeals. Parties use symbols to signal their inclusiveness to voters. With the saturation of symbolic politics, parties in Tamil Nadu and Maharashtra can no longer distinguish themselves through the use of ethnic symbols. On their part, Dalit voters are more attentive to party promises regarding public goods and which party can be trusted to deliver on them. In Tamil Nadu, Dravidian parties turn to different types of populist programs to mobilize Dalit voters. These include the provision of television sets to poor families, low-cost food grains, and public welfare initiatives such as the mid-day meal program, subsidized food canteens, and housing and insurance programs for the poor.[28]

In Maharashtra, the Congress Party used the cooperative movement and the employment guarantee program to bring the poor into the welfare net. This has been to the benefit of Dalits, who are disproportionately poor. The cooperative program became a mechanism for extending state patronage and for recruiting and retaining Dalit mobilization entrepreneurs.[29] Parties competed to capture cooperatives in order to consolidate electoral support among voters. Through banks, schools, and factories linked to the cooperatives, the Congress Party recruited and retained local Dalit notables.

From the perspective of a Dalit party in a movement state, the ubiquity of Dalit symbols and the presence of Dalit organizations pose a challenge. Unlike the BSP in Uttar Pradesh or the LJP in Bihar, a Dalit party in a movement state does not possess or benefit from the significance attached to being the only symbol of Dalit identity. As a result, the Dalit party's campaign slogans and symbols do not resonate with Dalit voters in the same way as they would in Uttar Pradesh or Bihar. A BSP district president in Nagpur acknowledged this problem: "Maharashtra is the *karm bhumi* [roughly "hub"] of Dalit politics. In this region, everyone wears a blue hat.[30] That makes it very difficult for us to establish an emotional connection with the voter." A Dalit MLA from the Congress Party expressed a similar view: "You cannot compare the Dalit voter in Maharashtra to the one in Uttar Pradesh. The voter in Maharashtra is looking for economic progress. We cannot mobilize our brethren in the name of Babasaheb [Ambedkar] alone. Babasaheb is everywhere. Everyone uses him." In Tamil Nadu, in Dalit localities, VCK party workers compete with workers from other

---

[28] Political parties rely on their party activists in the Dalit localities to ensure that Dalits are made aware of these programs and are able to access them.

[29] See D. W. Attwood, "Patrons and Mobilizers: Political Entrepreneurs in an Agrarian State," *Journal of Anthropological Research*, vol. 30, no. 4 (1974), pp. 225–241.

[30] The color blue is associated with Dr. B. R. Ambedkar and Dalit politics.

political parties. To mobilize Dalits, the VCK appeals to the ideology of Periyar and Dr. Ambedkar, with which many Dalits are already familiar.

Similarly, as the BSP has tried to expand its vote share among Dalits in Maharashtra, it has come up against two challenges. First, even as BSP workers appeared in Dalit neighborhoods, they had to compete against Dalit workers from other parties that were already present in the same locality. Second, the BSP mobilization in Maharashtra was not introducing Dalits to a new ideology of emancipation. The anticaste ideology was already well-entrenched in Dalit neighborhoods and localities.

In movement states, then, multiethnic parties built an exchange relationship that was based both on material transfers and on recognition of Dalits. Since multiple parties provide recognition (a pure public good), recognition is not an issue on which political parties can differentiate themselves in the eyes of the Dalit voter. Dalit party leaders and symbols have therefore failed to encourage the formation of Dalit electoral blocs.

When Dalits choose to affiliate with different parties, their electoral solidarity is not produced at the neighborhood level, to reinforce the shared caste identity; instead, the two cut across each other. Moreover, Dalit symbols and the demand for recognition are no longer able to act as a unifying force for Dalit voters. Among Dalits, consequently, at the locality level in movement states, the preference for bloc voting has remained relatively weak. As one VCK functionary complained before the 2006 Tamil Nadu state assembly elections, "One of our biggest problems is the lack of unity. There are fifty different voices and fifty different agendas within the community. Without coming together as a group, we cannot win elections."

Bloc Voting in Non-movement States

In Uttar Pradesh and Bihar, the Congress Party, which until the 1980s received a sizable Dalit vote, did not expand its base and recruit party workers in Dalit localities.[31] Even when the Congress Party began to mobilize voters directly, in the 1970s and 1980s, it had a very thin base of party workers among Dalits. This pattern of weak penetration of Dalit localities began to change with the emergence of the BSP. According to focus group participants and interview subjects, the appearance of Dalit party workers and social mobilization entrepreneurs in

---

[31] The undermobilization of Dalits in Uttar Pradesh and Bihar is reflected in the turnout figures for the group in the 1971 election. In Uttar Pradesh and Bihar, 50.5% of Dalits voted, whereas in Tamil Nadu and Maharashtra the Dalit turnout was 75.5%; see Samuel James Eldersveld and Bashiruddin Ahmed, *Citizens and Politics: Mass Political Behavior in India* (Chicago: University of Chicago Press, 1978).

these localities in Uttar Pradesh and Bihar was more recent, with this transformation having occurred only in the past generation. The responses to questions during the focus group discussions and interviews illustrate the undermobilization experienced by Dalits. The elderly interview subjects reported that when Congress Party candidates used to visit during campaigns, until the 1980s, they were accompanied by people from outside the village or by the prominent notables of the village. On the few occasions when Dalits had visited to campaign for the Congress, they were from the adjoining towns. One elderly voter observed, "Earlier, when parties campaigned in our village, everyone knew who was the master and who was the servant. The master was told to organize the vote. Nowadays, people from the party ask us for our votes. They all vanish after the polling, but during the election, party activists and local leaders make promises and plead with us for our votes." Another participant lamented, "Just because our people were not sitting on high chairs in high politics did not mean that we did not exist. We were represented by a class of people who still look down on us, even though they lived off our votes. That form of politics was wrong!" One more elderly villager recounted, "Those who ruled our daily lives also ruled our politics. But now those days are gone."

United behind a single party, or a local leader, Dalits, in Uttar Pradesh and Bihar, were more likely to view access to the state purely through a caste lens. The feeling among voters that the state views them through their caste identity, and they must make their claim on the state as a caste group is stronger in Uttar Pradesh and Bihar as compared to Tamil Nadu and Maharashtra. For example, interview subjects in Uttar Pradesh often cited instances of public projects that had stopped the moment the BSP had lost power in the state capital. Elections were often viewed as a contest among groups and focus group participants and interview subjects frequently justified their support for their caste parties by saying: "Every person votes with their community and their community's leader, so we do the same." Among party workers and candidates there was a strong perception that Dalit voters were most likely to vote as a caste bloc. In Uttar Pradesh, the Jatavs were viewed as a captive vote of the BSP, and in Bihar, the Dusadhs were viewed as strong LJP supporters.

In Uttar Pradesh and Bihar, as a subordinate group, Dalits were undermobilized during elections as vote blocs. Mostly tied to the Congress, Dalits came to support a single party. Voting for the Congress over a large number of elections reinforced the caste solidarity at the locality level among Dalit voters. The preference for bloc voting, especially prior to the rise of the BSP, is reflective of the undermobilization of Dalits in the electoral arena, but not of their social mobilization.[32] In non-movement states, Dalits were more likely to express high

---

[32] Bloc voting along caste lines is not the same as Dalit self-mobilization since this solidarity was local in nature (created at the locality level), externally motivated by political parties, and was restricted to elections.

interest in bloc voting, more likely to vote for a single party at the locality level, and more likely to rely on ethnicity to choose a political party.

Dalit preference for bloc voting in the non-movement states has remained high for decades and predates party system fragmentation in these states. Recall, in the 1971 Indian National Election Study, 60% Dalits in Uttar Pradesh and Bihar reported a preference for bloc voting, and in 2004, a majority (54%) were motivated similarly. A high proclivity for bloc voting does indeed make electoral success of an ethnic party more likely, but it does not guarantee it. A multiethnic party should just as easily be able to mobilize an ethnic bloc of voters as an ethnic party. In a fragmenting party system in the 1990s, then, why did Dalits shift their support from the Congress to the BSP and not other multiethnic parties? The promise of empowerment gave the Dalit and Backward-Caste parties an edge over multiethnic parties in the mobilization of Dalits.

In Uttar Pradesh and Bihar, after independence, the Congress saw itself as the sole benefactor of the marginalized. The party focused on the arithmetic of assembling the coalition of castes to maintain its hold on power in the two states. Congress Party's top-down attempt at mobilizing Dalits periodically relied on public programs. In the 1970s Congress gave a call to banish poverty and an attempt to redistribute land to Dalits. Congress-promoted programs for the poor were often named after members of the Nehru-Gandhi family, for example, the 'Indira housing program,' the 'Jawahar employment program,' and the 'Indira Gandhi old age pension program.' These were portrayed expressions of state benevolence and often viewed among the Congress Party elite as acts of noblesse oblige. During interviews, Congress politicians frequently mentioned these programs to highlight the party's contribution to Dalit uplift.

Although the economic deprivation of Dalits was acknowledged, their social exclusion, which left Dalits exposed to oppression and humiliation in rural areas, was not addressed. Without a prominent Dalit movement in the two states, Dalit mobilization remained restricted to the electoral cycle. The demands for equal treatment of Dalits were not made forcefully and did not enter the electoral arena. The day-to-day social indignities Dalits faced were reinforced by their absence from the public sphere. Dalits remained invisible in history, the arts, popular culture, and the mass media. Unlike in Tamil Nadu and Maharashtra, social discourse remained deeply entrenched in the norms of hierarchy.

In Uttar Pradesh and Bihar, without the social movements, non-Dalit attitudes on Dalit inclusion were slow to change, and the discursive shift required for the adoption of symbols had not occurred. Additionally, in the absence of Dalit social mobilization entrepreneurs and party workers, the Congress Party was not pressured to either create or borrow from other states' symbols that would honor Dalits and provide them public recognition.

The Congress Party was then unprepared to respond to the challenge of low caste assertion. By 1990, without symbols such as Dr. B. R. Ambedkar or Periyar to lean on, the Congress was bereft of any ideology of social justice in Uttar Pradesh and Bihar. Worse still, it was poorly represented in Dalit localities through Dalit party workers and mobilization entrepreneurs. The Hindu nationalist BJP, ascendant at the time of Congress' decline, suffered from the same deficiencies. The BJP broadened its social base in the 1990s to emerge as a multiethnic party, but it failed to mobilize Dalits in substantial numbers. It began to alter its mobilization strategy toward Dalits only by 2014.

When Dalit and other lower-caste parties emerged in the non-movement states, they turned out to be the first formidable collective statewide challenges to the caste system. These parties and their leaders developed enormous symbolic power. Cultural ideology and identity are always very precious gains for the socially deprived. The more pronounced the deprivation, the more socially sensitive, coveted, and contested are these gains generally.[33] Party rallies, slogans, and symbols signified self-assertion for Dalits.

Party workers from Dalit parties highlighted the symbolic significance of their parties for the voter. "We are an exploited people," one BSP worker said. "Dalits vote for us because we are their own *kheti* [crop]. Why would you plow someone else's field? We have never before had any organization of our own." "Where else can we compete with other groups?" asked one of my interview subjects in Bihar in 2006. He was then an LJP representative in his neighborhood. He said, "Other groups have more resources and are in a habit of dominating us . . . We have still not lost the habit of subservience . . . In elections, numbers matter. And as long as we are united we can compete. . . . Right now politics is the only place where my people can."

Dalit parties did not rely on newspapers and television to connect to their voters.[34] The information on the party, its ideology of lower caste assertion, and its rallies, slogans, and leaders spread through word of mouth. Party workers transmitted symbolic politics to the Dalit voter. They discussed the party leaders and mobilization slogans in their localities and neighborhoods.

The effect of this mobilization was visible during focus group discussions and interviews. Time and again in Uttar Pradesh and Bihar, interview subjects and focus group participants explained their support for Dalit parties by pointing out, "Who else do we have?" Some said, "The BSP gave us a voice."

---

[33] R. S. Khare, *The Untouchable as Himself: Ideology, Identity, and Pragmatism among the Lucknow Chamars* (New York: Cambridge University Press, 1984).

[34] Television channels provided scant coverage to Dalit parties, and the reach of the newspapers was narrow because a large number of Dalits in Uttar Pradesh and Bihar were unlettered.

Others said, "Thanks to leaders like Ram Vilas Paswan and Lalu Yadav, the Dalit community now has some presence." "Even at this age, I have to do back breaking work," said an old woman who was a landless worker in western Uttar Pradesh, "Mayawati cannot change my life. But it is good that a Chamaran sits on the heads of these big people in the village and in the government." "We are with Behenji," declared one Dalit college student during a focus group discussion, "Which other Chamar in this country do the Thakurs [the local dominant caste] bow down to?" Similar sentiments were echoed by a focus group participant in Bihar when he said, "Lalu and Paswan talk like us. In front of government officials we are *gawaar* [uneducated or rustic]. They gave the gawaar a voice by waving a stick at the government officers." In Uttar Pradesh and Bihar, the issue of recognition remained attached to caste. Lower-caste parties and their leadership arose as symbols with mass appeal in such environments. Caste was a powerful mode for mobilizing Dalits, and caste-based parties and their leaders were the primary vehicles for seeking self-pride and recognition.[35]

A key frame for mobilization of Dalits had remained missing from the non-movement states; that is, recognition of Dalits as social equals had not emerged as an electoral demand. But that was changed by the emergence, at the moment of opportunity, of the BSP in Uttar Pradesh. In Bihar, the Backward-Caste parties that preceded the emergence of Dalit parties had made the demand for recognition. The marginalized were using their political parties to stake their claim to rule, a right that the caste system had fundamentally denied them. Thus the parties and personalities leading them represented multiple promises—improved access to the state and its functionaries, but also a reversal of the social order so that someone from the lowly servant caste could rule over the higher caste of

---

[35] For Uttar Pradesh, see Pushpendra, "Dalit Assertion through Electoral Politics," *Economic and Political Weekly*, vol. 34, no. 36 (1999), pp. 2609–2618; Ian Duncan, "Dalits and Politics in Rural North India: The Bahujan Samaj Party in Uttar Pradesh," *Journal of Peasant Studies*, vol. 27, no. 1 (1999), pp. 35–60; Sudha Pai, *Dalit Assertion and the Unfinished Democratic Revolution: The Bahujan Samaj Party in Uttar Pradesh* (New Delhi: Sage, 2002); Vivek Kumar, *Dalit Leadership in India* (New Delhi: Kalpaz Publications, 2002); Christophe Jaffrelot, *India's Silent Revolution: The Rise of the Lower Castes* (New York: Columbia University Press, 2003); Chandra, *Why Ethnic Parties Succeed*. For Bihar, see Francine R. Frankel, "Caste, Land and Dominance in Bihar: Breakdown of the Brahmanical Social Order," in Francine R. Frankel and M.S.A. Rao, eds., *Dominance and State Power in Modern India: Decline of a Social Order*, vol. 1 (New Delhi: Oxford University Press, 1989) pp. 46–132; Jaffrelot, *India's Silent Revolution*; Hetukar Jha, "Promises and Lapses: Understanding the Experience of Scheduled Castes in Bihar in Historical Perspective," *Journal of Indian School of Political Economy*, vol. 12, nos. 3–4 (2000), pp. 423–444; Sanjay Kumar, Mohammad Sanjeer Alam, and Dhananjai Joshi, "Caste Dynamics and Political Process in Bihar," *Journal of Indian School of Political Economy*, vol. 20, nos. 1–2 (2008), pp. 1–32; Jeffrey Witsoe, "Bihar," in Atul Kohli and Prerna Singh, eds., *Routledge Handbook of Indian Politics* (London: Routledge, 2013), pp. 298–307.

masters. This was a powerful and potent appeal. Often it was reinforced by the only Dalit party worker or mobilization entrepreneur, who represented the Dalit party in the Dalit locality. It sharply distinguished the Dalit and lower-caste parties from the multiethnic parties in the eyes of Dalit voters. Dalits were drawn to these parties as a voting bloc.[36]

Confirmation of the Relationship between Mobilization and Bloc Voting

The relationship between mobilization by parties and the preference for caste-based bloc voting across movement and non-movement states turns on the difference in competition for Dalit votes across these states. To confirm this relationship, I test one of its implications. Since Dalits and non-Dalits are mobilized by approximately the same number of parties in Tamil Nadu and Maharashtra, the caste of the respondent—Dalit or non-Dalit—should not matter for his or her preference toward bloc voting. In Uttar Pradesh and Bihar, where Dalits are mobilized by fewer parties than non-Dalits, Dalit and non-Dalit attitudes toward bloc voting should vary. The attitude toward caste-based voting, then, is the key dependent variable in the analysis. The caste of the respondent, categorized as Dalit or non-Dalit, is the key independent variable.

A linear regression of the data from the 2004 Indian National Election Study provides evidence for this intuition. As Table 6.3 shows, as a determinant of the attitude toward bloc voting, the variable of caste (Dalit or non-Dalit) is statistically significant for Uttar Pradesh and Bihar, but not for Tamil Nadu and Maharashtra. Dalit and non-Dalit attitudes toward bloc voting, then, are similar in movement states.[37] By contrast, in the non-movement states, Dalits' attitudes differed from those of non-Dalits, with Dalits more likely to report the preference for bloc voting. For the Dalits in Uttar Pradesh and Bihar, lower social mobilization has meant less competition for Dalit votes. As a result, Dalits there have been more inclined toward bloc voting than non-Dalits living in the same states. Socially mobilized Dalits in Tamil Nadu and Maharashtra have access to a greater number of political parties, and therefore, for them, strong caste consciousness does not translate into large caste electoral blocs.

---

[36] The Backward-Caste and Dalit parties included the RJD, the LJP, and the BSP.
[37] The analysis controls for location (rural/urban), gender, age, and income.

Table 6.3. **Linear regression: Attitudes toward bloc voting in movement and non-movement states**

	Movement States		Non-movement States	
	t	*Standard Error*	*t*	*Standard Error*
Caste (Dalit or Non-Dalit)	−0.148	0.15	0.323 *	0.132
Education	−0.254 ***	0.072	−0.367 ***	0.056
Age	−0.004	0.054	−0.124 **	0.043
Location (rural or urban)	−0.458 **	0.171	−0.129	0.174
Socioeconomic status	−0.048	0.047	−0.107 **	0.038
Gender	0.380	0.398	0.410 **	0.126

$n = 5{,}292$; 2,341 in movement states and 2,951 in non-movement states.
$^{*}p < 0.1$; $^{**}p < 0.05$; $^{***}p < 0.01$

Reconsideration of Explanations for Dalit Mobilization

The analysis in this chapter has shown that multicaste parties are able to outcompete Dalit parties in the movement states of Tamil Nadu and Maharashtra, not because the Dalit voting bloc favors the former over the latter, but because the weak impulse for bloc voting among Dalits prevents the formation of such blocs. This, in turn, disadvantages the mobilization effort of the Dalit parties.

We know that Dalits in Tamil Nadu and Maharashtra vote in fewer numbers for Dalit parties than do Dalits in Uttar Pradesh and Bihar. A long-standing adage in Indian politics is that when Indians vote, they don't merely cast their votes; they actually vote their caste. The above analysis suggests that this adage applies only in some states and not in others. How voters come to be mobilized in a competitive party system influences their attitudes toward bloc voting. In the movement states of Tamil Nadu and Maharashtra, the multiple electoral solidarities that Dalits developed by supporting different parties have cut across the solidarity that social exclusion imposes on Dalits. In these states, despite a high degree of caste consciousness and persistence of social exclusion, Dalits are less likely to vote as a bloc than are Dalits in Uttar Pradesh and Bihar, who are more likely to vote their caste. Dalit parties—the VCK in Tamil Nadu and the BSP in Maharashtra, on the one hand, and the BSP in Uttar Pradesh and the LJP in Bihar, on the other hand—thus faced very different attitudinal terrain among Dalits in the moment of electoral opportunity in their respective states. Dalit parties in Uttar Pradesh and Bihar found it relatively easier to amass Dalit votes than did Dalit parties in Tamil Nadu and Maharashtra.

Both Tamil Nadu and Maharashtra have been home to strong regional movements. Did strong Tamil and Marathi regional mobilizations undermine Dalit ethnic politics in the two states? This is a plausible proposition. After all, a regional identity should subsume caste identity by offering a home to all social groups. The same is not true in practice, however. Regional or subnationalist movements are often led by members of dominant castes, and, therefore, they are not automatically inclusive. Inclusion rarely occurs without the agency of the excluded. In Tamil Nadu, Dalits found a home in the Dravidian movement because the movement strongly attacked the caste system, and as a result, it aligned itself with the nascent Dalit movement, which has always had its distinct appeal. By contrast, the Shiv Sena in Maharashtra that adopted the mantle of Marathi subnationalism was vehemently anti-Dalit in its early years. It attacked Dalits in 1978 when the state government decided to rename the Marathwada University after Dr. B. R. Ambedkar. Then again, in 1987, when the Maharashtra government published Dr. B. R. Ambedkar's complete works on the occasion of his birth centenary, the Shiv Sena made a major issue of a volume titled *Riddles of Hinduism* and attacked Dalits. Its mobilization was not centered on an anticaste discourse. In order to expand its vote share, the Shiv Sena opened its door to Dalits. But, to do this, it was forced to include Dalit symbols and recognize an anticaste discourse promoted by the Dalit movement. Today, the Shiv Sena supports the celebration of Dr. B. R. Ambedkar's birthday in Dalit localities.

Regional movements in Tamil Nadu and in Maharashtra became inclusive because of Dalit assertion. To assume that such movements are inherently inclusive toward socially marginalized groups is erroneous. Top-down nationalist movements rarely are. Take another example: compare the divergent fortunes of two identities proposed by two nationalist movements. The Dravidian movement and Periyar may have popularized the Adi-Dravida identity for Dalits. But, it was Iyothee Thasss, a Dalit social activist in the late nineteenth century, who first proposed and advocated for it. In my interviews, I found that the name Adi-Dravida is widely adopted in Tamil Nadu; a majority of my interview subjects preferred its use. Dalits have come to own the name because they had an agency in its creation. By contrast, the Harijan identity was proposed by Gandhi and adopted during the Congress-led Indian freedom movement, which was particularly strong in Uttar Pradesh and Bihar, but Dalits had no say in proposing the name. Over a period of time, as we have seen, the name Harijan has been discarded by Dalits in Uttar Pradesh and Bihar. Dalit movements have made multiple parties across the ideological spectrum, including the regional parties, more inclusive, and have thereby undermined the electoral prospects of emergent Dalit parties. It is also noteworthy that in Tamil Nadu and in Maharashtra, during the focus group discussions and interviews, Dalits rarely brought up the Tamil and Marathi regional identities as a reason for supporting a particular party.

Does the variation in the success of Dalit parties reflect the difference in the accommodation of Dalit elites across centralized multiethnic parties? Kanchan Chandra has argued that because the emergent Dalit elite could not be accommodated within the centralized Congress Party, this organizational blockage led to the rise of caste-based parties.[38] With the exceptions of the Communist Party and the BJP, almost all parties in India are centralized, which means that upward mobility is restricted for elites belonging to all ethnic groups across most parties. And yet, Dalit ethnic parties flourish only in some states?

On the whole, an organizational approach places the burden of causality for the rise of an ethnic party on the elite in the ethnic group. But an ethnic party's formation does not guarantee the party's success, which depends on the ability of the elite to persuade ethnic voters to support the party. How amenable ethnic voters are to such persuasion often depends on how they were previously mobilized. In fact, the last two chapters suggest that we need to revisit our understanding of inclusive parties. We often judge the inclusiveness of a multiethnic party by focusing on the votes that the party is able to garner from different groups, or by counting the number of elites from different groups. The above discussion points out that these may not be the most accurate indicators of inclusiveness, especially as it relates to marginalized groups such as Dalits.[39] The experience of Dalit mobilization suggests that in order to evaluate the inclusiveness of a political party, we must go beyond the party's vote share from different groups and the breakdown of the party elite, and instead probe the infrastructure in place for the mobilization of different groups. Recruiting party workers in a group's neighborhoods, using the group's symbols, and campaigning directly to the group's members are some of the instruments that a party uses to build credibility with and mobilize voters.

The role of money in electoral politics has been on the rise,[40] and it would be plausible to attribute the success of the BSP in Uttar Pradesh and the LJP

---

[38] Chandra, *Why Ethnic Parties Succeed*

[39] Findings from Latin America also come to a similar conclusion. Mala Htun shows that inclusion at the top, in legislatures and in cabinets, may not produce representation for marginalized groups. See Mala Htun, *Inclusion Without Representation in Latin America: Gender Quotas and Ethnic Reservations* (New York: Cambridge University Press, 2016).

[40] Devesh Kapur and Milan Vaishnav, eds., *Costs of Democracy: Political Finance in India* (New Delhi: Oxford University Press, 2018).

in Bihar on their access to more financial resources than VCK has been able to mobilize. Michael Collins, for example, has argued that to overcome its financial constraints, the VCK has had to ally with wealthier Dravidian parties in exchange for campaign support.[41] The difference in electoral performance of Dalit parties is not a function of financial resources at their command, however. The access to state power has indeed added to the resources of the BSP in Uttar Pradesh and the LJP in Bihar. Still, these parties did not begin their electoral journeys as wealthy organizations. To raise funds, they have turned to traditional as well as innovative solutions. The BSP and LJP have recruited wealthy candidates and asked them to contribute to party coffers. Such candidates are attracted to these Dalit-based parties because of the size of the electoral blocs these parties control. In its early days, the BSP turned to crowd funding, by requesting its Jatav supporters to contribute a small amount to party funds using the slogan "one rupee, one vote." Mayawati has asked her party workers to use the occasion of her birthday to make contributions to the BSP election funds.[42] And finally, the two parties are supposed to have raised funds through rent seeking while in government. In fact, their financial strength is the reflection of their electoral strength and not the other way around. Undoubtedly, finances matter to electoral campaigns, but if they were the determinants of electoral outcomes, incumbency in India would be an advantage for parties as well as candidates. That it is not points to the limited role of money in the process of mobilization.

Thus far, I have explored the effects of one type of collective action of Dalits—their social mobilization—on another type—their electoral mobilization by ethnic and multiethnic parties. Either by social movements or ethnic parties or multiethnic parties, Dalits have been mobilized in all four states. Still, do the forms that mobilization of the marginalized takes matter? The next chapter takes up this question and shows that the type of mobilization is consequential.

[41] Michael A. Collins, "Navigating Fiscal Contraints: Dalit Parties and Electoral Politics in Tamil Nadu," in Devesh Kapur and Milan Vaishnav, eds., *Costs of Democracy: Political Finance in India* (New Delhi: Oxford University Press, 2018), pp. 119–152.

[42] Milan Vaishnav, *When Crime Pays: Money and Muscle in Indian Politics* (New Haven: Yale University Press, 2017).

7

How Mobilization Type Shapes
Dalit Welfare

Mobilization is a means to an end. Dalits have mobilized to seek social and economic equality. They have turned to the Indian state, in particular, to address their poverty. The state is the major provider of welfare benefits and driver of human development. The national government operates a number of welfare schemes, but key services, including education, healthcare, electricity, etc., are delivered at the state level.[1]

Welfare indicators have improved substantially in India over time, but there has been considerable variation at the subnational level. The conventional explanation for this is that certain Indian states have outperformed others because of greater resource endowments and better quality public administration.[2] Thus, it is no surprise that Dalits in Tamil Nadu and Maharashtra are less poor overall than Dalits in Uttar Pradesh and Bihar. What is remarkable, however, and demonstrated here through a close analysis of welfare indicators over time, is that the *equality gap*, or disparity between Dalits and other groups in society, is considerably less in Tamil Nadu and Maharashtra than in Uttar Pradesh and Bihar. This speaks to how these states distribute welfare benefits, not their overall capacity to do so.

That Dalits have achieved greater welfare parity in movement states (where Dalits are not an electoral bloc and split their votes) than in non-movement states (where Dalits are an electoral bloc) are outcomes that need to be explained.

---

[1] With the transfer of additional financial powers from the federal government to the states in 2015, the role of the states in administering welfare programs has increased significantly.

[2] Scholars, in particular Jeffrey Witsoe, have argued that redistributive plans of lower-caste-based parties are thwarted by a reticent bureaucracy populated by higher caste functionaries. See Jeffrey Witsoe, *Democracy Against Development: Lower-Caste Politics and Political Modernity in Post-Colonial India* (Chicago: University of Chicago Press, 2013). The varied record of parties on redistribution raises the tantalizing question of why multiethnic parties are more adept at negotiating bureaucratic reticence than ethnic parties.

I argue the variation in welfare provision and subsequent human development outcomes turns on a distinction in types of mobilization. When Dalits act
collectively as a bloc, there are different consequences in the social sphere and
the electoral sphere. In the social sphere, collective action encourages petitioning and protests that put pressure on local bureaucrats, inform political parties of
Dalit issues, politicize Dalit concerns, and monitor state performance. Together
these can make parties as well as the state more responsive to Dalit needs.
Democratic accountability is thus increased. In the electoral sphere, however,
bloc behavior has two especially negative effects: (1) it transforms Dalits into
weak clients, meaning their ethnic party can take them for granted, and they are
unable to gain real political leverage in a multiparty system since their party is
not forced to compete for their votes; and (2) it increases the probability welfare schemes will be disrupted or dismantled with electoral transfers of power.
Democratic accountability is thus decreased.

Variation in Welfare Outcomes

I compare the welfare-related outcomes of Dalits with other social groups from
the early 1990s to the present. This period is marked by the onset of party system fragmentation and the rise of Dalit and other lower-caste ethnic parties to
power in Uttar Pradesh and Bihar. To assess welfare, I trace changes across three
indicators over time: (1) poverty rates; (2) literacy rates; and (3) the availability
of electricity in rural areas. Data on poverty rates provides an overall picture of
welfare. Data on literacy and electricity capture key aspects of development.[3]

Poverty Rates

I rely on poverty rates calculated by Arvind Panagariya and Vishal More and
based on National Sample Survey data to assess changes in poverty rates over
time for Dalits and other social groups.[4]

---

[3] Similar patterns are also found in National Family Health Survey data on infant mortality rates
and in a review of National Sample Survey data on availability of electricity in urban areas. These are
not presented here in deference to brevity.

[4] See Arvind Panagariya and Vishal More, "Poverty by Social, Religious and Economic Groups
in India and Its Largest States: 1993–1994 to 2011–2012," *Indian Growth and Development Review*,
vol. 7, no. 2 (2014), pp. 202–230. The authors standardize and re-estimate older Indian poverty rates
according to the Tendulkar line—a purchasing power parity measure. They rely on data from various
rounds of the National Sample Survey for their calculations. For a summary of debates around the
Tendulkar line, see Mihir Shah, "Understanding the Poverty Line," *The Hindu*, August 6, 2013.

In 1993–1994, Dalits in Tamil Nadu, Maharashtra, Uttar Pradesh, and Bihar were considerably poorer than other social groups. Dalits were not equally poor across states, but within states they were poorer than other groups by roughly the same degree. Across the four states, Dalit poverty ranged 15.6–19.6% points less than the state averages. (see Table 7.1.)

Between 1993–1994 and 2011–2012, poverty rates for Dalits and total poverty rates declined across all states. Yet, Dalits achieved varying levels of income parity across states. Tamil Nadu eliminated 62% of its gap between Dalits and the state average in this period. Maharashtra eliminated 86% of its gap between Dalits and the state average in this period. Both of these states, movement states where Dalits do not act as a strong electoral bloc and instead split their votes across parties, performed better than the national average (50%). Uttar Pradesh reduced its gap by 42%; this was less than the national average. Income parity between Dalits and other groups in Bihar was especially volatile; the difference in poverty rates between Dalits and the state as a whole actually increased from 15.6% to 16.9% over the full period.

Literacy Rates

I use Indian census data to examine changes in literacy rates for Dalits and other social groups between 1991 and 2011.[5]

In 1981, the majority of Dalits and Indians were unlettered. Literacy rates varied across states, but the gap between Dalits and other social groups within states was roughly similar. Dalit literacy rates ranged 18.4–24.7 percentage points less than the state averages. (see Table 7.2.) The disparity between Dalits and others shrank overall, but remained similar for Tamil Nadu, Uttar Pradesh, and Bihar in 1991; Maharashtra was an outlier in terms of its early increase in Dalit literacy

---

[5] Literacy is defined in the Indian Census as the ability to read and write in any one language. Literacy rates are calculated for the portion of the population aged seven years and older. Historically, the Indian government has been the major provider of education in the country, and literacy rates have closely reflected the public provision of education. Private schooling has expanded substantially in recent decades, however. Nearly 30% of children in rural areas now attend private schools. See Anita Joshua, "Over a Quarter of Enrolments in Rural India Are in Private Schools," *The Hindu*, January 16, 2014. But the poor have been the least likely to exit public schooling. Since the early 1990s in Uttar Pradesh, the World Bank has intervened directly in the state education system to improve it and remedy gender disparities. Literacy gains for the period studied (1981–2011) are thus tied to a combination of public, private, and, in the case of Uttar Pradesh, international organization-supported and monitored provision of education. Their precision as a proxy for the public provision of education has been somewhat reduced with time, but they likely remain generally accurate and the best indicator available. Literacy rates are a conventional proxy for assessing education, a key aspect of welfare.

Table 7.1. **Changes in poverty rates, 1993–2012**

		1993–1994	2004–2005	2009–2010	2011–2012	Absolute Change in Poverty Rate (-)	2011–2012 Gap/ 1993–1994 Gap (% Gap Reduction)
Split Vote	Tamil Nadu						
	Dalits	64.3	48.6	28.8	19.0	45.3	—
	Total	45.0	30.7	17.4	11.7	33.3	—
	Gap	**19.3**	**17.9**	**11.4**	**7.3**	—	0.38 (62)
	Maharashtra						
	Dalits	65.4	52.9	34.7	19.7	45.7	—
	Total	48.6	38.9	24.8	17.3	31.3	—
	Gap	**16.8**	**14.0**	**9.9**	**2.4**	—	0.14 (86)

Bloc Vote							
Uttar Pradesh	Dalits	68.2	55.2	52.3	40.9	27.3	—
	Total	48.6	41.0	37.8	29.5	19.1	—
	Gap	**19.6**	**14.2**	**14.5**	**11.4**	—	0.58 (42)*
Bihar	Dalits	76.4	77.3	67.7	51.0	25.4	—
	Total	60.8	54.6	53.7	34.1	26.7	—
	Gap	**15.6**	**22.7**	**14.0**	**16.9**	—	1.08
National Average	India						
	Dalits	60.5	50.9	40.6	29.4	31.1	—
	Total	45.7	37.7	29.9	22.0	23.7	—
	Gap	**14.8**	**13.2**	**10.7**	**7.4**	—	0.50 (50)

*Indicates gap was volatile and did not decline consistently over time.

Source: Arvind Panagariya and Vishal More, "Poverty by Social, Religious and Economic Groups in India and Its Largest States: 1993–1994 to 2011–2012," *Indian Growth and Development Review*, vol. 7, no. 2 (2014), pp. 202–230.

Table 7.2. Changes in literacy rates, 1981–2011

		1981	1991	2001	2011	Absolute Change in Literacy Rate, 1991–2011 (+)	2011 Gap/1991 Gap (% Gap Reduction)
Split vote	**Tamil Nadu**						
	Dalits	29.7	46.74	63.2	73.3	43.6	—
	Total	54.4	62.7	73.5	80.1	25.7	—
	Gap	**24.7**	**15.96**	**10.3**	**6.8**	—	0.43 (57)
	Maharashtra						
	Dalits	33.6	56.5	71.9	79.7	46.1	—
	Total	55.8	64.9	76.9	82.3	26.5	—
	Gap	**22.2**	**8.4**	**5.0**	**2.6**	—	0.30 (70)
Bloc vote	**Uttar Pradesh**						
	Dalits	15.0	26.85	46.3	60.9	45.9	—
	Total	33.4	41.6	56.3	67.8	34.4	—
	Gap	**18.4**	**14.75**	**10.0**	**6.9**	—	0.47 (53)**
	Bihar						
	Dalits	10.4	19.5	28.5	48.7	38.3	—
	Total	32.1	38.5	47.0	61.8	29.7	—
	Gap	**21.7**	**19.0**	**18.5**	**13.1**	—	0.69 (31)

National Average	India					
Dalits	21.4	37.4	54.7	66.1	44.7	—
Total	43.6	52.2	64.8	73.0	29.4	—
Gap	**22.2**	**14.8**	**10.1**	**6.9**	—	0.47 (53)

**The World Bank intervenes directly in the Uttar Pradesh education system. Literacy gains have occurred in this context and do not reflect the state's independent distribution of education across social groups.

Source: Census of India.

rates. Dalit literacy rates for the three states then ranged 14.75–19.0 percentage points less than the state averages in 1991. Disparities in Dalit literacy rates, then, were comparable as the party system fragmentation accelerated in the 1990s.

By 2011, the majority of Dalits (66.1%) and all Indians (73.0%) were counted as literate. For consistency in comparisons across indicators, I focus my data analysis on the period 1991–2011. During this time, Tamil Nadu eliminated 57% of its gap between Dalits and the state average, and Maharashtra eliminated 70% of its gap between Dalits and the state average. Both of these states, movement states where Dalits predominantly split their votes, performed better than the national average (53%). Uttar Pradesh's performance appears extraordinary and mirrors the national average.[6] Disparities in literacy rates in Bihar persisted through at least 2001 before dropping in 2011. Bihar eliminated just 31% of its gap between Dalits and the state average.

Electricity Usage

I rely on National Sample Survey data to track changes in the availability of electricity in rural areas for Dalits and other social groups between 1999 and 2010.[7]

In 1999–2000, disparities in the availability of electricity ranged from 16–100 homes per 1,000 distribution. (see Table 7.3.) This distribution is skewed, in part, by the extremely low provision of the service in Bihar. Disparities in Maharashtra (a movement state where Dalits split their votes) and Uttar Pradesh (a non-movement state where Dalits vote as an electoral bloc) were nearly identical, however, in spite of widely varying levels of service provision. Absolute increases in the availability of electricity for Maharashtra, Uttar Pradesh, and Bihar by 2009–2010 are also quite comparable.

In 2009–2010, more than 90% of all rural households in Tamil Nadu had access to electricity. This is a remarkable accomplishment and represents a 40% decrease in the disparity in availability of electricity between Dalits and the state average between 1999 and 2010. In the same period, Maharashtra reduced its

[6] It is difficult to tell how much the World Bank intervention in the state's education system has driven these results.

[7] The state plays a substantial and direct role in generating and delivering electricity, much more so than it does for other household amenities such as access to an improved water source or toilet, indicators that are sometimes used to assess the standard of living aspect of welfare. The state's commitment to providing electricity in rural areas also represents a significant challenge. Extending electricity to rural areas is costly, difficult practically, and selective. Power lines are built to some villages and not others; villages themselves remain highly segregated by social groups. For these reasons, it is useful to track changes in the availability of electricity in rural areas to gain a sense of how states balance their distribution of goods and services.

Table 7.3. Changes in availability of electricity in rural areas, 1999–2010

		NSS 55th Round, 1999–2000	NSS 61st Round, 2004–2005	NSS 66th Round, 2009–2010	Absolute Change in Availability of Electricity (+)	Round 66 Gap/ Round 55 Gap (% Gap Reduction)
Split vote	Tamil Nadu					
	Dalits	671	794	919	248	
	Total	741	846	961	220	
	Gap	**70**	**52**	**42**	—	0.60 (40)
	Maharashtra					
	Dalits	650	683	794	144	
	Total	750	762	842	92	
	Gap	**100**	**79**	**48**	—	0.48 (52)
Bloc vote	Uttar Pradesh					
	Dalits	136	151	242	106	
	Total	235	240	332	97	
	Gap	**99**	**89**	**90**	—	0.91 (9)*
	Bihar					
	Dalits	41	49	176	135	
	Total	57	101	183	126	
	Gap	**16**	**52**	**7**	—	0.44 (56)*

(continued)

Table 7.3. **Continued**

		NSS 55th Round, 1999–2000	NSS 61st Round, 2004–2005	NSS 66th Round, 2009–2010	Absolute Change in Availability of Electricity (+)	Round 66 Gap/ Round 55 Gap (% Gap Reduction)
National Average	India					
	Dalits	393	473	583	190	
	Total	484	549	657	173	
	Gap	**91**	**76**	**74**	—	.81 (29)

The variable traced is "primary source of energy used for lighting (electricity) in rural areas." NSS data is presented as a value per 1,000 households.

*Indicates gap was volatile and did not decline consistently over time.

Source: National Sample Survey.

Table 7.4. **Percentage change in gap between Dalits and state average across welfare indicators**

	Indicator	*Poverty rates*	*Literacy rates*	*Availability of electricity in rural areas*
	Period	*1993–2012*	*1991–2011*	*1999–2010*
Split vote	Tamil Nadu	–62	–57	–40
	Maharashtra	–86	–70	–52
Bloc vote	Uttar Pradesh	–42	-53**	–9*
	Bihar	+8	–31	–56*
	India	–50	–53	–29

*Indicates gap was volatile and did not decline consistently over time.
**The World Bank intervenes directly in the Uttar Pradesh education system. Literacy gains have occurred in this context and do not reflect the state's independent distribution of education across social groups.

gap between Dalits and the state average by 52%. Both states performed considerably better than the national average (29%) in the extent of gap reduction.

Uttar Pradesh and Bihar performed poorly, by comparison. Uttar Pradesh reduced its gap by just 9% over the period. More problematic is that the gap between Dalits and the state average was actually less in 2004–2005 than in 2009–2010.

In raw terms, Bihar reduced its gap by 56%, but this was not without considerable bias in how the service was provided in 2004–2005; the gap had actually increased 325% at that time. Bihar's volatility in service provision was much higher than Uttar Pradesh's and comes in the context of very low service provision overall. Notably, the data points in 2004–2005 measured service provision (and its intergroup distribution) under the RJD-controlled government.[8]

The performance of the four states across welfare indicators is summarized in Table 7.4.

These differences related to literacy and provision of electricity surfaced in my field observations in the four states. In Uttar Pradesh and Bihar during focus group discussions and interviews, I heard frequent complaints about Dalit children being treated poorly by higher-caste teachers at school. In the process of identifying my rural sample, I discovered villages where electricity had reached

---

[8] The Rashtriya Janata Dal (RJD), a lower-caste ethnic party supported heavily by Dalits, led the Bihar state government under Chief Minister Rabri Devi from March 11, 2000 to March 6, 2005.

upper-caste households, but not Dalit households. "Electricity arrived in our village in 1998," said a focus group participant in eastern Uttar Pradesh in 2004, "but it could not travel a hundred more yards to our houses." In 2009 in Bihar, I surveyed election campaigns in many villages where only the Dalit section of the village was without electricity connections. In the focus group discussions and interviews in Tamil Nadu and Maharashtra, the dominant grievances were qualitatively different and were common to Dalits and non-Dalits. Dalits wanted better quality teaching in government schools and demanded the conversion of primary schools into secondary schools so their children could continue their studies nearby. In some villages, focus group participants demanded computer training for their children, a concern that did not surface in the discussions in rural Uttar Pradesh and Bihar.[9] In these movement states, Dalits expressed anger about the duration of power cuts and not about power connections. But most importantly, Dalits shared these concerns with the rest of the village.

A pattern repeats itself across different indicators. Dalits experienced less relative deprivation vis-à-vis other social groups in states where they split their votes and their social mobilization enabled them to exert pressure on the state, than in states where they acted as an electoral bloc, and where in between elections, their weak social blocs were unable to put pressure on the state. Put another way, Dalit and lower-caste-based parties in Uttar Pradesh and Bihar were less effective in reducing the disparities between Dalits and non-Dalits than multiethnic parties in Tamil Nadu and Maharashtra.[10]

Social Mobilization and Welfare
Social Blocs and Democratic Accountability

For the marginalized and powerless to have any chance of working a political system to their advantage, they need to have in their midst individuals who know where and how to engage the political system as well as how to effectively mobilize the group. The process of social mobilization produces such capacity among the marginalized. Mobilization in the social sphere is beneficial for a number of reasons—the marginalized can voice their concerns, claim their entitlements, protest their neglect, and monitor the quality of public services provided to

---

[9] They could not always explain why computer training could help children; however, they had heard that there were good jobs to be had if children could use a computer.

[10] The causal link between Dalits' relative deprivation and electoral and social blocs is suggestive not definitive. See David Collier, "Understanding Process Tracing," *PS: Political Science and Politics*, vol. 44, no. 4 (2011), pp. 823–883.

Table 7.5. **Variation in Dalit petitioning at district offices across states**

	States	Total Petitioners
Movement States	Tamil Nadu	23
	Maharashtra	25
Non-movement States	Uttar Pradesh	15
	Bihar	9

them. These activities put pressure on parties and representatives seeking the vote of the marginalized to act in response.

A higher density of Dalit mobilization entrepreneurs, party workers, and NGOs in Tamil Nadu and Maharashtra are responsible for sustaining higher levels of petitioning and protest activities in these states. In Uttar Pradesh and Bihar, the density of such actors is much lower; most of the mobilization activity is carried out by political parties, and this is largely confined temporally to electoral campaigns. Mobilization entrepreneurs and party workers often connect Dalits to their elected representatives and the state. In between elections, these individuals show up to the offices of the elected representatives or the block-level bureaucrat with problems and concerns in their neighborhoods and localities. Often these petitions are related to access to public services, including reliable roads and transportation links, water and electricity, and schools, hospitals, and fair-priced shops. Sometimes petitioners request interventions with the police or members of the dominant community to resolve conflicts.

In 2006, I observed petitioning behavior of citizens over two days in two districts in each of the four states. (see Table 7.5.) I found that Dalits in Tamil Nadu and Maharashtra were far more likely to approach their elected representatives and local bureaucrats in movement states than in non-movement states. I counted twenty-three Dalit petitioners in Tamil Nadu, twenty-five in Maharashtra, fifteen in Uttar Pradesh, and nine in Bihar. Across all four states, roughly half the petitioners were seeking assistance for collective rather than individual concerns.[11]

Mobilization entrepreneurs and Dalit social organizations are also at the forefront of protest activities. These are aimed at local or statewide concerns ranging from raising minimum farm wages to protesting atrocities against Dalits to demanding proper implementation of programs meant for Dalits. Protest aims

---

[11] The observations were made on the same two days of the week. Petitioners were approached outside the offices of the sitting MP, MLA, and the block officer. Across all four states, Dalits were a small minority of the total number of petitioners.

may vary, but combined, protests demonstrate Dalits' strength and attract the attention of politicians. Most Dalit protest activity is small in scale, and large-scale shutdowns, strikes, and marches are rare.

Protests by a disadvantaged minority can favorably shift government behavior and policy.[12] When it comes to protests, scope matters; large protests by thousands that are backed by a political organization are more effective than small ones.[13] Still, the value of small protests in applying pressure on local and district-level government officials should not be discounted. "Even if thirty to forty people protest on a highway or outside a government office," a Dalit activist in Tamil Nadu explained, "it can create a law and order situation." He was referring to the threat of escalation of a protest into a violent standoff, a prospect government officials are eager to avoid. A protest can turn into a spectacle if it draws police and journalists, not to mention rival politicians. A police official confirmed this: "These days everyone has a cell phone [referring to the camera on the phone], and TV channels look for sensational videos." Dalit activists are eager to politicize their protests to draw maximum attention to their demands and themselves. They try to inflict disruptive costs on state officials to compel them to intervene on their behalf.[14] During fieldwork, I encountered few protests that were related to access to schools or electricity; still, protests have an indirect effect on the provision of such public services. Protests compel party and state officials to turn their attention to an area, and they embolden Dalits in their interaction with public officials.

In 2008–2009, over a period of six months, I tracked Dalit protest activities as reported in vernacular and English dailies in the four states. (see Table 7.6.) In Tamil Nadu, I recorded twenty-four protests and, in Maharashtra, twenty-one. In Uttar Pradesh and Bihar, the number of protests were far lower, just fourteen and six, respectively.

[12] A number of scholars have made this argument in their work. See Frances Fox Piven and Richard A. Cloward, *Poor People's Movements: Why They Succeed, How They Fail* (New York: Pantheon Books, 1977); James W. Button, *Blacks and Social Change* (Princeton: Princeton University Press, 1989); Richard C. Fording, "The Conditional Effect of Violence as a Political Tactic: Mass Insurgency, Welfare Generosity, and Electoral Context in the American States," *American Journal of Political Science*, vol. 41 (1997), pp. 1–29; Joseph E. Luders, *The Civil Rights Movement and the Logic of Social Change* (Cambridge: Cambridge University Press, 2010); David Q. Gillion, *The Political Power of Protest: Minority Activism and Shifts in Public Policy* (Cambridge: Cambridge University Press, 2013); S. Laurel Weldon, *When Protest Makes Policy: How Social Movements Represent Disadvantaged Groups* (Ann Arbor: University of Michigan Press, 2011).

[13] Gillion, *The Political Power of Protest*.

[14] A protest can inflict disruptive cost by upsetting the routine activity of the target and causing it material and reputational harm; see Luders, *The Civil Rights Movement and the Logic of Social Change*.

Table 7.6. **Variation in Dalit protests across states**

	States	Total Protests
Movement States	Tamil Nadu	24
	Maharashtra	21
Non-movement States	Uttar Pradesh	14
	Bihar	6

In the movement states, Dalits joined in protests with members of other groups on issues of common concern. I observed Dalit participation in a number of such protests: villagers protested in Tamil Nadu to demand improved bus service to their cluster of villages, labor protested in Tamil Nadu to demand better safety provisions at work, and peasants protested in Maharashtra to demand an increase in minimum wages for daily wage workers. In Uttar Pradesh and Bihar, I did not witness the same level of cross-caste participation in protests. Movement states, in general, are home to more protest activity than is the case in non-movement states.[15] Dalits in the movement states are more socially mobilized and have more opportunities to participate in protests than Dalits in non-movement states.

Dalits in movement states are also more vocal about the problems they face in accessing basic public services in their localities and neighborhoods. During my interviews and focus group discussions in Dalit localities, I inquired about the problems related to public services in the localities and neighborhoods. Across the four states, Dalits complained about public service delivery, but I noticed that the frequency and intensity of complaints were much higher in Tamil Nadu and Maharashtra than in Uttar Pradesh and Bihar. Out of the 203 Dalit interview subjects in Tamil Nadu and Maharashtra, 69.4% complained about public services. In Uttar Pradesh and Bihar out of the 206 Dalit interview subjects, only 51.9% by comparison mentioned a public-service-related grievance.

Dalits in the movement states also complained about more public services than Dalits in the non-movement states. But on the whole, Dalit neighborhoods and localities in Tamil Nadu and Maharashtra, the movement states, had access to a higher quantum of state provisions than localities and neighborhoods in Uttar Pradesh and Bihar.

---

[15] For example, according to the data released by the Indian Bureau of Police Research and Development, between 2011 and 2014 Tamil Nadu recorded a little over 78,000 protests and Maharashtra 27,000 protests. In the same period Bihar recorded 2,800 protests and Uttar Pradesh fewer than 500 protests.

When I probed this puzzling behavior further, I found that the expression of voter discontent regarding public service delivery reflected the politicization of these shared concerns in the neighborhoods and localities. Mobilization entrepreneurs and party workers often contribute to this process of politicization. In all four states, in localities with multiple party workers, I found that Dalit party workers frequently held each other responsible for failures such as bad sanitation facilities, the poor state of roads, electricity shortages, and uneven implementation of government programs. By contrast, they competed to take credit when such concerns were addressed. Blame games between local rivals and attempts to outbid rivals' promises politicize public service delivery and raise expectations regarding their quality. It is not surprising then, that Dalit discontent related to public services was more pronounced in the movement states of Maharashtra and Tamil Nadu where the density of mobilization entrepreneurs and party workers in Dalit neighborhoods and localities was higher. The more mobilized Dalit voters in Tamil Nadu and Maharashtra, despite relatively better access to public services, also have higher expectations about these services than their less mobilized counterparts in Uttar Pradesh and Bihar.

Marginalization-related constraints notwithstanding, Dalits in movement states are more likely to hold their political representatives accountable than Dalits in non-movement states. As compared to Uttar Pradesh and Bihar, Dalits in Tamil Nadu and Maharashtra are (1) more likely to protest their neglect by the state and discrimination by dominant groups; (2) more likely to petition their representatives and bureaucrats; and (3) more critical of public service delivery. Dalits in movement and non-movement states are situated differently in their ability to hold political parties and local bureaucrats accountable. This difference in their capacity to make demands on parties and state officials influences the day-to-day responsiveness of the state. But, these differences are further augmented by differences in the electoral incentives to remain attentive to Dalit welfare faced by ethnic and multiethnic parties in movement and non-movement states. Next, I outline these incentives and explain why they differ.

Electoral Mobilization and Welfare

Electoral Blocs and Democratic Accountability

Historically, marginalized groups are disproportionately poor. In practice, democratic accountability in the case of the poor is already constrained. We know that the poor as potential clients of political parties find it more difficult than those from middle- and upper-income brackets to hold their representatives accountable. The poor are less likely to protest, more vulnerable to intimidation, reluctant to turn to the courts, and their concerns rarely draw the attention of the news media. As citizens, the poor are especially prone to being invisible. "Poor people," claims Stuart Corbridge, "often see the state when the state decides to see them."[16] As elections approach, the state opens its eyes to the poor. But electoral blocs of the marginalized group can further exacerbate this problem. Bloc voting among a marginalized ethnic group hurts its welfare outcomes for two reasons: First, it makes the marginalized even weaker clients of their ethnic party. Second, it results in welfare policy disruption each time the marginalized's ethnic party is voted out of office.

Weak Clients

In the states of Uttar Pradesh and Bihar, until the 1990s, Dalits were a captive vote bloc of the Congress Party. Today, the same trend continues—the Jatavs in Uttar Pradesh are tied to the BSP while the Dusadhs in Bihar are attached to the LJP. Although Dalit voters take pride in their ethnic parties and that Mayawati and Ram Vilas Paswan have become leaders of national stature, they also complain their party workers take their support for granted and they have few choices other than the Dalit parties. "Other parties do not trust us," I heard frequently during interviews conducted in 2004 and 2009. "Even if we vote for them, they will not believe that we supported them. We see campaign vehicles from different parties on the highway, and we also get to see their posters. In the markets, we see their party workers. But, they do not come to our localities to ask for our votes." Party workers of other multiethnic and ethnic parties confirmed this view. I often heard comments like this: "What's the point of campaigning among Chamars? Everyone knows they only have eyes for the elephant [the BSP's electoral symbol]. There's no sense wasting time and resources to campaign among them." Sometimes even the BSP and the LJP did not campaign extensively in Dalit areas, so confident were these parties of obtaining Dalit support. "We know the Dusadh vote is behind us," said one LJP candidate. "So we must reach out to other groups to improve our prospects." A BSP party worker separately admitted, "The Jatavs are our people, so sometimes we don't even campaign in their localities. Instead, we spend our time and resources on localities where we are trying to pull more voters."[17]

With fewer parties competing for Dalit votes in Uttar Pradesh and Bihar, it was more difficult for Dalit voters to hold the party they supported accountable when it was in office. A party may even deliberately undersupply its core voters (most

---

[16] Stuart Corbridge, Glyn Williams, Manoj Srivastava, and René Véron, *Seeing the State: Governance and Governmentality in India* (Cambridge: Cambridge University Press, 2005), p. 10.

[17] For example, when the BSP was trying to mobilize upper-caste Brahmin voters in the 2007 state assembly election, the party's workers formed *bhaichara* (brotherhood committees) across different constituencies. These committees always had a substantially larger number of Brahmins than Dalits.

loyal supporters) with programs and focus primarily on swing voters (those who are not firm supporters of the party, but whose support is crucial to winning an election). An ethnic party can do this because its core supporters lack an effective mechanism for punishing the party or defecting.[18] Indeed, in Uttar Pradesh, BSP representatives have been found to focus on swing voters rather than on core supporters when it comes to providing villages access to electricity.[19]

In Uttar Pradesh and Bihar, an accountability mechanism does seem to be in place for higher-ranked groups, since competition for their votes is high, but not for Dalit voters.[20] In this sense, Dalits end up being weak clients in states where Dalit parties have had electoral success.[21] In the absence of strong competition for the Dalit vote, there are fewer incentives for Dalit parties to be responsive to Dalit voters. This does not mean that Dalit parties do not design policies for Dalits; they do.[22] But an ethnic or multiethnic party backed by a captive voting bloc is likely to undersupply its supporters with expected benefits. The BSP, for example, during its tenure in government, implemented a series of policies targeted specifically at Dalits. Its flagship program was the *Ambedkar Gram Vikas Yojana* ("Ambedkar Village Progress Program"; AGVY). Under this program, funds were allocated for public works in villages where Dalits made up more than 30% of the population. The party also distributed small plots of land and provided occupancy rights to land previously distributed to Dalits. Yet, the leakage of funds is rampant in premier programs launched by ethnic parties. For instance, a government audit of the AGVY found that one-third of the spending (USD $50 million) could not be accounted for. The money was presumably lost to fraud. With respect to corruption and welfare programs for the poor, Dalit ethnic parties are no different from other political parties. More often than not, the marginalized, who are either the actual or the potential beneficiaries of these public programs, are not in any position to protest corruption actively.

Nevertheless, there are two mechanisms by which voters can in fact punish a party: they can abstain from voting or they can support a rival

---

[18] See Susan C. Stokes, "Political Clientelism," in Carles Boix and Susan C. Stokes, eds., *The Oxford Handbook of Comparative Politics* (New York: Oxford University Press, 2007), pp. 604–627.

[19] See Brian Min, "Distributing Power: Electrifying the Poor in India," unpublished paper, 2010, available at http://www-personal.umich.edu/~brianmin/Min_UP_20101019.pdf.

[20] Such competition could also exist within a party, with more responsive patrons or representatives replacing less responsive ones. Typically, however, and apart from a few exceptions, Indian political parties are highly centralized organizations that lack transparent internal elections.

[21] See Steven Wilkinson, *Votes and Violence: Electoral Competition and Ethnic Riots in India* (Cambridge: Cambridge University Press, 2004).

[22] See Sudha Pai, *Dalit Assertion and the Unfinished Democratic Revolution* (New Delhi: Sage, 2002); Santosh Mehrotra, "Well-Being and Caste in Uttar Pradesh: Why UP Is Not Like Tamil Nadu," *Economic and Political Weekly*, vol. 41, no. 40 (2006), pp. 4261–4271.

party.[23] Parties that rely on Dalit voting blocs undersupply them with programs and patronage. Why, then, do Dalits not resort to these two punishment mechanisms?

During interviews, a number of reasons surfaced to explain such an outcome. Dalits were rarely aware of the large-scale corruption that occurred in the distribution and implementation of government contracts. The Dalit voter, I found, was more interested in the actual benefit of the program than in the amount of public money lost to corruption. Only when public services are delivered to them, do they experience and form a strong opinion on corruption related to programs. Public service delivery-related concerns came up regularly during interviews and focus group discussions in Uttar Pradesh and Bihar in 2004 and 2009, and the highest frequency of responses suggested that once a party transforms itself into a vehicle for group dignity and respect, then the voter-party relationship no longer operates on material transactions. Their weak record in delivering public services to Dalits notwithstanding, the support for the BSP among the Jatav and for the LJP among the Dusadhs remains steadfast. One interview subject in Uttar Pradesh said, "The BSP should fulfill its responsibility towards us. I fulfill my duty towards the community by voting for the party." Another focus group participant in the same state echoed the sentiment, "The party is like our mother. Do I stop respecting my mother if she does not feed me delicious food every day? We will not stop supporting the BSP." A focus group participant in Bihar asked, "No political party does anything for the poor, so why should I punish my party?" Older voters who acknowledged the deficiencies in how their ethnic parties treated them were still committed to the party, because they felt that parties such as BSP and LJP treated them better than the Congress Party had in previous decades. But Dalits were also conscious that they could do little to change the ways of their parties. Only when a child cries, will a mother listen, a focus group participant in Uttar Pradesh lamented. "We are poor. We do not have a say. Our voice dies inside us."

In Tamil Nadu and Maharashtra, where Dalits are less likely to vote as an electoral bloc, there are more incentives for political parties, even multiethnic parties, to be responsive to Dalits' concerns.[24] Multiethnic parties in Tamil Nadu and Maharashtra have been more inclusive, especially at the base; these parties have networks among all groups, including Dalits, and these networks have made the parties more attentive to the well-being of the poor. Multiple parties campaign in Dalit localities, and party workers in Dalit localities do not take the

---

[23] See Gary Cox, "Swing Voters, Core Voters, and Distributive Politics," in Ian Shapiro, Susan C. Stokes, Elisabeth Jean Wood, and Alexander S. Kirshner, eds., *Political Representation* (New York: Cambridge University Press, 2009), pp. 342–357.

[24] A number of scholars have pointed to differences between Uttar Pradesh and Tamil Nadu with respect to indicators of well-being. See Amartya Sen and Jean Drèze, *India: Economic Development*

Dalit support for granted. Dalit voters, on their part, are willing to shift their allegiances during elections based on the appeals made by parties and leaders. Welfare programs begun in the two states by multiethnic parties reflect this cross-group mobilization strategy. These states gave birth to two of India's best-known pro-poor programs: the mid-day meal scheme, developed in Tamil Nadu, and the Employment Guarantee Scheme (EGS), developed in Maharashtra.

In 1960, the Congress Party government in Tamil Nadu began to provide mid-day meals to elementary schoolchildren in districts with high concentrations of poor people. In 1982, the All India Anna Dravida Munnetra Kazhagam (AIADMK) government extended the program to all the districts in the state. The program's objectives were to expand school enrollment among children belonging to the poorest families and to improve student retention in the schools. The program also aimed to reduce rates of malnutrition among schoolchildren. Since the inception of the program, its scope and breadth have been upgraded under the tenures of different governments. It has been extended to the secondary schools, and there have been improvements in the caloric and nutritional content of the meals served. Tamil Nadu has recorded rapid growth in its literacy rates and has also reduced malnutrition among children. The program was so successful that in 2001 the Indian Supreme Court ordered it extended to all government-run schools in the country. It is the largest such program in the world, feeding 120 million children in India every day.

The Employment Guarantee Scheme (EGS) was begun by the state government in Maharashtra in 1970. Its initial objective was to guarantee at least one hundred days of annual employment to the poorest households in the state during a drought, but the EGS was extended. It not only increased the sense of entitlement among the poor in Maharashtra but also contributed to a reduction in the poverty rate. Given the successes of the EGS in Maharashtra, in 2005 it was launched across India's one hundred most economically distressed districts, and in 2008 it was extended nationwide.

It is no coincidence that these two pioneering poverty-alleviation programs appeared in Tamil Nadu and Maharashtra. They reflect the social-mobilization-generated compulsion of political parties in those states to respond to the

and Social Opportunity (New Delhi: Oxford University Press, 1999); Jean Drèze and Amartya Sen, *An Uncertain Glory: India and Its Contradictions* (Princeton: Princeton University Press, 2013). See also Mehrotra, "Well-Being and Caste in Uttar Pradesh," pp. 4261–4271 where the author shows that indicators of nutrition, reduced infant mortality, literacy, and access to electricity, sanitation, and clean water are higher in Tamil Nadu than in Uttar Pradesh. Mehrotra argues that Tamil Nadu's higher indicators of well-being are related to the social mobilization of the lower castes in that state, by contrast with the electoral mobilization of the lower castes in Uttar Pradesh, but his perceptive observation does not outline the mechanism that produces these different mobilization-related effects.

material distress of the poor, including Dalits. Caste-based mobilization among the poorest groups increased the competition for these groups' votes among political parties. Dalits divided their support among different parties. In fact, during the phase of party system fragmentation, most parties in these states came to view Dalits as supporters or potential supporters. Since the Dalit voters even among the largest and politically influential subcastes, Adi-Dravidas in Tamil Nadu and Mahars in Maharashtra, mostly do not vote their caste, political parties cannot take their support for granted. This is why multiethnic parties have developed welfare programs in order to cement their support among these groups. Such programs are caste-neutral, since they target the poor irrespective of caste.

Policy Disruption

During my visits to Dalit localities in the early stage of my fieldwork in Uttar Pradesh, I often encountered half-built community halls, roads, and electric poles that were without wires. These were projects that were begun during BSP rule in 2002–2003, and then were left incomplete when the BSP government had lost power. Governments changed hands from one party to another even in Tamil Nadu, but I did not observe public services in Dalit localities suffering a similar fate.

The electoral blocs of the marginalized influence their welfare outcomes adversely in yet another way. Each time the ethnic party is voted out of office and a rival party that is not tied to the marginalized group takes office, the welfare policies for the marginalized will be disrupted, and members of the group will lose their access to the state.[25] When the marginalized do not vote as a bloc, competition for their votes ensures policy continuity even as parties get voted in and out of office. When parties view a segment of voters as supporters or potential supporters, they are less likely to discontinue welfare programs for that segment begun by the rival party.

With the success of lower-caste-based ethnic parties, it became commonplace for policies to target particular ethnic groups. In non-movement states, where welfare programs came to be associated with particular ethnic groups, programs catering to those groups' needs were designed and implemented only when those groups' chosen parties were in power. As a result, Dalits in Uttar Pradesh experienced disruption of the welfare programs that were designed for them by the Congress and the BSP. The programs to redistribute land to landless Dalits implemented by both parties came to a stop when they were voted out of office. This pattern is anecdotally well known. During my

---

[25] The same argument would hold true if the marginalized voted as a bloc at the state level for a multiethnic party instead of an ethnic party.

interviews with party workers, I was repeatedly told that when the BSP is not in power in Uttar Pradesh, Dalit-focused programs lose their budgetary support. In Uttar Pradesh, Samajwadi Party rule is assumed to be beneficial to Yadavs and Muslims, whereas BSP rule is assumed to benefit Dalits; in Bihar, Yadavs (Bihar's most politically prominent OBCs) are supposed to have benefited disproportionately during Lalu Yadav's three terms in government, whereas Kurmis and upper-caste citizens are said to benefitted after 2006 from the Janata Dal United–BJP coalition government. BSP-initiated welfare programs were suspended as soon as the government changed. Similarly, the BSP has discontinued targeted programs begun by other ethnic parties. These disruptions have increased wastage because very often projects are left incomplete at the moment the government collapses or is voted out.

The implication here is that when a group votes as a bloc and is viewed as the captive bank of a particular party, the group is likely to experience disruption in its access to welfare-related programs when that party is voted out of office. Furthermore, in non-movement states, Dalits are tied to fewer parties and are therefore likely to lose contact with the state when their ethnic party is not in office. These disruptions perpetuate the absolute deprivation facing Dalits. They also prevent the narrowing of disparities between Dalits and non-Dalits.

Populist welfare policies in the movement states of Tamil Nadu and Maharashtra did not target specific ethnic groups. As a result, some welfare programs continued when governments changed; other programs disappeared, but new ones were begun in their place. Moreover, in the movement states, where there are more party workers from more parties and more campaign visits to Dalit localities, Dalits do not lose contact with the state when the state government changes.

At its very minimum, the electorally successful ethnic parties of a marginalized group represent higher levels of descriptive representation for the group. But we would expect these descriptive representation related gains to also translate into material gains for the marginalized. After all, the material needs of the marginalized are urgent. Parties mobilize voters on the promise of representing their interests; they connect the voters to the state. Scholars from around the world report that ethnic group mobilization, when it occurs, seeks access to the state for material benefits.[26] Caste mobilization, it is argued, seeks state patronage.[27] Caste-based "narrow" ethnic parties tend to divert scarce state resources towards coethnics instead of focusing on the provision of public

---

[26] See Robert Bates, "Ethnic Competition and Modernization in Contemporary Africa," *Comparative Political Studies*, vol. 6, no. 4 (1974), pp. 457–484; Donald Horowitz, *Ethnic Groups in Conflict* (Berkeley: University of California Press, 1985); Paul Collier, *Wars, Guns, and Votes: Democracy in Dangerous Places* (New York: Harper, 2009).

[27] See Kanchan Chandra, *Why Ethnic Parties Succeed: Patronage and Ethnic Head Counts in India* (Cambridge: Cambridge University Press, 2004).

goods.[28] Ethnic party success, then, should result in the relative welfare gains for the allied ethnic group.

The rise of lower-caste parties in Uttar Pradesh and Bihar during the 1990s was viewed as a revolutionary moment in Indian politics.[29] And yet, scholars and commentators have long lamented that the politics of recognition promoted by lower-caste-dominated (Dalit or OBC) parties in the two northern states has not produced a politics of redistribution.[30] The rise of the BSP, the *Samajwadi Party* ("Socialist Party"; SP), RJD, and LJP has not reliably advanced the well-being of the marginalized supporting them according to several indicators; instead, citizens and groups with more resources have cornered the benefits of government programs.[31] In addition, ethnographic work in rural Uttar Pradesh finds that the rise of new Dalit political actors at the village level has not been accompanied by an improvement in the group's economic standing. Thus, political change is not seen as having been translated into economic improvement, and where there is evidence of economic improvement, it is attributed not to political factors but rather to changes in the economic environment that have improved Dalits' livelihoods.[32]

[28] See Tariq Thachil and Emmanuel Teitelbaum, "Ethnic Parties and Public Spending: New Theory and Evidence From the Indian States," *Comparative Political Studies*, vol. 48, no. 11 (2015), pp. 1389–1420.

[29] See Pai, *Dalit Assertion and the Unfinished Democratic Revolution*; Christophe Jafferlot, *India's Silent Revolution: The Rise of the Lower Castes*; Vivek Kumar, *India's Roaring Revolution: Dalit Assertion and New Horizons* (New Delhi: Gagandeep, 2006) .

[30] Scholars who focus on issues of governance view the rise of caste-based political parties with substantial skepticism. For them, the rise of such parties encourages policies based on patronage rather than programmatic policies. See Philip Keefer and Stuti Khemani, "Why Do the Poor Receive Poor Services?" *Economic and Political Weekly*, vol. 39, no. 9 (2004), pp. 935–943. One scholar sees lower-caste parties not as heralding a new era in pro-poor policies but rather as plundering the treasury while claiming to follow in the footsteps of the upper-caste-dominated parties that were previously in control. See Pranab Bardhan, "Sharing the Spoils: Group Equity, Development, and Democracy," in Atul Kohli, ed., *The Success of India's Democracy* (Cambridge: Cambridge University Press, 2001), pp. 226–241. Other scholars claim that the quality of governance becomes a low priority for poor voters when identity drives their choice of political parties. See Pratap Bhanu Mehta, *The Burden of Democracy* (New Delhi: Penguin, 2003); Ashutosh Varshney, "Democracy and Poverty," in Deepa Narayan, ed., *Measuring Empowerment: Cross-Disciplinary Perspectives* (Washington, DC: World Bank, 2005), pp. 383–401. An opposing view holds that state resources in the form of programmatic policies do not amount to much for poor and marginalized Dalits anyway, since government programs do not even reach the group in the absence of Dalit parties and elected Dalit representatives. See Kumar, *India's Roaring Revolution*.

[31] See Mehrotra, "Well-Being and Caste in Uttar Pradesh," pp. 4261–4271.

[32] See Devesh Kapur, Chandra Bhan Prasad, Lant Pritchett, and D. Shyam Babu, "Rethinking Inequality: Dalits in Uttar Pradesh in the Market Reform Era," *Economic and Political Weekly*, vol. 45, no. 35 (2010), pp. 39–49.

The above analysis suggests the need for deeper and more systematic inquiry across Indian states into how the mobilization of a marginalized group actually influences the creation and implementation of programmatic policies benefiting the group. An ethnic party allied with a marginalized ethnic group represents one form of group assertion. In this sense, the party embodies the political equality that democracy promises to all groups irrespective of their social standing. As the evidence presented in this chapter demonstrates, however, the electoral success of Dalit parties is not a prerequisite for Dalit welfare. Dalits' welfare outcomes are better when they are able to form social blocs to petition party and state officials, protest state neglect, and divide their votes between parties instead of voting as an electoral bloc. In terms of welfare outcomes, Dalits are worse off when they form electoral blocs to support parties.

Party competition is supposed to be beneficial for the poor.[33] We need to be careful when we assess the degree of party competition in a party system, however. We rely on vote shares of political parties to draw these conclusions. The above discussion on effects of Dalit mobilization suggests that a high degree of party competition in the system and low competition for a group's support can go hand in hand. As a result, such groups that are a captive vote bloc for a party end up being underserved by the benefits of competitive politics. To understand and evaluate the benefits of competitive politics in diverse societies, it is therefore important to dig deeper into vote shares and inquire whether parties are actually competing for the votes of all the groups equally or if the competition for some groups is higher than others.

The mobilization of a marginalized group, when it occurs, is no small feat. Whether it is in the social or the electoral sphere, or both, the collective action of the marginalized already represents the overcoming of serious constraints. So, then, why does it matter what form this mobilization takes? In this chapter, I have shown that social and electoral blocs of the marginalized have very different effects, and therefore, the form that mobilization takes is consequential for welfare outcomes for the marginalized.

---

[33] Rina Agarwala, in her work on urban poor in India, highlights the benefits of competitive politics; see Rina Agarwala, *Informal Labor, Formal Politics, and Dignified Discontent in India* (New York: Cambridge University Press, 2013). Also, Pradeep Chhibber and Irfan Nooruddin, through a cross-state analysis, show that in India party competition within bounds produces public policy benefits; see Pradeep Chhibber and Irfan Nooruddin, "Do Party Systems Count? The Number of Parties and Government Performance in Indian States," *Comparative Political Studies*, vol. 37 (2010), pp. 152–187. Timothy Besley, Persson Torsten, and Daniel M. Strum similarly exploit variation in party competition across U.S. states to show that lack of political competition hinders economic growth; see Timothy Besley, Persson Torsten, and Daniel M. Strum, "Political Competition, Policy and Growth: Theory and Evidence from the US," *The Review of Economic Studies*, vol. 77, no. 4 (2010), pp. 1329–1352.

8

The Identity Trap

We eat, drink, live, and die in our community. Our community is the
only thing we have.
> —A Dalit agricultural worker in Mawana Uttar Pradesh.[1]

As long as people don't know that you are a Dalit, things are fine. The
moment they find out your caste, everything changes. . . . Why is my
caste my only identity?
> —Omaprakash Valmiki, Hindi author and poet.[2]

The bottom line always stood out: I was a mere Mahar, a Dalit, a
Harijan, and a Scheduled Caste, belonging to the lowest stratum of
society. It was as if I was tainted with a singular blemish—a tragic
flaw inherited through birth. No matter what I did, where I went, or
what success I achieved, I would always be looked upon as a Mahar, an
untouchable . . . albeit one who had achieved success. It was as if being
a Mahar was an apology for a human being!
> —Narendra Jadhav, former Chairman of the Reserve Bank of India[3]

He used to tell us, there is so much pressure because of my caste. When
I become a doctor I will leave this country. That is the only way to
escape my caste.
> —Family of Balmukund Bharti, a student at the prestigious All India
> Institute of Medical Sciences who committed suicide on March 3, 2010,
> following caste-based bullying.

We often view the decision to identify with a social collective as a choice that individuals make. Amartya Sen, among others, reminds us that history and background are not the only prisms through which to see ourselves and the groups to which we belong:

I can be, at the same time, an Asian, an Indian citizen, a Bengali with
Bangladeshi ancestry, an American or British resident, an economist,

[1] Focus group discussion, 2004.

[2] See Omaprakash Valmiki, *Joothan: An Untouchable's Life*, trans. Arun Prabha Mukherjee (New York: Columbia University Press, 2003), p. 154.

[3] See Narendra Jadhav, *Untouchables: My Family's Triumphant Journey out of the Caste System in Modern India* (New York: Scribner, 2005), p. 239.

a dabbler in philosophy, an author, a Sanskritist, a strong believer in secularism and democracy, a man, a feminist, a heterosexual, a defender of gay and lesbian rights, with a nonreligious lifestyle, from a Hindu background, a non-Brahmin, and a nonbeliever in an afterlife (and also, in case the question is asked, a nonbeliever in a "before-life" as well). This is just a small sample of diverse categories to each of which I may simultaneously belong.[4]

Thus, ethnic identity, for Sen, is only one among the wide repertoire of identities to which he has access. Other scholars argue that ethnic identity can be fluid, multidimensional, and endogenous to politics, since the individual, generally born into more than one identity group, has a choice about which one to identify with at any given time.[5] But the conceptualization of ethnic identity as something fluid and chosen stands in sharp contrast to the lived experience of the Dalit agricultural worker and his fellow focus group participants in Uttar Pradesh, because their discovery of new and different social identities is foreclosed by their poverty. Nor would it have resonated with Omaprakash Valmiki, a renowned Hindi litterateur; Narendra Jadhav, an economist and former Chief Economist of the Reserve Bank of India; and Bal Mukund Bharti, the medical student whose distress led him to take his own life, even though all three appear to have access to a substantial repertoire of identities, for they continue to be viewed as holders of a single identity, one that is inextricably bound up with an indelible stigma. Dalits are marginalized because of their caste identity across all the states. Their identity is widely evoked in their mobilization. In this chapter, I explain the confinement of the Dalit identity.

The expectation that ethnic identity will compete with many other identities is based on the assumption that all the members of a given society, regardless of their ethnicity, will enjoy access to multiple and meaningful social identities. But access to social identities is mediated; it depends on one's social standing. And that is especially the case in an ethnically ranked society in which historically, low-ranked ethnic groups have been subjected to social exclusion. Not only does the exclusion of a marginalized group deny its members the resources needed to discover the repertoire of identities accessible to other groups, but members of the marginalized group also face the larger society's refusal to recognize them in their new identities, even when the opportunity to choose a new identity

---

[4] Amartya Sen, *Identity and Violence: The Illusion of Destiny* (New York: Norton, 2006), p. 19.

[5] This is the view presented by Kanchan Chandra, "Ethnic Parties and Democratic Stability," *Perspectives on Politics*, vol. 3, no. 2 (2005), pp. 235–252.

appears. For a society's marginalized members, then, the choice of social identities is constrained.[6]

Marginalization, Stigma, and Identity

Prominent explanations for the durability of identity point to three factors. First, if the state categorizes a people in a certain way, they view themselves in the same way. Second, political mobilization of identity, and the accompanying promise of state patronage draw people to identity categories. Third, individuals seek security, credit, information, and assistance in their identity networks; this strengthens the hold of identity on their lives. The durability of Dalit identity, however, is not fully explained by recognition from the state, promises of electoral benefits, or the advantages associated with belonging to a caste network.[7] Dalit identity, instead, owes its persistence to Dalits' economic marginalization, which limits their access to opportunities for developing new social identities, and to Dalits' social marginalization, which obstructs recognition of new identities for Dalits even when there are opportunities for Dalits to adopt new identities. Dalits, as one of the most marginalized groups in India, generally lag behind non-Dalits across key indicators of human well-being. These gaps between Dalits and non-Dalits reveal Dalits' relative lack of economic opportunity and economic freedom, disadvantages that in turn constitute more of an obstruction for Dalits than other caste groups in terms of the ability to develop diverse interests and discover possibilities for adopting new social identities. In a ranked

[6] Scholars suggest that individuals can instrumentally adopt identities for economic and political reasons; see Robert H. Bates, "Ethnic Competition and Modernization in Contemporary Africa," *Comparative Political Studies*, vol. 6, no. 4 (1974), pp. 457–484; Kanchan Chandra, *Why Ethnic Parties Succeed: Patronage and Ethnic Head Counts in India* (Cambridge: Cambridge University Press, 2004); Michael Hechter, *Principles of Group Solidarity* (Berkley: University of California Press, 1987); Alvin Rabushka and Kenneth A. Shepsle, *Politics in Plural Societies: A Theory of Democratic Instability* (Columbus: Charles E. Merrill, 1972). Unable to adopt new identities through self-identification, the marginalized, then, are constrained in the instrumental use of identities.

[7] These are three popular explanations for the durability of caste identity. For the state recognition-based explanations, see Oliver Mendelsohn and Marika Vicziany, *The Untouchables: Subordination, Poverty, and the State in Modern India* (Cambridge: Cambridge University Press, 1998); Susan Bayly, *Caste, Society and Politics in India from the Eighteenth Century to the Modern Age* (Cambridge: Cambridge University Press, 1999); Nicholas Dirks, *Castes of Mind: Colonialism and the Making of Modern India* (Princeton: Princeton University Press, 2001). For the electoral benefits-based explanations, see Paul R. Brass, *The Politics of India since Independence* (Cambridge: Cambridge University Press, 1990); Chandra, *Why Ethnic Parties Succeed*. And for the caste network-based explanation, see Kaivan Munshi and Mark Richard Rosenzweig, *Why Is Mobility in India So Low? Social Insurance, Inequality, and Growth* (Cambridge: National Bureau of Economic Research, 2009).

society marked by social and economic inequality, the available set of identities and affiliations is severely restricted for marginalized citizens.

Why is this so? In part, it has to do with what has been called a "capability" or "freedom" gap for individuals of lower social and economic status.[8] For marginalized citizens, this gap represents unequal access to opportunity-producing freedoms, including education, better health, or greater access to information. The gap also represents the higher likelihood of the presence of opportunity-denying causes, including humiliation or daily oppression.

Restriction in life choices, induced by poverty and social stigmatization, exists across many aspects of the lives of members of a marginalized group. As a group, apart from their lower rates of literacy and higher school drop out rates, marginalized individuals have lower life expectancy and higher infant mortality rates. Members of a marginalized group may be denied access to public spaces such as schools, markets, restaurants, and religious sites. It may be more difficult for marginalized individuals than for others to marry across group boundaries, since the members of a marginalized group are less likely to be accepted as marriage partners. The marginalized may enjoy less access to credit, elected representatives, state officials, and state benefits and may be treated poorly by state institutions. For example, their incarceration rates may be higher, and they may be more vulnerable to mistreatment at the hands of state authorities. Additionally, they may be more likely to get bullied and humiliated across a range of social situations because of their low-ranked identity.

In these ways, material deprivation and social exclusion curtail access to multiple freedoms and restrict the choices that marginalized individuals can make in their lives, choices that include developing and selecting among a number of available social identities. For example, education opens doors to multiple occupational paths, each of which can form the basis of a social identity later in life. Education may also expand an individual's awareness and thus offer more choices besides ethnicity when it comes to alignment with interests and issues. Economic resources, by facilitating travel, can encourage interaction with new ideas and engagement with new identities. In other words, if the number of affiliations and loyalties, including new ethnic affiliations, that an individual can potentially acquire is a function of the number of opportunities accessible to that individual and if the number of such opportunities is in turn a function of the capabilities and freedoms that the individual enjoys, then an endowment of fewer freedoms and opportunities will imply access to fewer social identities. Members of a lower-ranked, stigmatized group because they are likely to be endowed with fewer resources, less information, and less social acceptance,

---

[8] Amartya Sen, *Development as Freedom* (Oxford: Oxford University Press, 1999).

are therefore also less likely to discover new interests and less likely to be introduced to multiple collectives. This restraint of choice means that the members of a marginalized group are more likely to be confined exclusively to their stigmatized identity. In this way, poverty induced and maintained by a legacy of social exclusion restricts the size of a marginalized individual's repertoire of identities.

But it is not just how we see ourselves that matters; how others see us matters as well. Apart from the available repertoire of identities and the individual choices contained in that repertoire, the acquisition of a new identity depends on the acceptance of that identity by others. Charles Taylor has explained that the process of acquiring any identity is dialogical and that stigmatization or "misrecognition" can be damaging: "Our identity is partly shaped by recognition or its absence, often by the misrecognition of others, and so a person or group of people can suffer real damage, real distortion, if the people or society around them mirror back to them a confining or demeaning or contemptible picture of themselves.... Non-recognition or misrecognition can inflict harm, can be a form of oppression, imprisoning someone in a false, distorted, and reduced mode of being."[9] And Axel Honneth has similarly held, "[We] owe our integrity ... to the receipt of approval or recognition from other persons."[10] Herein lies the problem for Dalits and similarly stigmatized groups—others' recognition of a new identity is not a given when it comes to the experience of an individual who is eager to move away from a stigmatized identity that has been socially assigned. When a Tamil Dalit physician is rejected by a Tamil patient from a higher caste for reasons of ritual purity and pollution or when non-Dalit students from poor families refuse a midday meal at a government school because it was prepared by a poor Dalit cook or when a Bengali building society rejects a tenant just because he happens to be a Bengali Muslim and not a Bengali Hindu, the individual's chosen identity is undermined by others' lack of recognition. With respect to her patient, the physician may see herself as a fellow Tamilian and also identify strongly with her professional identity. The cook in the public school may see herself as a poor person similar to the parents of the children who are refusing the meal cooked by her. And the tenant may identify far more strongly with his Bengali identity than his religious identity. But self-identification does not matter; all that matters is others' perceptions.[11] This is the social identity trap—the

[9] See Charles Taylor, *Multiculturalism: Examining the Politics of Recognition* (Princeton: Princeton University Press, 1994), p. 25.

[10] See Axel Honneth, "Integrity and Disrespect: Principles of a Conception of Morality Based on the Theory of Recognition," *Political Theory*, vol. 20, no. 2 (1992), pp. 187–201, p. 188.

[11] Another example is the experience of Simon P. Owens, labor organizer and member of a late-twentieth-century Detroit-based Marxist-humanist collective: "Because generations of white people had defined him and all other blacks first and foremost as 'Negroes,' he had no alternative but to acknowledge—or, rather, react to—that spurious identity;" see Jacqueline Jones, *A Dreadful*

fact of being marked by a primary stigmatized identity, which was chosen by others and which continues to be imposed by others regardless of one's own choices. The struggle against this trap is often at the heart of a marginalized individual's life experience.

For much of Indian history, of course, caste and socioeconomic status have reinforced each other.[12] In recent years, however, caste and socioeconomic status have gradually begun to become decoupled. The last six decades have seen the outlawing of caste discrimination and the establishment of affirmative action policies in government employment, educational institutions, and state and national legislatures. These changes have opened up avenues for upward mobility for people from the lower castes. In addition, there has been steady improvement in the political representation of the Backward and Scheduled Castes. Meanwhile, the Indian economy has been growing at an average annual rate of above 6% since 1991, thus creating opportunities for upward economic mobility, and allowing Dalits to trickle up into the Indian middle-income brackets.[13] Moreover, urbanization, it is important to note, is increasing in India, and so all the changes mentioned have had even more far-reaching effects in urban areas.[14]

Deceit: The Myth of Race from the Colonial Era to Obama's America (New York: Basic Books, 2013), p. 265.

[12] Ashwini Deshpande as well as Sukhdeo Thorat and Katherine Newman find continued linkage between caste and economic status. See Ashwini Deshpande, "Does Caste Still Define Disparity? A Look at Inequality in Kerala, India," *The American Economic Review*, vol. 90, no. 2 (2000), pp. 322–325; and Sukhdeo Thorat and Katherine Newman, eds., *Blocked by Caste: Economic Discrimination in Modern India* (New Delhi: Oxford University Press, 2009).

[13] On the outlawing of caste discrimination and the establishment of affirmative action policies, see Marc Galanter, *Competing Equalities: Law and the Backward Classes in India* (Delhi: Oxford University Press, 1984). On increased upward mobility for lower-caste citizens, see Rohini Pande, "Can Mandated Political Representation Increase Policy Influence for Disadvantaged Minorities? Theory and Evidence from India," *American Economic Review*, vol. 93, no. 4 (2003), pp. 1132–1151; Nishith Prakash, "The Impact of Employment Quotas on the Economic Lives of Disadvantaged Minorities in India," unpublished paper, 2009, available at http://www.dartmouth.edu/~prakash/ Prakash_Job_Market_2010.pdf; Viktoria Hnatkovska, Amartya Lahiri, and Sourabh B. Paul, "Breaking the Caste Barrier: Intergenerational Mobility in India," *Journal of Human Resources*, vol. 48, no. 2 (2013), pp. 435–473. On improvements in the political representation of the Backward and Scheduled Castes, see Christophe Jaffrelot and Sanjay Kumar, *Rise of the Plebeians? The Changing Face of Indian Legislative Assemblies* (New Delhi: Routledge India, 2009). On annual economic growth and opportunities for upward economic mobility, see Viktoria Hnatkovska and Amartya Lahiri, "The Post-Reform Narrowing of Inequality across Castes: Evidence from the States," Working Paper No. 2012–22, Columbia Program on Indian Economic Policies, School of International and Public Affairs, Columbia University, 2012; Hnatkovska, Lahiri, and Paul, "Breaking the Caste Barrier," pp. 435–473.

[14] Indeed, by 2030, it is predicted 40% of Indians will reside in cities, and 70% of net new employment will be generated in urban areas; see Shirish Sankhe, Ireena Vittal, Richard Dobbs, Ajit Mohan, Ankur Gulati, Jonathan Ablett, Shishir Gupta, Alex Kim, Sudipto Paul, Aditya Sanghvi, and

In many ways, the link between occupation and caste—the very basis of the caste system—continues to break. Nevertheless, social mobility remains relatively uncommon for lower-caste Indians.[15] Together, Dalits' low income and their rank as India's lowest caste group continue to place severe limits on Dalits' access to Indian society's repertoire of social identities.

New Identities, Old Stigmas

Do the constraining effects of low income and low social rank appear only when these two factors work in conjunction or do such constraints also appear when one of the factors is absent? One way to separate the effects of socioeconomic status and social rank is to ask what happens when income and social rank are decoupled so that higher socioeconomic status opens the door to new social identities for Dalits. Put another way, can Dalits successfully adopt new social identities successfully when the economic constraints on their access to the social identity repertoire are removed?

To assess the relative levels of prejudice faced by Dalits, I investigated the preferences of women in the urban middle-class arranged-marriage markets in three Indian states—Uttar Pradesh, Maharashtra, and Tamil Nadu.[16] I used a

Gurpreet Sethy, "India's Urban Awakening: Building Inclusive Cities, Sustaining Economic Growth" (Mumbai: McKinsey Global Institute, 2010). In addition, urban areas do not observe the rural norms and customs governing interactions between members of different castes, and so urban individuals who come from different caste backgrounds but have the same socioeconomic status are more likely to interact as social equals than would be the case in rural areas. People in cities, being less dependent on caste networks in their day-to-day lives, are also less influenced by caste-based preferences and customs, and the threat of excommunication from a particular community holds less sway for them.

[15] See, for example, E. Wayne Nafziger, "Class, Caste and Community of South Indian Industrialists: An Examination of the Horatio Alger Model," *Journal of Development Studies*, vol. 11, no. 2 (1975), pp. 131–148; Kaivan Munshi and Mark R. Rosenzweig, "Traditional Institutions Meet the Modern World: Caste, Gender and Schooling Choice in a Globalizing Economy," *American Economic Review*, vol. 96, no. 4 (2006), pp. 1225–1252; Munshi and Rosenzweig, *Why Is Mobility in India So Low?*; Rajeshwari Deshpande and Suhas Palshikar, "Occupational Mobility: How Much Does Caste Matter?" *Economic and Political Weekly*, vol. 43, no. 34 (2008), pp. 61–70; Surinder Jodhka, "Dalits in Business: Self-Employed Scheduled Castes in North-West India," *Economic and Political Weekly*, vol. 45, no. 11 (2010), pp. 41–48.

[16] See Amit Ahuja and Susan L. Ostermann, "Crossing Caste Boundaries in the Modern Indian Marriage Market," *Studies in Comparative International Development*, vol. 51, no. 3 (2016), pp. 365–387. For the purposes of our study, we defined the term *urban middle class* in keeping with that term's use in popular discourse rather than relying on classifications based strictly on income percentiles. Most of the participants in our study had earned a college degree, resided in an urban area, had access to the internet, and reported an annual family income of at least Rs. 200,000 or $4,000 (at the time of the study, in 2011–2012, individuals with earnings below that level were exempt from paying income tax). For a wide-ranging discussion of the modern Indian middle class, see Amita Baviskar and Raka

correspondence-based, semi-experimental design.[17] Working with matrimonial agencies, I initially made contact with 2,358 women from various castes and sent each one an expression of matrimonial interest from each of three prospective grooms across all three states.[18] I examined women's preferences, rather than men's, because marriage of women, especially, is policed strictly by family members, local communities, and, at times, rural caste councils. Honor killings are the most extreme form of this policing.[19] According to a 2013 National Council of Women study of 560 recent honor killings, intermarriage, often between a higher-caste woman and a lower-caste man, had occurred in 89% of the cases in which people were killed or threatened. A woman adopts the caste of her husband and, therefore, either stands to gain or to lose through intermarriage. The potential grooms who contacted the women were nearly identical in terms of age, height, skin color, education, and family characteristics; all were from upper-middle-income, high-status backgrounds. They held similar graduate degrees and were in lucrative careers. But each of these otherwise similar men belonged to a different caste category—either Dalit, Backward Caste, or upper caste. All the grooms were open to intercaste marriage. The Dalit grooms clearly indicated that they identified with their professional and educational identities far more strongly than their caste identity, and this informed their search for a marriage partner. This is not to say that these Dalit grooms were embarrassed by their caste identity in any way. In their search for a marriage partner, the potential bride's professional, educational, and family status profiles mattered much more to them than her caste identity.

I had two principal reasons for focusing the study on the arranged-marriage market. First, in ethnically and racially divided societies, social distinctions survive when social boundaries continue to be reinforced from one generation to the next. Most scholars agree that ethnic, racial, and caste identities are defined by descent-based attributes.[20] This way of thinking about caste identity places endogamy, or the practice of marrying within one's own group, at the heart of those attributes' reproduction. Indeed, the conventional wisdom on caste in

---

Ray, *Elite and Everyman: The Cultural Politics of the Indian Middle Classes* (New Delhi: Routledge India, 2011).

[17] For details about the study design, see Appendix C.

[18] I selected three prospective grooms from each of the three states, for a total of nine.

[19] According to a widespread tradition, women are vested with honor by their families and communities; a woman's sexual behavior then has broad ramifications. By marrying into a lower caste, a woman can be said to bring dishonor to her family and/or community, a shame that can only be remedied through her death.

[20] See Kanchan Chandra, "What Is Ethnic Identity and Does It Matter?" *Annual Review of Political Science*, vol. 9 (2006), pp. 397–424; Kanchan Chandra and Steven Wilkinson, "Measuring the Effect of Ethnicity," *Comparative Political Studies*, vol. 41, nos. 4–5 (2008), pp. 515–563.

India suggests that a strong preference for endogamy, along with the associated policing of caste boundaries, is common to all castes, with the result that caste identity is reproduced from one generation to the next. Since marriage is one mechanism by which ethnic identity is reproduced, scholars view intermarriage as a sign of social integration and assimilation.[21] Consequently, an interest in intercaste marriage in the arranged marriage market indicates a weakening of caste boundaries. Second, even though the private sphere is difficult to access, it is essential to study behavior in that sphere in order to assess individual choices since an individual's public embrace of ethnic diversity often coexists with prejudice against out-groups in the private sphere. In fact, it can be argued that the private sphere—where decisions are made about who will be one's next-door neighbors, who will study with one's children, who will be one's friends, and who will be considered an eligible marriage partner for one's children—is where the true nature of prejudice is revealed. I studied interest in intercaste marriage in cities because urban life is relatively anonymous, by contrast with life in a village, and urban couples are less embedded in the multigenerational power structure that characterizes a village—two factors that would seem to allow a mixed-caste couple to avoid the worst forms of discrimination, at least to some degree.[22] In addition, people in cities, who have access to matrimonial newspaper pages and websites, are exposed to a larger number of choices in the marriage market than are people in the countryside, who even now rarely use these media to find marriage partners.[23]

So, what did I find? Of the initial group of 2,358 women, 1,702 responded to the expressions of matrimonial interest sent to them on behalf of the prospective grooms. I found that a groom who belonged to the woman's caste elicited the most positive response. Among the upper-caste women, 99.3% responded positively to the upper-caste groom, 54% to the Backward-Caste groom, and only 28% to the Dalit groom; among the Backward-Caste women, 84% responded positively to the Backward-Caste groom, 61% to the upper-caste groom, and

[21] See David D. Laitin, *Identity in Formation: The Russian-Speaking Populations in the Near Abroad* (Ithaca and London: Cornell University Press, 1998); D. A. Coleman, "Trends in Fertility and Intermarriage among Immigrant Populations in Western Europe as Measures of Integration," *Journal of Biosocial Science,* vol. 26, no. 1 (1994), pp. 107–136.

[22] See Center for the Study of Developing Societies, *Indian National Election Study, 2004* (New Delhi: Center for the Study of Developing Societies, 2004), which bears this intuition out. Survey data from the study show that 53% of city residents rejected a proposed ban on intercaste marriage, but only about 36% of rural residents rejected the proposed ban.

[23] Matrimonial advertisements in newspapers and matrimonial website memberships are expensive and typically beyond the reach of low-income Indian families. In recent years, however, sections for Backward and Scheduled Castes have been appearing in the matrimonial pages of Indian newspapers, and more individuals from these groups have been using matrimonial websites.

37% to the Dalit groom. Among the Dalit women, 94% responded to the Dalit groom, 53% to the upper-caste groom, and 62% to the Backward-Caste groom. I found that 71% of the Dalit women—who, again, would have stood to improve their social rank by marrying outside their caste—had an interest in intermarriage, as compared to 62% of the non-Dalit women. More specifically, and from the standpoint of the prospective grooms, the out-of-caste positive response rate was 54% for the three upper-caste grooms, 50.5% for the three Backward-Caste grooms, and 33.5% for the three Dalit grooms, and this was the case even though the profile of the Dalit groom was almost identical to, if not marginally better than, the other two profiles.[24]

Thus, no matter how I looked at the semi-experimental results, they clearly showed that the prospective Dalit grooms were the least preferred marriage prospects. These findings suggest that Dalit identity, even though it was associated in the marriage market study with a variety of very positive markers, was sufficient to lower the acceptability of the Dalit grooms, and that others in the marriage market viewed the Dalit grooms as Dalits first and foremost, regardless of the grooms' economic class or their professional and regional identities. In other words, Dalit grooms remain trapped in their caste identity because others' choices were constrained by the stigma attached to that identity.

I also conducted 15 one-on-one interviews with women who participated in the study, and these, too, revealed social bias against Dalits. The non-Dalit women I interviewed reported that their immediate or extended families would object to their marriage into a Dalit family, and they feared being ostracized within their communities. Nevertheless, some non-Dalit women were willing to consider such a match; for them, the prospective Dalit groom's income, level of education, and professional status were more important than his caste. Others, in order to improve their own class standing, were willing to consider marriage to a wealthier lower-caste husband. As the observational data suggest, these women are still in the substantial minority, but the interviews suggest there may be more change in this area as caste ties and social policing weaken in the urban environment. The fact that a relatively large number of upper-caste women responded positively to the matrimonial interest of the Backward-Caste grooms also points in this direction.[25]

---

[24] For the upper-caste grooms, the out-of-caste responses came from Backward-Caste and Dalit women; for Backward-Caste grooms, from upper-caste and Dalit women; and for Dalit grooms, from upper-caste and Backward-Caste women. Out-of-caste response rates to the Dalit grooms were similar across all three states.

[25] Not so long ago, the Backward Castes were also regarded as lowly, but their higher social rank has facilitated greater social mobility for them than Dalits have experienced.

Next, in collaboration with Susan Ostermann, I checked for the independent effects of socioeconomic status on the behavior of the Dalit women. All 1,702 women who participated in the study were from the urban middle class, but they were divided by a status difference that was based on family income, and some were wealthier than others. We already knew that 71% of the Dalit women had expressed a preference for intermarriage, whereas only 62% of the women in the upper- and Backward-Caste groups had done so. We also knew that among the Dalit women there was a significant and positive relationship between socioeconomic status and preference for out-of-caste marriage, with the preference for intermarriage expressed more often in the upper-middle-income subset of Dalit women than in the middle- and lower-middle-income subset of Dalit women.[26] In our interviews with the middle- and lower-middle-income Dalit women who did not aspire to improve their social status by marrying outside their caste, I often heard that they saw intermarriage as likely to put them at a substantial disadvantage, since they had no experience of living in a higher-caste world and would need to make the adjustment not only to a new caste but also to the substantial gap between their current class and the new, higher one. Therefore, even though the stigma of Dalit identity might have been expected to lead all the Dalit women to seek a change of caste identity through marriage, we found that lower socioeconomic status acted as a constraint on this aspiration in the middle- and lower-middle-income subset. This finding reflects the independent role of socioeconomic status as a constraint on the aspirations of Dalits in general, and as a factor that keeps Dalits trapped in their stigmatized identity even when the acquisition of a new identity becomes possible.

The Dalit experience of nonrecognition and misrecognition is not unique to the marriage market. Individuals and groups alike have been known to change their identities, including their ethnic identities, as a way of improving their social status. This is a common reason for learning a new language, and for Dalits' increasing efforts to master English.[27] Many Dalit activists today recommend the embrace of English as a means of avoiding discrimination, breaking

---

[26] Given the semi-experimental design and randomization, Susan and I turned to t-tests to determine whether a given treatment (or variable) would have a significant effect on the preference for out-of-caste marriage. Before conducting t-tests on the Dalit women, we created two subsets of them on the basis of socioeconomic status, one for the wealthy Dalit women and the other for the middle-income Dalit women. When we compared each subset's preference for out-of-caste marriage, we found that the two subsets were distinct ($t = 1.982$, $p < 0.05$) and that the relationship between socioeconomic status and preference for out-of-caste marriage was significant and positive.

[27] See Laitin, *Identity in Formation*. Indeed, Chandrabhan Prasad, a prominent Dalit intellectual and activist, has been involved in the project of building a temple to the goddess of English; see Geeta Pandey, "An 'English Goddess' for India's Down-Trodden," *BBC News/South Asia*, February 15, 2011.

out of menial jobs, and gaining access to more lucrative and more prestigious jobs in the cities, since a command of English is viewed as a marker of higher socioeconomic status in India. But even when Dalits do learn English, they continue to face discrimination in the white-collar job market. Employers discriminate against them while screening résumés for interviews, Dalit candidates are treated with less fairness than candidates from other castes during the interview process for entry-level white-collar jobs, and employers believe that job candidates' merit is a function of caste and religion.[28]

When the opportunity presents itself, people from marginalized groups also look to military service as a means of achieving upward mobility and claiming a higher martial status, as in the case of the Mahars of Maharashtra and the Mazhabi Sikhs of Punjab, two prominent Dalit communities that take this route.[29] Nevertheless, in spite of Dalits' distinguished record of valor on the battlefield, other soldiers in the Indian army sometimes express reluctance to mingle as equals with their Dalit counterparts. For example, the higher-ranked Jat Sikh soldiers of the Sikh Regiment are eager to maintain separation from their coreligionists, the Mazhabi Sikh soldiers of the Sikh Light Infantry.[30] Soldiers in general are highly respected in India, but when Dalit soldiers return to their villages and towns after retirement, they sometimes struggle to find homes in non-Dalit residential localities and book rooms in hotels.[31]

Religious conversion, another path toward higher status, has been a way for Dalits both to leave the Hindu faith, which assigns their lowly status, and to protest the lack of reform within the Hindu community.[32] But here, too, even when Dalits have adopted faiths that profess equality among believers, others in these new faiths have not viewed them as equals—they are still seen as Dalit Sikhs, Dalit Christians, and Dalit Muslims, not simply as Sikhs, Christians, and

---

[28] Sukhadeo Thorat and Paul Attewell, "The Legacy of Social Exclusion," *Economic and Political Weekly*, vol. 42, no. 41 (2007), pp. 4141–4145; Ashwini Deshpande and Katherine Newman, "Where the Path Leads: The Role of Caste in Post-university Employment Expectations," *Economic and Political Weekly*, vol. 42, no. 41 (2007), pp. 4133–4140; Surinder S. Jodhka and Katherine Newman, "In the Name of Globalisation: Meritocracy, Productivity, and the Hidden Language of Caste," *Economic and Political Weekly*, vol. 42, no. 41 (2007), pp. 4125–4232.

[29] Stephen P. Cohen, "The Untouchable Soldier: Caste, Politics, and the Indian Army," *Journal of Asian Studies*, vol. 28, no. 3 (1969), pp. 453–468.

[30] Amit Ahuja, "India," in Ron E. Hassner, ed., *Religion in the Military Worldwide* (New York: Cambridge University Press, 2013), pp. 159–178.

[31] See Gopal Guru, "The Indian Nation in its Egalitarian Conception," in Ramnarayan S. Rawat and K. Satyanarayana, eds., *Dalit Studies* (Durham and London: Duke University Press, 2016), pp. 31–52.

[32] Johannes Beltz, *Mahar, Buddhist, and Dalit: Religious Conversion and Socio-political Emancipation* (New Delhi: Manohar, 2005); Milind Wakankar, *Subalternity and Religion: The Prehistory of Dalit Empowerment in South Asia* (Abingdon: Routledge, 2010).

Muslims. Higher-caste Muslims do not marry lower-caste Muslims as a general custom. Dalit Christians are not allowed to bury their dead alongside higher-caste Christians. And, higher-caste Sikhs will not share the management of Sikh temples with Dalit Sikhs.

Dalits can also make lifestyle changes in order to lay claim to a higher status. Apart from intermarriage, which gives Dalit women a route to higher social status, such lifestyle changes include the adoption of new names, new customs, and upper-caste cultural and religious practices for the purpose of moving up the ladder of rank.[33] Again, though, Dalits who have made such changes have not been accepted as equals among upper-caste Hindus, especially in rural India, where practices of untouchability, if reduced, continue to be seen.[34]

Life in politics, it is reasonable to expect, could enable leaders from marginalized groups to find acceptability among different sections of society. As a result, over time, the popularity of these leaders would transcend caste boundaries. The effects of identity-based stigma, however, are not limited to the Dalit commoner, but also extend to Dalit leadership across India. Dalit leaders find themselves caged in an identity trap. Perceptions about Mayawati, Ram Vilas Paswan, Thol. Thirumavalavan, Prakash Ambedkar, and other leaders are limited to them functioning solely as representatives of Dalits. Despite their commentary on a wide array of issues, these leaders have seldom been given the respect for contributing to a broader social and political discourse. Perceptions of upper caste leaders, by contrast, are not similarly constrained by their caste identities, and they are more routinely accepted as representatives beyond their own caste groups.[35]

It is striking that all these mechanisms for status improvement through identity change turn on individual choices. As such, they highlight the agency among Dalits in the construction of their identities. Equally striking, however, is the fact of others' refusal to recognize Dalits in their new identities. Agency alone, in an environment where identity change is disrupted by prejudice and discrimination, cannot mitigate the effects of stigmatization.

Dalits in India—and, for that matter, the Burakumin in Japan, or African Americans in the United States, or the Roma in Europe—do not enjoy the same ability to acquire new identities and affiliations as other members of their societies. All the members of a marginalized group also do not enjoy the same degree

---

[33] M. N. Srinivas, *Caste in Modern India and Other Essays* (Bombay: Asia Publishing House, 1962).

[34] See Balmurli Natrajan, *The Culturalization of Caste in India: Identity and Inequality in a Multicultural Age* (Abingdon: Routledge, 2012); Ghanshyam Shah, Harsh Mander, Sukhadeo Thorat, Satish Deshpande, and Amita Baviskar, *Untouchability in Rural India* (New Delhi: Sage, 2006).

[35] TM Krishna, "The TM Krishna column: Why are India's Dalit thought leaders always reduced to their caste identity?" *Scroll.in*, December 16, 2018.

of choice in selecting a new identity.[36] The very fact that individuals and groups cannot choose new social identities has powerful implications for a ranked society that is defined by disparities among ethnic groups. It raises questions about the efficacy of incentives and benefits that have been put in place to reduce ethnic disparities.[37] Even when these policy measures improve the representation of marginalized groups in different sectors, they cannot undermine the power of stigma associated with a marginalized identity. This is why individuals' access to new identities, not to mention the larger society's acceptance of individuals' choices in this matter, raises questions that are consequential for a marginalized group such as India's Dalits.

As things stand, poverty and social stigmatization continue to trap a large number of Dalits in their caste identity. Dalits share the experience of marginalization with other Dalits. It binds them to one another and arguably makes them easier to mobilize as a caste. Dalits can also be mobilized around issues related to social recognition, respect, acceptance, and inclusion, since the group cannot take these fundamental entitlements for granted. Because the elements of ethnic solidarity are common to the entire Dalit community, we might reasonably expect the shared experience of marginalization and exclusion to forge not just social but also electoral solidarity within the group (as has been observed among African Americans,[38] for example) and to encourage the development of a Dalit voting bloc—the creation, in effect, of a political identity trap to accompany the Dalit social identity trap.

At the same time, however, social relations and political mobilization follow two distinct logics. Social relations, especially in the case of Dalits, are still largely governed by the logic of hierarchy, with caste rank continuing to define how the members of different groups relate to one another. Electoral mobilization, by contrast, follows the logic of numerical preponderance—what is consequential

---

[36] See Courtney Jung, *The Moral Force of Indigenous Politics: Critical Liberalism and the Zapatistas* (Cambridge: Cambridge University Press, 2008), p. 55: "Membership [in a group] may . . . have the appearance of permanence, as doubtless it does for many African Americans who have lived their whole lives under the shadow of race. . . . The fact that this . . . dimension of identity has the potential for fluidity does not mean that the potential is realized. Constructivists should be interested to explain when it changes and when it does not." See also Courtney Jung, *Then I Was Black: South African Political Identities in Transition* (New Haven: Yale University Press, 2000), the author's earlier work on South African political identities.

[37] See Laitin, *Identity in Formation*; Kanchan Chandra, ed., *Constructivist Theories of Ethnic Politics* (New York: Oxford University Press, 2012).

[38] This is the idea of "linked fate" among the marginalized African American community. According to it, the experience of racial discrimination sustains group solidarity among the black community. On election day, blacks rely on a utility heuristic of voting their race. See Michael C. Dawson, *Behind the Mule: Race and Class in African-American Politics* (Princeton: Princeton University Press, 1994).

in electoral politics is the size of a group, not its rank. Therefore, in a competitive multiparty system, a political party striving to build the largest possible coalition of voters cannot afford to treat Dalits as anything other than the political equal of every other segment of the electorate, notwithstanding the question of social status, especially when Dalits form a sizable share of voters. In this way, the Dalit social identity trap does not have to be mirrored in electoral politics. Others in society may not recognize Dalits' adoption of new social identities, but the same should not be true when it comes to the adoption of a political identity. Therefore, we might reasonably expect competition for the Dalit vote among multiple parties not only to make multiple political identities available to Dalits but also, for that very reason, to undermine the prospects for bloc voting on the part of Dalits. The historical reality, though, is that political parties mobilized Dalits in some states while undermobilizing them in others. Where Dalits have been mobilized by multiple parties in the electoral arena, Dalits have been less inclined to vote as a bloc, but where Dalits remained electorally undermobilized, social and electoral exclusion reinforced each other and, as a result, Dalits have voted as a bloc.

|| 9 ||

Conclusion: Whither Dalit Politics?

The marginalized have been mobilized across many democracies by social movements and political parties, yet few studies systematically investigate the relationship between their social and electoral mobilization. This book, by comparing the mobilization of Dalits by multiethnic and ethnic parties in states that have been home to strong anti-caste movements and in states where such movements have been weak, has outlined and illustrated a set of arguments related to the mobilization of the marginalized by political parties and social movements. First, the book shows that the mobilization of the marginalized is distinct. It seeks both social and political inclusion. Unless the marginalized mobilize themselves, political parties do not mobilize them. Second, the book demonstrates that the act of self-mobilization for seeking social equality alters the salience of ethnicity in electoral politics. In a competitive multiparty system, the social mobilization of a marginalized ethnic group brings political parties to their localities and diffuses ethnic symbols and demands into the party system. Together, these undermine bloc voting among members of the ethnic group, thereby curtailing the success of ethnic parties and instead enabling multiethnic parties' success. The electoral performance–related outcomes of caste and multicaste parties that these mechanisms have produced are contingent on such institutional factors as a competitive multiparty system and a single-member-district plurality electoral system made up of ethnically mixed districts. These arguments join the growing literature on the democratic mobilization of marginalized groups and on the relationship between social movements and political parties. They inform our understanding of a number of issues related to ethnic mobilization. This chapter explores some of the implications of the arguments presented in this book.

Marginalization and Mobilization

Marginalization, as this book has argued, must be taken seriously by scholars of ethnicity and mobilization. Ethnicity has been a means of social exclusion across many societies around the world. For excluded groups, lower social status often corresponds with lower economic status. Even as societies historically ordered by hierarchical or ranked relationships between groups come to be governed democratically, members of excluded groups continually struggle to access the full panoply of their legal, political, and social rights.[1]

A focus on marginalization and its effects allows us to draw a distinction between marginalized groups and other groups. One effect of marginalization is that it traps individuals in a group identity. The discussion in Chapter 8 illustrates how Dalits, because of their inability to access alternate identities, and because of others' refusal to look past the stigma attached to Dalit identity, can remain confined to their caste identity. This denial of access to alternate identities for marginalized groups extends to social identity, including professional, associational, religious, regional, and sometimes even national identity. So far, the literature on ethnic politics has viewed ethnic identity as a matter of individual choice. In the case of marginalized groups such as African Americans, Dalits, Europe's Roma, and Japan's Burakumin, this may not be so true, since they lack a real choice in the process of shaping their identity. Marginalization has a profound influence on the mobilization of a group. At the same time, self-mobilization holds the potential to release the members of a group from their social and political identity traps.

Participation without Mobilization

We often equate participation with mobilization in a democratic political system, the underlying intuition being that without contacting and organizing voters, parties cannot bring them to the polls. If the marginalized possess franchise, it should be in parties' interest to mobilize them. We know empirically, however, that the poor and marginalized face a large number of constraints when they try to mobilize themselves. Catch-all or multiethnic parties will seldom challenge existing structural relations to mobilize marginalized voters. Therefore, marginalized voters are likely to be undermobilized. Despite the possession of franchise, they may not be free to participate, and even if they are able to vote, their demands and interests may not be reflected in electoral politics. In India, the state registers marginalized voters, is attentive to providing them access to polling stations, and has reserved electoral districts for them.

---

[1] For distinction between ranked and unranked societies, see Donald Horowitz, *Ethnic Groups in Conflict* (Berkeley: University of California Press, 1985).

In addition, parties campaign in poor localities. By contrast with the situation in Western democracies, today, India's poor, including Dalits, vote in the same numbers as the well-to-do.[2] And yet possession of the franchise has not always translated into electoral mobilization for the marginalized. This book has demonstrated that, for the marginalized, the mere possession or exercise of the franchise does not necessarily imply political mobilization. Unless the marginalized mobilize themselves, they are either not mobilized or are undermobilized by political parties.

The early experience of Dalits' electoral participation in states such as Uttar Pradesh and Bihar highlights the danger of viewing electoral participation as a sign of electoral mobilization. The above account also suggests that democratic participation by members of a group and their marginalization in the political process can go hand in hand. Even as the members of a marginalized group participate, their demands and symbols can remain absent from the electoral process. Compare, for example, Dalits' support for the Congress Party in Uttar Pradesh and Maharashtra until the 1980s. In both states, Dalits turned out to support the same party, but the Congress Party mobilized Dalits in Maharashtra and undermobilized them in Uttar Pradesh. In Maharashtra, the Dalit movement and the relative freedom of Dalits from the dominant castes compelled the Congress Party to mobilize Dalits on the basis of their demands and to acknowledge and honor Dalit symbols. By contrast in Uttar Pradesh, the weakness of Dalit social mobilization and the dependence of Dalits on members of dominant castes made it possible to garner Dalit support with the assistance of the members of those dominant castes. Meanwhile, with limited social mobilization within their community, Dalits could not compel the Congress Party to alter its behavior. These findings remain broadly relevant to the mobilization of marginalized groups.

Although Dalits' self-mobilization and monitoring by the Election Commission have enabled Dalit electoral mobilization across Indian states, these findings still remain broadly relevant to the mobilization of marginalized groups. Take the example of women. Gender-related issues have been neglected in Indian politics. Across every indicator related to basic needs and well-being, women lag behind men. Crime against women—in a variety of forms, including sexual assault and rape, domestic violence, and female foeticide—remains rampant. Women form half of the Indian electorate, and they vote in numbers equal to those of men, yet their issues are not

---

[2] See Sanjay Kumar, "Patterns of Political Participation: Trends and Perspective," *Economic and Political Weekly*, vol. 44, no. 39 (2009), pp. 47–51; Amit Ahuja and Pradeep Chhibber, "Why the Poor Vote in India: 'If I Don't Vote, I Am Dead to the State,'" *Studies in Comparative International Development*, vol. 47, no. 4 (2012), pp. 389–410.

prominently featured on the political agenda. When they are, women seldom have a say in selecting the issues. During the locality-based campaign survey and observations of large public rallies, I found that women's issues were rarely raised. Both weak self-mobilization among women and their continued dependence on men within the Indian family unit have limited the direct outreach of parties to women.[3] Among the party workers I counted across neighborhoods and localities in 2004 and 2009 in the four states, only 11% and 14%, respectively, were women. Where parties have begun to mobilize women, the change has often been triggered by women's organizational activities, through Self Help Groups for example.

This discussion highlights the significance of a group's status endowments to the process of its electoral mobilization. Marginalization influences the goals, resources, constraints, and opportunities of a group's mobilization. It also shapes the group's identity. And yet we know little about how marginalization comes to influence a group's behavior across a number of important questions that the subfield of ethnic politics studies.[4]

Social Movements and Political Parties

By comparing Dalit mobilization across movement and non-movement states, this book has highlighted the electoral consequences of social mobilization of a marginalized group. But the effects of social mobilization can also be examined in the context of the social and electoral mobilization of a dominant group. How, for example, does the Tea Party movement in the United States influence the electoral prospects of the Republican Party?[5] Similarly,

---

[3] See Sanjay Kumar and Pranav Gupta, "Changing Patterns of Women's Turnout in Indian Elections," *Studies in Indian Politics*, vol. 3, no. 1 (2015), pp. 7–18.

[4] Apart from ethnic movements and ethnic parties, for example, we need to know more about how marginalization of an ethnic group affects its participation in ethnic violence, insurgencies, ethnic networks, and so on. The participation of marginalized Dalits and Adivasis in ethnic violence against Muslims has recently come to light; see Jagpal Singh, "Communal Violence in Muzaffarnagar: Agrarian Transformation and Politics," *Economic and Political Weekly*, vol. 5, no. 31 (2016), pp. 94–101. This behavior is puzzling, since traditionally these groups have not been in conflict with Muslims. One possible explanation for their participation is that the marginalized, given their vulnerability and identity trap, may be susceptible to recruitment for ethnic violence on behalf of dominant groups in return for the promise of security and entry into a new, unstigmatized identity.

[5] In the United States, for example, social movements have played a role in radicalizing the Republican Party. In the medium to long run, an extreme ideological turn is damaging for the Republican Party's electoral prospects. See Doug McAdam and Karina Kloos, *Deeply Divided: Racial Politics and Social Movements in Postwar America* (New York: Oxford University Press, 2014).

how does the Hindu nationalist movement influence the mobilization of and electoral prospects of the Hindu nationalist Bharatiya Janata Party (BJP)? These inquiries are likely to unearth different mobilization mechanisms from those that explain Dalits' mobilization. Movements of dominant groups may be less amenable to political compromise because their members are less reliant on state services, are better networked with the state, and are less fearful of the state's retributive response than the marginalized. More important, the insight, that interests of ethnic movements and ethnic parties do not always line up to reinforce each other,[6] and may be aligned only contingently, or even work at cross purposes, forces us to think about movement-party relations in new ways.

Both parties and movements play an important role in the articulation of citizen demands and in decision-making by aggregating preferences and providing information. When a party emerges from long-standing movements, such movements can support as well as challenge the allied party. Under specific conditions, as the experience of Dalit parties and movements suggests, a prior movement curtails the success of the allied party. The Dalit mobilization experience points to an additional aspect of movement-party relations. An electorally successful ethnic party can stifle the emergence of a vibrant ethnic movement if the party views the movement as a potential threat. Autonomous movements can credibly criticize a party and its leadership, compromise its agenda, direct ethnic voters elsewhere, and generate rival leaders. For these reasons, successful ethnic parties are often wary of parallel ethnic movements. Such fears are likely heightened for the leader-centric parties frequently seen in India. It is no surprise then that both Mayawati and Ram Vilas Paswan have refrained from supporting Dalit protest movements—fearing movement leaders might eventually supplant them—and the BSP in Uttar Pradesh and the LJP in Bihar have done very little to foster Dalit social mobilization.[7]

We should take the representational role of social and protest movements seriously. As a form of collective action with a lower threshold of mobilization than political parties, social and protest movements remain a more accessible form of demand articulation. At a historical moment in which protest movements across the world are shaping party politics, this book joins the call for renewing interest in movement-party relations. For the marginalized, ethnic

---

[6] Doug McAdam and Sidney Tarrow, "Ballots and Barricades: On the Reciprocal Relationship between Elections and Social Movements," *Perspectives on Politics*, vol. 8, no. 2 (2010), pp. 529–542.

[7] The BSP and the LJP are not internally democratic, a characteristic they share with most other Indian political parties.

party as well as ethnic movement success represents voice. But do voice and democratic choice always go together?

Voice without Choice

The normative debate on ethnic parties is made up of two opposing views. One view is that in democratic politics, the recognition of group rights and freedoms often comes at the expense of individual freedoms. In this sense, the mobilization of an ethnic group is seen as undermining the democratic process.[8] The opposing view is that since all the groups in a society are not equal, the politics of different ethnic groups should not all be judged by the same criteria. In many instances, according to this view, a marginalized group's identity is the very reason the group has been underrepresented, and so members of the group must mobilize around their group identity in order to attain their rights and freedoms. Ethnic mobilization, then, is seen as enabling the participation of hitherto excluded groups and enhancing the democratic process versus undermining it.[9]

Those who study the effects of lower-caste parties' emergence in India have largely taken a positive view of these parties' appearance because of their representational benefits. For these scholars, lower-caste-based parties affirm the promise of democracy and political equality for marginalized groups.[10] As

---

[8] See George Kateb, *The Inner Ocean: Individualism and Democratic Culture* (Ithaca: Cornell University Press, 1994). From this perspective, the central concern is that even when the members of the ethnic group have shared interests, they may not share all their interests, and so giving primacy to ethnic identity means ignoring those individual interests that are not shared by all the members of the ethnic group. For example, work on intersectionally marginalized communities has illuminated some of the contradictions that arise when group identity is given primacy; more marginalized people within the group, including poor people and women, are often neglected. See Dara Z. Strolovitch, *Affirmative Advocacy: Race, Class, and Gender in Interest Group Politics* (Chicago: University of Chicago Press, 2007).

[9] See Will Kymlicka, *The Right of Minority Cultures* (Oxford: Oxford University Press, 1995).

[10] See Ashutosh Varshney, "Is India Becoming More Democratic?," *Journal of Asian Studies,* vol. 59, no. 1 (2000), pp. 3–25; Myron Weiner, "The Struggle for Equality: Caste in Indian Politics," in Atul Kohli, ed., *The Success of India's Democracy* (Cambridge: Cambridge University Press, 2001), pp. 193–225; Sudha Pai, *Dalit Assertion and the Unfinished Democratic Revolution: The Bahujan Samaj Party in Uttar Pradesh* (New Delhi: Sage, 2002); Yogendra Yadav, "Understanding the Second Democratic Upsurge: Trends of Bahujan Participation in Electoral Politics in the 1990s," in Francine R. Frankel, Zoya Hasan, Rajeev Bhargava, and Balveer Arora, eds., *Transforming India: Social and Political Dynamics of Democracy* (New Delhi: Oxford University Press, 2000), pp. 120–145; Zoya Hasan, "Conflict Pluralism and the Competitive Party System in India" and "Representation and Redistribution: The New Lower-Caste Politics of North India," in Zoya

discussed in Chapters 5 and 6, the Bahujan Samaj Party (BSP), the Lok Janshakti Party (LJP), the Viduthalai Chiruthaikal Katchi (VCK), and the like have given Dalits a presence beyond the realm of electoral politics. A Dalit political party and influential Dalit leaders provide descriptive and symbolic representation for the average Dalit voter, given the long reality of Dalits' almost total absence from the public sphere, not to mention from the historical and cultural fabric of Indian society.

Ethnic parties that focus on mobilizing marginalized groups bring new voters into the political process. They mobilize voters who have not been previously mobilized by political parties. These parties represent symbolic citizenship for the members of groups that are invisible in a society, and they represent demands that the political process has ignored. These are all valuable contributions in their own right.[11]

Dalit ethnic parties have mobilized Dalits across Uttar Pradesh and Bihar, and this has been an empowering experience for Dalits in those states. Besides the psychological benefits of electoral mobilization by Dalit ethnic parties, Dalits are more assertive about challenging entrenched caste norms. Dalits have gained a degree of protection from the coercive and disrespectful practices of state officials and members of dominant groups. Parties such as the BSP have altered the culture of Indian politics by introducing Dalits as rulers—a sharp contrast to the group's ritual status.[12] Dalit parties have also become a symbol of pride and aspiration for Dalits. Often during my fieldwork, when I came across young party workers belonging to the BSP, they enthusiastically showed me the party's blue flag. It represented *Bhim Shakti* or "Dalit power" to them.[13] Dalits as a historically marginalized group are

Hasan, ed., *Parties and Party Politics in India* (New Delhi: Oxford University Press, 2002), pp. 1–36; 370–396; Christophe Jaffrelot, *India's Silent Revolution: The Rise of the Lower Castes* (New York: Columbia University Press, 2003); Hugo Gorringe, *Untouchable Citizens: Dalit Movements and Democratization in Tamil Nadu* (Thousand Oaks: Sage, 2005); Ajoy Bose, *Behenji: A Political Biography of Mayawati* (New Delhi: Penguin India, 2008); Badri Narayan, *The Making of the Dalit Public in North India: Uttar Pradesh, 1950–Present* (New Delhi: Oxford University Press, 2011).

[11] See Owen M. Lynch, *The Politics of Untouchability: Social Mobility and Social Change in a City of India* (New York: Columbia University Press, 1969); Donna Lee Van Cott, *From Movements to Parties in Latin America: The Evolution of Ethnic Politics* (Cambridge: Cambridge University Press, 2005); Courtney Jung, *The Moral Force of Indigenous Politics: Critical Liberalism and the Zapatistas* (New York: Cambridge University Press, 2008).

[12] See Jane Mansbridge, "A 'Selection Model' of Political Representation," *The Journal of Political Philosophy*, vol. 17, no. 4 (2009), pp. 369–398; Eva-Maria Hardtmann, *The Dalit Movement in India: Local Practices, Global Connections* (New Delhi: Oxford University Press, 2009).

[13] The phrase incorporates Dr. B. R. Ambedkar's nickname (Bhim).

vulnerable not only to feelings of social alienation but also to direct coercion by dominant castes and by state instruments such as the police. The electoral success of Dalit parties begins to address these concerns—by raising the group's social profile, on the one hand, and by protecting the group from coercion, on the other hand. Among my Dalit interview subjects, 37.5% in Uttar Pradesh acknowledged feeling safer during the tenure of the BSP, even though their economic deprivation remained unaddressed; in Bihar, 27.4% made similar claims about the tenure of the RJD government. In a 2009 interview in eastern Uttar Pradesh, a BSP worker told me, "Most of our voters are poor, so they generally hesitate to approach government officials and the police. They have little confidence in them. During Behenji's [Mayawati's] rule, there has been at least some assurance that government officials and the police will not mistreat us when we turn to them." Dalits' increased confidence regarding their dealings with dominant groups and the state has been a consequence of the BSP's electoral victories. A dominant-caste police official in western Uttar Pradesh said in an interview: "When the BSP is in power, Dalits come alive. When that government falls, they go back to playing dead." A focus group participant felt that even when the BSP was out of power, it had a lingering effect: "The BSP's strong showing over two decades has meant that now, even if the party is not in power, government officials hesitate to treat us disrespectfully. They know that if Behenji [Mayawati] returns to power, they could be punished." Ethnographic work conducted in rural Uttar Pradesh has found the rise of the BSP has been accompanied by the emergence of Dalit political activists and a discourse of empowerment.[14] A similar discourse is beginning to emerge in Bihar, although the LJP has not been in government in the state. "Under Lalu Yadav," one interview subject in Bihar observed, "the poor have remained poor, but the atmosphere for the downtrodden has changed. Earlier, any upper-class person could threaten, abuse, or even hit me, and I could do nothing. During Lalu's rule that behavior changed." "The LJP does not run the government in Bihar, but we have been in the government in Delhi [federal level]," explained an LJP party worker in Bihar, "Paswanji has been in the cabinet. Our party has influence. Today, the Dusadhs cannot be trampled over. Those times are over."

Dalit parties, then, can increase Dalits' political and social voice, especially when the party has political power. This voice comes at a price, however. It relies on Dalits being without electoral choice, which has serious unintended consequences. Since successful ethnic parties of marginalized groups are able to

---

[14] See Craig Jeffrey, Patricia Jeffery, and Roger Jeffery, "Dalit Revolution? New Politicians in Uttar Pradesh, India," *Journal of Asian Studies,* vol. 67, no. 4 (2008), pp. 1365–1396.

capture a large section of their ethnic vote bloc, they, as Chapter 7 has discussed, are inherently less accountable to their core supporters. The lack of choice also hurts Dalits in another way. Dalits, otherwise ignored and neglected by the state machinery, political organizations, and the media, value political parties' visits to their localities during electoral campaigns as a rare, but predictable moment when those with influence show up at their doorsteps. The exercise of being asked for their votes matters to Dalits and other marginalized groups. It is a reversal of their otherwise subordinate status with respect to the state and the rest of society. When fewer political parties ask for poor voters' support, those voters' status as political equals, and the momentary efficacy that accompanies it, is undermined.[15] So when poor voters are neglected during the campaign, they feel aggrieved. During the interviews in Uttar Pradesh and Bihar, voters in Jatav and Dusadh localities complained bitterly about being ignored by political parties who did not campaign among them because they assumed they were supporters of their group's ethnic party. "Are we so lowly that they will not even try to persuade us?" complained one interview subject. Referring to her locality, another subject asked, "Who knows, if the other parties campaigned here, a few voters would be persuaded to vote for them. Don't parties need votes to win? So why would they write us off?"

Today, indigenous people in Latin America, African Americans, and Dalits in India end up voting as ethnic or racial blocs in support of ethnic and multiethnic parties. Bloc voting has drawn the attention of scholars of marginalized groups because it represents successful collective action of the marginalized in electoral politics. Yet, the broader consequences of bloc voting for the marginalized require a more careful assessment. Since the marginalized rely disproportionately on electoral politics to access the state through political parties, bloc voting makes them vulnerable in new ways. By throwing their weight behind a single party, as Chapter 7 has shown, the marginalized unintentionally turn the election into an absolute win or lose proposition—if their ethnic party gets elected to office, they have access to the state, but if their party loses, they are shut out.

Ethnic and Multiethnic Politics in a Diverse Society

Ethnic mobilization in a diverse society has always been viewed with concern. Scholars of multiethnic democracies point to the failure of democratic

---

[15] See Ahuja and Chhibber, "Why the Poor Vote in India," pp. 389–410; Mukulika Banerjee, *Why India Votes* (New Delhi: Routledge India, 2014).

accountability, the poor provision of public goods, and electorally driven eth-nic violence.[16] Cohesion is often regarded as a prerequisite for the efficacy of democratic institutions.[17] But how is a multiethnic society to achieve cohesion or come close to it? More specifically, what is a low-income democracy such as India to do in the face of ongoing contention in the name of caste, religion, and so forth? On a related note, do fears related to ethnic diversity apply to soci-eties defined by ranked ethnic relations? The evidence presented in this book suggests that ethnic diversity does not necessarily translate into ethnic polar-ization. It also suggests that although ethnic diversity may sometimes have an adverse influence on welfare policies, ethnic mobilization in a ranked society is the means by which a marginalized ethnic group finds its voice in the political system.

When ethnic cleavages are crosscut by party cleavages in the electoral arena, ethnic polarization is checked from spilling over into the electoral arena, and the success of multiethnic party politics is enabled at the expense of ethnic party politics. In such an instance, members of an ethnic group support different parties, and a multiethnic party garners support from different ethnic groups. By contrast, when the two cleavages reinforce each other, ethnic polarization is exacerbated and ethnic party politics succeeds at the expense of multiethnic party politics. In this case, members of an ethnic group vote as a bloc for one party and it becomes easier for an ethnic party to mobilize its ethnic group using ethnic appeals. But even when ethnic parties representing marginalized groups succeed, their success does not necessarily become the harbinger of violent con-flict.[18] In Bihar and Uttar Pradesh, the rise of caste-based parties has not been accompanied by a concomitant rise in caste violence. These parties have not

[16] For how identity-based voting can undermine democratic accountability, see Ashutosh Varshney, "Democracy and Poverty," in Deepa Narayan, ed., *Measuring Empowerment: Cross-Disciplinary Perspectives* (Washington, DC: World Bank, 2005), pp. 383–401. For how ethnic diver-sity undermines public service provision, see Alberto Alesina, Reza Baqir, and William Easterly, "Public Goods and Ethnic Divisions," *Quarterly Journal of Economics*, vol. 114, no. 4 (1999), pp. 1243–1284 and Philip Keefer and Stuti Khemani, "Why Do the Poor Receive Poor Services?" *Economic and Political Weekly*, vol. 39, no. 9 (2004), pp. 935–943. For how ethnically diverse societies are prone to electoral violence, see Paul Collier, *Wars, Guns, and Votes: Democracy in Dangerous Places* (New York: Harper, 2009).

[17] See Charles Taylor, "The Dynamics of Democratic Exclusion," *Journal of Democracy*, vol. 9, no. 4 (1998), pp. 143–156. Democracy has been seen as working best when "the people" represents the members of a cohesive group who have the capacity to deliberate together for the achievement of consensus. "To some extent," Taylor writes, "the members must know one another, listen to one another, and understand one another" (p. 144), and he observes that "democratic states need some-thing like a common identity" (p. 143).

[18] In this connection, see Weiner, "The Struggle for Equality," pp. 193–225; Kanchan Chandra, "Ethnic Parties and Democratic Stability," *Perspectives on Politics*, vol. 3, no. 2 (2005), pp. 235–252.

targeted out-groups during their rule. In fact, in my interviews with workers from the BSP, Lok Janshakti Party (LJP), and Rashtriya Janata Dal (RJD), they often made it clear that their mobilization work had checked the spread of left-wing guerilla groups in their states by channeling lower-caste protests against landed upper castes away from violent insurgency and toward electoral politics.[19] The ethnic mobilization of marginalized groups is, then, a prerequisite for multiethnic parties to become inclusive in ranked societies. It is ethnic mobilization that provides the political system with symbols, demands, and leaders to represent a marginalized identity. When ethnic mobilization takes the form of a successful ethnic party, it results in the mobilization of otherwise undermobilized marginalized voters. Indeed, as the experience of Dalit mobilization suggests, ethnic mobilization can gradually facilitate social change through democratic politics.

Democratic Mobilization and Social Change

The survival of the democratic state in India, more than any other factor, has undermined the moral legitimacy of the hierarchically-organized Hindu caste system.[20] In a democratic society, it is impossible to shut "downstairs" interests permanently out of power arrangements.[21] The Indian Constitution, by granting all members of Indian society the same set of political rights, set in motion the process of making citizens out of subjects through the intervention of democratic institutions. This process continues.[22] The pattern of Dalits' social and electoral mobilization is reflective of the process of social transformation whereby a severely marginalized group is able to reverse, at least partially, centuries-old social and political exclusion. Indian society is still transforming from a society that adheres to caste hierarchy to one that demands equality between castes. For India's democracy, midwifing this transformation has been one of the primary challenges from the outset.[23]

Today, caste in India continues to be implicated in atrocities, violence, and discrimination, and yet the caste system is no longer defended in the public sphere.[24] No political party lends its explicit support to the old order.

---

[19] Mayawati often emphasizes this point in her speeches.

[20] See Weiner, "The Struggle for Equality," pp. 193–225.

[21] See Robert A. Dahl, *On Political Equality* (New Haven: Yale University Press, 2006).

[22] See Varshney, "Is India Becoming More Democratic?" pp. 3–25.

[23] Gopal Guru provides a very thoughtful assessment of the limitations of Dalit electoral politics. See Gopal Guru, "The Indian Nation in Its Egalitarian Conception," in Ramnarayan S. Rawat and K. Satyanarayana, eds., *Dalit Studies* (Durham and London: Duke University Press, 2016), pp. 31–52.

[24] Andre Beteille and C.J. Fuller point out that justifications provided for caste inequality are a thing of the past and the ideas of social equality have come to be accepted in the public sphere at least

Constitutionally mandated policies that reserve electoral districts for Dalits have ensured representation for Dalits across all tiers of governance. Atrocities and discrimination against Dalits are condemned by all political parties. Dalits, as voters, protesters, organizers, party workers, and representatives, have collectively contributed to shaping the democratic challenge to the social order. They have also wholeheartedly embraced democracy—even more than any other group in India, as some would argue. They are enthusiastic voters.[25] The responses that Dalits provided to questions regarding democratic institutions in the 2004 Indian National Election Study are consistent with the above discussion. A large majority of Dalits (67.5%) stated a preference for democracy over authoritarian rule; 70.6% expressed faith in electoral institutions; and 62.2% believed that their votes made a difference.[26] According to the 2004–2005 round of the India Human Development Survey, Dalits are more likely to join civic organizations and attend political meetings than their upper-caste counterparts.[27]

Dalit social mobilization has begun to alter how Dalits are mobilized electorally. These changes are consolidating the democratic gains made by the group. With an increase in Dalit social mobilization, for example, the Hindu nationalist BJP has had to alter its mobilization strategy for Dalits. In the past, the BJP's strategy focused on mobilizing Dalits only as Hindus. Today, the party mobilizes Dalits both as Dalits and as Hindus. Thus, instead of telling Dalits which symbols to revere and which gods to pray to—something that the BJP affiliate Seva Bharati has been doing for decades—the party is recognizing Dalit icons like Dr. B. R. Ambedkar. Even in Uttar Pradesh and Bihar, the BJP is using Dalit symbols popularized by Dalit parties to mobilize Dalits, an effort that has been accompanied by a drive to recruit social mobilization entrepreneurs across Dalit localities. Consider the appeals made by Narendra Modi, the BJP's prime ministerial candidate in the 2014 national election. During his campaign, Modi regularly declared that the coming decade belonged to Dalits and the lower castes. In his victory speech after the election, he evoked Dr. B. R. Ambedkar. To

in principle if not in practice. See Andre Beteille, *Society and Politics in India: Essays in a Comparative Perspective* (London: Athlone Press, 1991); and C.J. Fuller, *Caste Today* (New Delhi: Oxford University Press, 1997).

[25] See Javeed Alam, *Who Wants Democracy?* (New Delhi: Orient Longman, 2004); Kumar, "Patterns of Political Participation," pp. 47–51.

[26] See Center for the Study of Developing Societies, *Indian National Election Study, 2004* (New Delhi: Center for the Study of Developing Societies, 2004).

[27] Sonalde Desai and Amaresh Dubey find that education and income are positively correlated with membership in civic organizations and participation in political meetings, but once they control for these factors, they find that Dalits are more politically engaged than upper castes. See Sonalde Desai and Amaresh Dubey, "Caste in 21st Century India: Competing Narratives," *Economic and Political Weekly*, vol. 46, no. 11 (2012), pp. 40–49.

Dr. Ambedkar himself, this would have been an anathema, since he was not only opposed to Hindu nationalism but also converted to Buddhism in protest. The historical antipathy was mutual; the Hindu nationalists rejected Dr. Ambedkar's ideas and image for decades. However, nationwide, among Dalits, the popularity of Dr. Ambedkar has increased over the years, and eager to expand its vote share among Dalits, the BJP has begun to co-opt him as a part of the pantheon of great Indian leaders it recognizes. Dr. Ambedkar's image appeared alongside those of current BJP leaders on the party's posters during the 2014 campaign. Since then, to shed its upper-caste image, the party has sent its legislators to dine with Dalits at their homes, expanded the memorialization of Dr. Ambedkar, and backed the election of Ram Nath Kovind, a Dalit, as the 14th President of India. The BJP's courting of the Dalit vote has been somewhat successful. In the 2014 national election, the BJP's vote share among Dalits stood at 25% after having being stuck at 10% across previous elections. Whether the party can sustain or even increase its vote share among Dalits remains to be seen.

Even if the BJP's campaign activities amount to nothing more than symbolic politics, they further the ongoing process of mainstreaming Dalit symbols and demands for inclusion. These activities also represent an increase in the nation-wide competition for Dalit votes, a large majority of which have typically been captured by Dalit ethnic or social justice-oriented multiethnic parties. The competition for Dalit votes and the accompanying acknowledgment of Dalits' concerns and recognition of their symbols empower the Dalit leaders within political parties. Unlike their predecessors, the younger cohort of Dalit leaders are far more likely to challenge their party leadership to address Dalit concerns. In March 2018 when a two-judge panel of India's Supreme Court altered provisions of the 1989 Prevention of Atrocities Act—landmark hate crimes legislation protecting Dalits and Adivasis, widespread street protests rocked a number of states.[28] Despite the absence of a Dalit caucus within the Indian parliament, Dalit legislators across political parties aggressively pushed their parties and the ruling BJP to enact legislation to override the Supreme Court's judgment.

This is not to say that there exists a consensus around the state policies mandating Dalits' inclusion. How could there be? The upper castes, who stand to lose from the upending of the old order, have resisted the transformation. The

---

[28] This law has required Indian public officials to respond promptly to complaints of caste-based discrimination and violence by filing criminal charges and pursuing proper investigations. In their order, the Supreme Court justices asserted the act had been misused in a few instances and that a delayed and a more complex approval process for filing hate crimes charges was needed. But the Indian government's own data belies the court's concern. The National Crime Records Bureau reports that only 10% of the total cases filed under the act have been classified as false, and that the rate of false reporting has declined in recent years.

party system reflects this ideological tension. Drawing on data from the Indian National Election Study, scholars have thus shown that in politics there is greater ideological consensus across the political spectrum on economic policies, but they failed to find the same agreement around social policies.[29] Specifically, there is a clear ideological division among supporters of political parties on the question of whether the state should or should not intervene to improve the social status of minority and marginalized groups. Members of the upper castes who support the Hindu nationalist BJP are opposed to such policies, but these policies are favored by members of marginalized groups and by religious minorities who support the Congress Party and the regional parties. As Hindu nationalist parties like the BJP and Shiv Sena try to mobilize Dalit support, this ideological gap will be less likely to find expression in party politics.

As Dalits' support for Hindu nationalist parties has increased, it has also become more difficult for these parties to oppose caste-based reservations. For example, the *Rashtriya Swayamsevak Sangh* ("National Volunteer Corps"; RSS), the ideological fountainhead of the Hindu nationalist movement, has been forced to support reservation policies for disadvantaged groups. This is not at all surprising, since RSS-affiliated political parties such as the BJP and Shiv Sena already rely on the support of disadvantaged groups, namely, Dalits, Adivasis, and Other Backward Castes, all of whom enjoy reservations in state institutions. In this sense, Dalits' social mobilization in a competitive multiparty system, by increasing the competition for Dalits' votes, can make political parties more inclusive and force them to moderate their stands on polarizing issues.

Whither Dalit Politics?

In 2014, the 16th Indian parliament had thirty-two political parties. But, apart from the LJP, hardly any Dalit parties were represented. The BSP, despite obtaining 19.6% of the total vote share and a majority of the Dalit vote in Uttar Pradesh, was unable to win a single one out of eighty seats in the state. No Dalit parties from either Tamil Nadu or Maharashtra won seats there either. Meanwhile, the national vote share of the BSP declined from 6.1% in 2009 to 4.1% in 2014. The BSP still remains the third-largest national party, and in all likelihood will improve its seat share in the 2019 parliamentary elections. But the presence or absence of Dalit parties in legislatures is increasingly an insufficient indicator of the vibrancy of Dalit politics.

---

[29] See Pradeep Chhibber and Rahul Verma, "The BJP's 2014 'Modi Wave': An Ideological Consolidation of the Right," *Economic and Political Weekly*, vol. 49, no. 39 (2014), pp. 50–56.

Today, internal as well as external constraints against mobilization are continuing to relax for Dalits. Altering social relations, especially in rural India, ongoing rural-to-urban migration, and improving economic opportunities have all played a role in these changes. Increasing literacy rates are also contributing to self-awareness among Dalits, and the number of Dalit social and political entrepreneurs in Dalit localities and neighborhoods is increasing across Indian states.

New Dalit mobilization entrepreneurs and new Dalit movements are beginning to reflect this transformation. Consider two recent examples of high-visibility protests. In 2015, Chandrashekhar Azad formed the Bhim Army to promote education and security for Dalits in Uttar Pradesh. The Bhim Army protested the violence of upper-caste Thakurs against Dalits. In 2016, Jignesh Mevani led a Dalit protest to highlight the flogging of Dalits in Gujarat. Large-scale Dalit protests against atrocities in movement states such as Maharashtra or Tamil Nadu are routine. But the appearance of such strong protests in weak movement states like Uttar Pradesh and Gujarat reflects the nascent ability of Dalits there to stand up to dominant castes and state machinery. As has been the case with previous Dalit movements, these movements will shape the electoral mobilization of Dalits. But they will also put pressure on ethnic and multiethnic parties and state officials to respond to Dalit's concerns.

Furthermore, Dalit politics is taking root in new dimensions of the public sphere: organizations in new sectors, an online Dalit public sphere, and a Dalit diaspora. On campuses of public universities, Dalit study circles have emerged, and their participants are often at the forefront of Dalit students' assertion. Dalit entrepreneurs have come together to launch the Dalit Chamber of Commerce to support the fledgling class of Dalit businesses in India.

A Dalit counterpublic sphere is not new. So far, it has been limited to the locality: it exists in teashops, in *chaupals* (seating under shade trees), in Ravidas and Buddhist temples, and in celebrations of Dalit icons. Occasionally, it extends beyond the locality, for example, during Dalit protests and larger festivals. Today, on Dalit websites and discussion forums, Dalits from India and its diaspora are building a digital counterpublic sphere to exchange ideas, share information, and present a perspective on issues from their vantage points. Round Table India, the Dalit and Adivasi Students' Portal, Ambedkar.org, and Savari have emerged as some of the prominent Dalit websites. There are YouTube channels widely watched by Dalits, including National Dastak, Bahujan TV, Awaaz India, Dalit Dastak, Dalit Camera, and the Dalit News Network. Besides these platforms, there are a number of Facebook groups and Twitter accounts that share commentary and news on Dalits, highlight Dalit experiences, commemorate histories and leaders, discuss Dalit literature and cultural materials, and mobilize Dalit popular opinion. Across India, numerous Dalits have joined WhatsApp groups to share, discuss, and learn about Dalit social and political concerns. As safe spaces, these platforms allow Dalits to express opinions they would otherwise be reluctant to share directly with higher caste friends or colleagues. The effects of this connectivity are strengthening a national Dalit consciousness and democratizing Dalit politics.

In the past, Dalit political assertion in different parts of India has often failed to spread beyond linguistic and cultural boundaries to develop into a cohesive national movement. Today, the imagination of the Dalit community is no longer restricted by city or state boundaries. Exposed to online Dalit discourse from different parts of the country, Dalit youth have begun to imagine themselves as a community across language and cultural boundaries. When Rohith Vemula, a Dalit graduate student at the University of Hyderabad, committed suicide in 2016 to protest his ill-treatment by his university administration, his suicide note went viral on social media, and the outpouring of anger in response to his death generated nationwide protests across university campuses. Recent Dalit movements led by Jignesh Mevani and Chandrashekhar Azad in Gujarat and Uttar Pradesh, respectively, instead of remaining confined to their states of origin, attained national prominence and widespread Dalit following because of the pictures and videos shared by organizers on online platforms.

Besides amplifying Dalit protests, social media has lowered the barriers to entry into political discourse for Dalits. Political parties have traditionally held veto power over the content and timing of Dalit political messaging. Digital politics has disrupted this pattern. Online campaigns and conversations begun outside political parties are able to disturb the calculus of party messaging to Dalits. By highlighting acts of atrocities and discrimination against Dalits, as well as spreading the word on Dalit protests, digital Dalit activists put pressure on both Dalit and multicaste parties. Not regimented behind a single party, Dalit online commentary is also not shy of critiquing prominent Dalit politicians. The power to set the Dalit political agenda, then, has begun to shift from parties to Dalit activists and voters.

Without a doubt, social media has enhanced the voice of Dalits in the public discourse, but experiences of digital empowerment from other parts of the world offer important lessons. One such lesson suggests that unequal access to the digital universe can privilege some voices over others. A large majority of Dalits remain untouched by the growth of social media. Three-fourths of Dalits, even today, reside in rural India, and among those who are urban residents, many lack internet access and rely on text messaging groups to learn about community issues. The digitally empowered Dalits are more likely to be city dwellers and with a higher socioeconomic status. With availability of cheaper smart phones and accompanying internet service packages, these constraints will lift.

For all their advantages, digital ties are limited in their durability; this is the other lesson worth remembering. Unless people interact face-to-face and form personal bonds while working together, they are unlikely to be able to sustain collective action. Digital collectives, then, inform the Dalit agenda, but they cannot replace grassroots-level organization. For this reason, Dalit movements, activists, politicians, and parties will continue to remain at the center of Dalit politics.

The caste system has migrated with South Asians. The persistence of caste-based distinctions has led to the appearance of Dalit organizations and groups in the Indian diaspora. These organizations aim to spread awareness about caste-based discrimination and find allies in their adopted home societies. They respond to the acts of discrimination that Dalits experience at the hands of other members of the Indian diaspora. They also highlight the poor record of the Indian state in responding to the needs of Dalits.[30] Dalit assertion in online communities and within the diaspora is an extension of the Dalit social mobilization that began in the movement states. Today, its message and symbols have diffused across Indian states and internationally through the diaspora population. Dr. B. R. Ambedkar is read and revered under street lamps and libraries in small towns and large cities in India as well as on websites that are accessed across the world. A higher degree of Dalit consciousness and self-mobilization, however, is unlikely to bolster the success of Dalit-based caste parties because it will enable Dalit mobilization by multiple parties. In a competitive multiparty system, the BSP, LJP, VCK, and RPI may not be the beneficiaries of these changes in the coming years.

In competitive politics no voter is an untouchable. As more political parties try to mobilize Dalits directly, the group's vote is likely to be divided among different parties rather than being concentrated behind a single multicaste or caste-based party. What is noteworthy, however, is that today, even in non-movement states, Dalits are being drawn through direct mobilization into multicaste parties such as the BJP. The rise of the BSP and the LJP has ensured that, even in non-movement states, a party that wants to mobilize Dalit voters has to recruit party workers in Dalit localities or neighborhoods instead of relying on non-Dalit intermediaries. Scholars have lamented the failure of the politics of recognition, as represented by the rise of lower-caste parties, to produce a politics of redistribution, especially in favor of the most marginalized supporters of these parties. This outcome of the politics of recognition was born of the caste-based voting blocs in Uttar Pradesh and Bihar. As Dalits come to be included in different

---

[30] For instance, nineteen international Dalit organizations approached the United Nations to declare atrocities against Dalits as genocide. Dalit organizations active in the UK have run a campaign for the introduction of laws against caste discrimination in the Indian diaspora. In the United States, the Dalit diaspora has approached the White House to put pressure on the Indian government to respond more effectively to the acts of discrimination and atrocities committed against Dalits. In Japan, Dalit organizations expressed their anger against the presentation of the Bhagwat Gita, a religious Hindu text, by the visiting Indian prime minister to his Japanese counterpart in 2014. Passages in the Gita outline the caste system and legitimize the social order.

parties, and as political parties cease viewing Dalits as a single bloc, competition for Dalits' votes will increase. As long as such competition is sustained, it will benefit Dalits by drawing more attention to their deprivation, thereby raising the likelihood of redistributive policies even in non-movement states. At the same time, however, the gains arising from this mobilization are likely to be incremental. They also may not immediately benefit the most marginalized Dalits, for the simple reason that this segment of the group is least likely to be able to hold the state machinery and its elected representatives accountable.

Appendix A

FOCUS GROUPS AND
FOLLOW-UP INTERVIEWS

I conducted eighty focus groups, twenty each across the four states of Tamil Nadu, Maharashtra, Uttar Pradesh, and Bihar. Focus groups were especially helpful, since I was a stranger and thus not automatically trusted by the subjects in the localities visited. The Dalit subjects I came in contact with were mostly poor. Even when I presented them with documentation clearly outlining our project's aims and my institutional affiliation, they worried about whom they might be speaking to, and they often asked which political party or governmental department I was from. Interacting in a group setting enabled me to reassure my respondents and allowed them to speak to me with greater confidence. The use of a focus group, as compared to something such as participant observation, also allowed for the replication of questions across different areas, enabling some generalizability.

The number of participants in each focus group ranged from twelve to fifteen. Each focus group discussion lasted from ninety minutes to two hours. I tabulated all the responses of the participants. For a particular focus group to be coded for a particular response, that response had to be used by at least one-third of the participants in that discussion. Given multiple opinions in a focus group, it could sometimes be coded for multiple responses. The figures take such overlap into account. There was much less overlap in responses in the one-to-one interviews that supplemented the focus group discussions.

The focus group discussions with Dalit voters were centered on the following questions:

- What problems regarding basic services did they face in their area?
- Did they face caste-based discrimination in their area?
- Was it important to vote on Election Day? Why?
- Was it important to vote with members of their caste community?

- Was caste a consideration in deciding which party to support?
- Did members of their caste living in their locality support the same party or different parties in the last election? Why was this the case?
- In a time of need, whom did they turn to for assistance?
- Which party did they support?
- Why did they support that particular party?
- Have you heard of Babasaheb Ambedkar?
- Why is Babasaheb important to you?
- Can you name his achievements or contributions to the community and the country?

Within an electoral district, localities and neighborhoods were randomly selected. First, I randomly selected localities from the list of polling booths used by the Electoral Commission. Next, I confirmed the income and caste profiles of localities and neighborhoods through multiple sources, all independent of one another. I turned to government officials, journalists, and party functionaries for this information. When a locality fit my required profile, I selected it. For neighborhood and locality selection, my income parameters included upper-, middle-, and lower-income households.

In urban as well as rural areas, I was comfortable selecting localities instead of households. Neighborhoods and localities are good proxies for income levels and caste status in rural and urban India, especially in small towns. In both types of settings, there exists segregation along class lines and very often along caste lines, too. Within a given locality, there may be household-income differentials within a certain range. Dalit localities are separate from localities of other castes in rural as well as urban areas. The distance between Dalit localities and other localities in rural India varies across states. I found this distance to be greatest in Tamil Nadu, whereas Dalit localities were closer to localities of higher castes in Uttar Pradesh and Maharashtra. A minority of Dalits belongs to the upper- and middle-income category, and so I oversampled on poor Dalit localities. Similarly, I oversampled on rural localities, since this is where the majority of Dalits reside. Even in large urban slums, Dalit hutments and housing are separate from those of other groups.

I used an income-based criterion to classify the survey and interview respondents and the focus group participants as poor or non-poor. Using the same classification as the surveys conducted by Lokniti (a program for comparative democracy administered by the Centre for the Study of Developing Societies, in New Delhi), I classified as poor anyone with an income of less than Rs. 2,000 per month.

Each focus group was constituted of individuals who had similar class and caste backgrounds. To select focus group participants and interview subjects in a

locality, I relied on a systematic sampling design. Using the voter list for a particular locality, I selected every sixth individual for participation in the focus group.
When occasionally the individual did not fit the income or caste parameter, or
when the individual was not available, or when our request for participation was
declined, I continued down the list. Since I had deliberately picked large localities to work in, I was able to deal with the problem of low response rates when
it arose.

Focus group discussions and interviews were conducted in the appropriate
local language; in Tamil Nadu, I required the support of a translator. In some
rural and urban localities, the focus groups were conducted with men and
women separately. I conducted the focus groups and interviews either early in
the morning or late in the evening, when most residents in the locality were at
home. In urban areas and in middle-class localities, focus groups and interviews
were conducted on weekends. The same method was used for the follow-up
one-to-one interviews. These interviews allowed me to check the validity of the
responses obtained during the focus group discussions. In addition, the questions related to choice of party were administered in a private setting.

The focus groups allowed me to establish my credibility in the communities. The focus groups also allowed me to demonstrate to the participants that
I was genuinely interested in finding out more about their lives and their engagement with politics. I discovered that the discussions created goodwill for me
even among those members of a community who had not participated in the
discussion. That said, people often felt constrained about what they could say
in a public discussion, and I found that interview subjects spoke to me far more
freely in private. Focus group participants felt wary of criticizing party workers
or members of dominant castes. Privately, however, interview subjects spoke
more frankly about the roles of these actors.

As is the case where other subaltern groups are concerned, there are limited
accounts of the democratic participation and mobilization of Dalits. The popular press and histories have poorly documented Dalits' political behavior. Focus
groups and interviews proved to be a useful instrument for partially addressing
this information gap. They were used to collecting oral histories on issues related
to the political participation and mobilization of Dalits in a particular area.

One concern about the validity of focus group data must be addressed
here: Does it privilege group opinion over individual opinion, and how representative are the opinions that can sometimes dominate a discussion? My field
observations tell me that individuals in rural India still gather political information through group discussions. In this sense, individual opinion is already contaminated with group opinion. That said, I took the precaution of conducting
five open-ended interviews in each locality to supplement the focus group discussions, and I report the findings of these two instruments separately. Finally,

I use focus group and interview findings in conjunction with findings of the survey data. The eighty focus groups and 409 follow-up interviews were conducted over a period of nineteen weeks.

The focus groups and the follow-up interviews were conducted in the parliamentary electoral districts listed in Table A.1 below.

Table A.1. **Lok Sabha constituencies that were sites of focus groups**

Tamil Nadu	Maharashtra	Uttar Pradesh	Bihar
Chennai	Mumbai	Azamgarh	Hajipur
Chidambaram	Nagpur	Lalganj	Patnasahib
Madurai	Sangli	Lucknow	Vaishali
Ramanathapuram	Wardha	Mawana	
		Meerut	

Appendix B

LOCALITY-BASED CAMPAIGN SURVEY

I conducted a locality-level survey just before the 2009 parliamentary election. Despite more than seventy years of electioneering, very few systematic studies of electoral campaigns exist in India.[1] The aim of this observational survey was to compare the intensity and content of electoral campaigns across localities in the four states of Tamil Nadu, Maharashtra, Uttar Pradesh, and Bihar.

Electoral Campaigns

Elections are often associated with a festive atmosphere, and parties discover innovative ways to campaign to voters. Party flags, badges, hats, and other items with party electoral symbols are distributed; posters are put up; and parties and candidates organize neighborhood walk-throughs and public meetings. Additionally, parties use television, radio, newspaper, and social media ads to get their message out to voters. Voters, too, look forward to the period of campaigning when party workers visit their areas to inquire about their concerns, make promises, and campaign for their party and candidate. Sometimes voters are taken to public meetings where, in addition to listening to party leaders, they are also provided food, entertainment, and a daily allowance. While direct campaigning is not the only method that parties use to mobilize voters, neighborhood-level campaigning remains an important mobilization strategy for poor voters who typically rely less on mass media for their information. The

---

[1] The Indian National Election Study conducted by Lokniti tracks some aspects of electoral campaigns. Examples of ethnographic work include Mukulika Banerjee, "Sacred Elections," *Economic and Political Weekly*, vol. 42, no. 17 (2007), pp. 1556–1562; Mysore Narasimhachar Srinivas and A. M. Shah, *The Grassroots of Democracy: Field Studies of Indian Elections* (Delhi: Permanent Black, 2007).

poor voters do not live in gated communities, and as such they are more accessible to political parties for direct contact as compared to middle- or upper-class
voters, who can more easily ignore the campaign because of the types of communities they live in. Neighborhood-level campaigning also has an interactive
aspect that mass media campaigns do not. A neighborhood-level campaign is
one of the few occasions when political parties come face to face with voters in
their locality. Typically, given the population size of an electoral district in a parliamentary election, it is impossible for candidates to attend neighborhood-level
meetings or undertake door-to-door campaigning; instead they focus more on
larger public meetings. Party workers therefore mostly undertake the locality or
neighborhood campaigning.

Observational Study Design

For this study, I observed the campaign in the locality for two days during the
final week of campaigning. This is when the campaigning is at its most intense
stage. Two researchers observed the campaign in every locality. For the purpose
of comparison, I observed the campaign along a general set of parameters in all
four states. For every locality, I recorded the number of parties that visited, who
was visited on behalf of the party and the candidate, what issues were raised, what
promises were made, what types of appeals were used, and what types of campaign
activities were relied upon. In addition, in each locality, I interviewed five voters
selected from the voter list using a stratified random sampling method. These voters were asked if it was important for them to vote with fellow caste members,
what factors mattered to them while selecting political parties, and whether caste
was a consideration while choosing to support a political party. In Dalit localities
and neighborhoods, I also asked the subjects if Dr. B. R. Ambedkar's birth and
death anniversaries were observed in their locality and which other festivals and
anniversaries were observed. Finally, I counted the number of political parties
that were represented in these neighborhoods and localities through their party
workers.

   The observations were made on different dates across different states, since
the 2009 parliamentary elections were staggered over six phases, and the four
states went to the polls on different dates. For example, in Uttar Pradesh, different parts of the state went to the polls over five separately timed phases, while
the entire state of Tamil Nadu went to the polls on the same day. I selected large
localities (over two hundred households) because they were most likely to be
targeted by parties. I also conducted follow-up interviews with voters and party
workers in each district. The survey was conducted in a total of 138 localities; 82

Table B.1. **Lok Sabha constituencies that were included in the locality-based campaign survey**

Tamil Nadu	Maharashtra	Uttar Pradesh	Bihar
Chennai	Chandrapur	Azamgarh	Hajipur
Chidambaram	Latur	Gautam Buddha Nagar	Munger
Madurai	Mumbai	Lalganj	Patnasahib
Mayiladuthurai	Nagpur	Lucknow	Vaishali
Ramanathapuram	Pune	Mawana	
Tiruchirappalli	Sangli	Meerut	
	Wardha	Pratapgarh	
		Sitapur	

of these were in general electoral districts, and 56 in electoral districts reserved for Dalit candidates.[2]

I first randomly selected localities from the list of polling booths used by the Election Commission. Next, I confirmed the size, income, and caste profile of localities and neighborhoods through multiple sources, all independent of each other. I talked to party functionaries, newspaper correspondents, the local station House Officer, and the officials in the local election commission office to identify the caste and income profile of a locality. When the locality fit the required profile, I selected it. For neighborhood and locality selection, the income parameters included upper-, middle-, and lower-income households. When I was not sure about the profile of a locality, I picked another one from my pool of locality names. Caste parameters included upper, Backward (or intermediate), and Dalit households. In rural and urban settings, I conducted locality-level surveys in nine types of neighborhoods. In large villages and urban localities, members of different castes can live together. But within these areas, there exist clear demarcations that separate clusters of houses belonging to different castes. These boundaries can get blurred in urban pockets, especially as the social distance between Backward and upper caste is shrinking. Dalits, I found, are still residentially segregated.

The locality-based electoral campaign survey and voter interviews were conducted in the parliamentary electoral districts listed in Table B.1.

---

[2] The Indian Constitution provides for reserved seats in the national parliament, state assemblies, and village and municipal bodies to guarantee representation for Dalits. The quota of seats is based roughly on population estimates of Dalits.

Appendix C

AN OBSERVATIONAL STUDY ASSESSING CASTE BOUNDARIES IN THE INDIAN MARRIAGE MARKET

Following well-tested designs for examining discrimination in the labor market, I used a correspondence-based design to study discriminatory behavior of upper-caste, Backward-Caste, and Scheduled-Caste women toward potential marriage partners from other caste categories.[1] I did this by conducting an observational study on three of India's largest matrimonial websites: Shaadi. com, Bharatmatrimony.com, and Jeevansathi.com.[2] The study was conducted across three of India's largest states: Uttar Pradesh in the north, Maharashtra in the west, and Tamil Nadu in the south.[3] The resulting data set covers a wide

---

[1] On designs for examining discrimination in the labor market, see Marianne Bertrand and Sendhil Mullainathan, "Are Emily and Greg More Employable than Lakisha and Jamal? A Field Experiment on Labor Market Discrimination," *American Economic Review*, vol. 94, no. 4 (2004), pp. 991–1013.; Sukhadeo Thorat and Paul Attewell, "The Legacy of Social Exclusion," *Economic and Political Weekly*, vol. 42, no. 41 (2007), pp. 4141–4145.

[2] Such website memberships cost up to $100 for a six-month package, a price that compares favorably with running newspaper ads, many of which cost as much as $75 for three weekend appearances. On the growing role of matrimonial websites, see Mukta Sharangpani, "Browsing for Bridegrooms: Matchmaking and Modernity in Mumbai," *Indian Journal of Gender Studies*, vol. 17, no. 2 (2010), pp. 249–276; Fritzi-Marie Titzmann, "Medialisation and Social Change: The Indian Online Matrimonial Market as a New Field of Research," in Nadja-Christina Schneider and Bettina Gräf, eds., *Social Dynamics 2.0: Researching Change in Times of Media Convergence* (Berlin: Frank & Timme, 2011), pp. 49–66; Snigdha Poonam, "Casting the Net," *The Caravan*, vol. 4, no. 3 (2012), pp. 48–59; Ravinder Kaur and Priti Dhanda, "Surfing for Spouses: Marriage Websites and the 'New' Indian Marriage?" in Ravinder Kaur and Palriwala Rajni, eds., *Marrying in South Asia: Shifting Concepts, Changing Practices in a Globalising World* (Telangana: Orient Blackswan, 2014), pp. 271–292.

[3] I chose to conduct this study on online platforms instead of responding to newspaper ads because the latter medium did not provide us with standard information about the respondents and their families. Online platforms require members to provide information about themselves and their backgrounds in a standard format.

variety of different upper-caste, Backward-Caste, and Scheduled-Caste jatis, or subcastes. My study focused on women because the taboos against intercaste marriage are stronger for women than for men: a woman's caste status, unlike a man's, changes when she marries outside her own caste and assumes the caste of her husband.

Before I could implement the correspondence-based aspect of my study, I had to identify a set of prospective grooms who were willing to work with us, and for whom caste presented no bar in the selection of a marriage partner. To do so, I turned to cooperating marriage bureaus. The bureaus delivered profiles for a set of potential grooms who were nearly identical in terms of my control variables: educational background, appearance, age, skin color, family status, income level, and profession. All the prospective grooms had very similar upper-middle-income/ high-status backgrounds, were between five feet nine inches and five feet ten inches tall, were twenty-seven or twenty-eight years old, possessed an MBA degree from a reputable Indian business school, reported an annual income that was the equivalent of approximately \$17,500 to \$18,500, and were fair in skin color.[4] From this set of prospective grooms, and from each of the three states, I then randomly chose one upper-caste man, one Backward-Caste man, and one Scheduled-Caste man, for a total of nine prospective grooms.

I registered these nine grooms with all three matrimonial websites. Then, I assembled a list of women who were also registered with at least one of the websites, and from this list I drew up a random sample of upper-caste, Backward-Caste, and Scheduled-Caste women from each state. I contacted each of these women on behalf of the three prospective grooms from her state—one man from each of the three caste categories. Every woman received one profile from a man belonging to her own caste category and two profiles from men belonging to the other two caste categories. I randomized both the timing of these transmissions and the order in which the prospective grooms' profiles were sent.[5] The

---

[4] The range of attributes was even narrower when it came to the set of profiles for a particular state. For example, in all three profiles from the northern state of Uttar Pradesh, the man was twenty-seven years old, had nearly the same annual income as the other two men, was five feet nine inches tall, and belonged to a family headed by a senior civil servant. Nevertheless, although these prospective grooms were above average on most attributes, they were by no means among the most desirable in terms of income, which for other prospective grooms in their age bracket went as high as Rs 3.5 million per year.

[5] An individual who registers with a matrimonial website typically receives many expressions of interest. Therefore, the prospective grooms featured in the nine study profiles offered just three of the many expressions of interest that each of the subjects would have received. In order to avoid any bias that might have arisen from the order in which the profiles were received, I randomized different components of the process of expressing interest—sometimes the Scheduled-Caste prospective groom was the first to express interest, sometimes it was the upper-caste, and at other times it was the Backward-Caste prospective groom who first made contact. The prospective grooms also sent their

women respondents were contacted by the prospective grooms through messages of interest, which I thought most of the women would have considered indicative of the willingness to explore a possible relationship. This message was standardized and prominently displayed, among other attributes, the caste of the individual expressing interest. No photographs of the prospective grooms were made available to the women who were contacted. Omission of photographs allowed us to ensure that the nine profiles used in the study would be almost identical across all the parameters revealed in the profiles. The introduction of a photograph would have contaminated the study and removed an important control related to beauty. Moreover, the absence of photographs was not at all unusual; in many matrimonial searches, photos are exchanged only after an initial level of mutual interest has been established.

Having either controlled for or randomized potential confounding variables, I was able to conclude that, for the women who responded to the three expressions of matrimonial interest by indicating interest in pursuing further contact, variations in the response rates were related to the caste status of the prospective grooms. The response rate overall was 72.1%, or 1,702 responses from the 2,358 upper-caste, Backward-Caste, and Scheduled-Caste women I contacted.[6] I recorded the caste of each woman who responded, in addition to other information typically deemed important in the process of matchmaking, such as the woman's height, her skin color, her age, her educational background, and her socioeconomic status.[7]

To gather more information about the data that I had collected through correspondence on the matrimonial websites, I also conducted fifty-six individual interviews with a subset of these women, from different regional and caste backgrounds (I spoke with eighteen upper-caste subjects, fifteen Backward-Caste subjects, and twenty-three Dalit subjects). The interviews were conducted by phone and in person. Since the interviews were of a deeply personal nature, I had to rely on the snowballing technique to construct my sample; that is, before a

---

expressions of interest at different times during the week and at different times of day; no women received expressions of interest from all three of the prospective grooms at the same time.

[6] I checked for bias in the response rates but did not find a statistically significant difference in the rates at which the upper-caste, Backward-Caste, and Scheduled-Caste subjects responded (or failed to respond) to the expressions of interest within a particular state.

[7] I also collected data on the women's professions but decided not to code and analyze this information. I made this decision in part because my qualitative research indicated that education and socioeconomic status, but not profession, are important parameters on which prospective grooms consider prospective brides—and, unsurprisingly, education and socioeconomic status are the same parameters on which brides try to impress prospective grooms. I also reasoned that profession is, in many ways, redundant with respect to educational background and socioeconomic status.

subject would agree to an interview, another subject, one or more of her family members, or one of my acquaintances had to vouch for me.

In the interviews, I asked each subject to define her ideal partner, to describe the process of searching for him, to explain the significance of caste in her personal life and in the search for a partner (her own search and the searches of her friends and family members), to state her reasons for wanting or not wanting an intercaste marriage, to tell us about how the degree of openness to intercaste marriage varied between the city where she lived and the rural area where she still had family members, and to describe how openness to intercaste marriage varied between women and men. I also asked her to tell us how she expected to view intercaste marriage by the time any eventual children of hers were ready to marry.

My study was motivated by the objective of studying variations in behavior as they related to caste boundaries in the arranged-marriage market. I chose to focus on the behavior of urban middle-income participants because, in theory, those individuals (and their immediate family members, who are often heavily involved in any search for a marriage partner) should have been exposed to less community-level policing than would have been the case for their rural counterparts. Moreover, instead of implementing an experimental design, I opted to estimate the effect of observable individual characteristics on behavior in the marriage market, for two reasons. First, although similar correspondence-based studies in the labor market have used fake résumés to gauge discrimination on the part of potential employers, I decided that sending fake letters of matrimonial interest to women who were in the process of looking for life partners would be unacceptable in terms of the costs that the subjects would have been forced to bear. An experimental design also would have wasted the time of women who had not consented to be involved in my research, and emotional stress might have been added to an already taxing process when the subjects eventually discovered that they were not corresponding with actual prospective grooms.[8] Second, there were at least six variables in addition to caste that affected the women's responses, with each parameter taking multiple values, and so I would have had to find an impossibly high number of prospective grooms and women respondents in order to implement a completely randomized experimental design. Given my desire to work only with prospective grooms for whom caste presented no bar to matrimony, and given the fact that caste discrimination remains rampant in India's marriage markets, I was virtually certain not to have been able to find enough sets of prospective grooms to execute a

---

[8] Such deception also would have undermined the credibility of the major matrimonial agencies that I was working with.

truly randomized experiment. In the circumstances, then, the design I chose was the one that offered the most ethical and practical way for us to proceed while still collecting meaningful behavioral data on interest in intercaste marriage in India's arranged-marriage markets.

My study departs from other studies of India's marriage market in that I focused on subjects' interest in intermarriage, as captured by women's positive responses to prospective out-of-caste grooms' profiles, whereas other studies have often used actual marriage outcomes as the basis of conclusions about behavior in India's marriage market.[9] I chose to focus on subjects' interest in intercaste marriage because I believed that such interest would serve as a better indicator of social distance than marriage outcomes could have done. During the matchmaking process, a number of confounding variables may work alongside an individual's caste to influence eventual marriage outcomes. For example, a woman who is open to marrying a man from another caste may actually decide against marrying him, not because of his caste, but because of one or more other factors, including his educational background, his income, his profession, his family background, his personality, his appearance, and so on. Therefore, studies of marriage outcomes are likely to underestimate the social distance between castes.[10]

[9] See Abhijit Banerjee, Esther Duflo, Maitreesh Ghatak, and Jeanne Lafortune, "Marry for What? Caste and Mate Selection in Modern India," *American Economic Journal: Microeconomics*, vol. 5, no. 2 (2013), pp. 33–72; Srinivas Goli, Deepti Singh, and T. V. Sekher, "Exploring the Myth of Mixed Marriages in India: Evidence from a Nationwide Survey," *Journal of Comparative Family Studies*, vol. 44, no. 2 (2013), pp. 193–206.

[10] This section draws from Amit Ahuja and Susan L. Ostermann, "Crossing Caste Boundaries in the Modern Indian Marriage Market," *Studies in Comparative International Development*, vol. 51, no. 3 (2016), pp. 365–387.

GLOSSARY

Adi-Dravida: A term used in Tamil Nadu to denote Dalits, its literal meaning is "Original natives or indigenous people of Dravida land."

Adi-Hindu: A newer identity proposed and embraced by literate Dalits in Uttar Pradesh in the 1920s to contest their lowly ritual status. It asserted that untouchables were pure or original Hindus robbed of their power and status by Aryan invaders.

Adi-Shudra: Refers to untouchable castes that are classed as outside of the varna, therefore, "untouchable."

Arya Samaj: A modern Indian Hindu reform movement founded in 1875 by Dayananda Sarasvati that seeks to reestablish Vedic values and practices.

Baba: "Father."

Babasaheb: "Respected Father." Dr. B. R. Ambedkar is frequently called Babasaheb by Dalits.

Bahujan: Literally means "the common people," especially the majoritarian grouping of Dalits, Backward Castes, Adivasis, and religious minorities. As an ideological construct, Bahujan refers to organizing those social groups into a political community that can challenge the minority dominant castes' power.

Buddha Purnima: A Buddhist festival commemorating the birthday of Gautam Buddha.

Chambhar: A Dalit caste in Maharashtra, the same as Chamars in North India. They are associated with leatherwork.

Dusadh: The most politically prominent Dalit caste in Bihar.

Dravidian: Relating to the family of languages common in South India and Sri Lanka, or those who speak them.

Jai Bhim: Means "victory to Dr. B. R. Ambedkar;" and followers of Dr. B. R. Ambedkar prefer to greet each other with "Jai Bhim" instead of the Hindu ways of greeting such as "Ram Ram."

Jatav: Also known as Chamars, they are the largest Dalit caste in Uttar Pradesh and in North India in general. A social group considered to be part of the Chamar caste of Dalits, now classified as a "Scheduled Caste" under India's modern system of positive discrimination.

Jati: A pan-Indian word to which the English usage "caste" most often refers. In very broad terms, jatis are local endogamous groups ranked hierarchically in comparison with other jatis.

Jatiwad: Casteism or communalism.

Jayanti: Birth anniversary, jayanti is used to refer to annual birthday celebrations of political and socio-religious leaders.

Lok Sabha: House of the People, members of which are directly elected.

Mahapurush: Literally means "great men." A term used in Dalit movements to refer to "great men" who challenged indignities of caste.

Mahar: A Dalit caste in Maharashtra. A majority of Marathi Dalits belong to this caste.

Mang: A Dalit caste in Maharashtra.

Maratha: Peasant community of Maharashtra.

Marathi: Language spoken in Maharashtra.

Namantar/Namantar Movement: Namantar means changing of name. The terms are associated with Dalit mobilization that ensued from the late 1970s till the mid-1990s in Maharashtra to rename Marathwada University.

Naxalites: A movement that first coalesced after a violent 1967 uprising led by a section of the Communist Party of India (Marxist) CPIM over a land dispute in a West Bengal village called Naxalbari, hence the name Naxalites. Theoretically the armed left-wing movement is committed to the overthrow of the Indian state. In 2004, the merger of the different factions of the movement produced the CPI (Maoist) faction. The movement fights in the name of the poor and dispossessed. The Maoists' footprint stretches across 16 Indian states, mostly in the central and eastern regions.

Pallar: A Dalit caste from Tamil Nadu largely made up of agriculturalists and laborers.

Pasi: A Dalit caste in Bihar and Uttar Pradesh.

Paraiyar: A Dalit caste in Tamil Nadu and Sri Lanka. Numerically, the largest "Scheduled Caste" in Tamil Nadu. Also known as Adi-Dravida.

Ravidas: A venerated northern Indian mystic poet, spiritual figure, and social reformer of the fifteenth and sixteenth centuries, known for his devotional songs that spoke to the ideas of equality in the eyes of God. Ravidas taught in Punjab, Uttar Pradesh, Rajasthan, and Maharashtra.

Ryotwari: Agrarian tax system used during colonial rule in southern India. The colonial government collected the taxes directly from the cultivators instead of relying on intermediaries. This system was conducive to the formation of a more egalitarian peasantry.

Samaj: "Society;" a term varyingly used to refer to social groupings, including castes and collective identities like Dalit or Bahujan.

Sangh Parivar: The family of Hindu nationalist organizations begun by members of the Rashtriya Swayamsevak Sangh. It includes the Bharatiya Janata Party and Vishwa Hindu Parishad.

Sanskritization: A process by which a lower caste attempts to raise its status and to rise to a higher position in the caste hierarchy. Sanskritization may take place through the adoption of vegetarianism, abstention from alcohol, the worship of "Sanskritic deities," or engaging the service of Brahmins for ritual purposes. Its essential ingredient is the imitation of behavior and beliefs associated with ritually high-status groups. The term was first coined by M. N. Srinivas in 1952.

Shiv Sena: An Indian far-right political party founded on Hindu nationalism and pro-Marathi ideology, based primarily in Maharashtra.

Shuddhi: Sanskrit for "purification." Refers to converting to Hinduism and is a part of Hindu worship.

Shudra: It is the fourth and lowest varna, and castes under Shudra varna are considered ritually impure.

Seva Bharati: An organization founded by the RSS focused on providing social activities and welfare services to the poor and marginalized.

Varnas: These are the four castes of the Hindu social order: Brahmin, Kshatriya, Vaishya, and Shudra. Each varna is further subdivided in to a number of jatis or subcastes. As outcastes, Dalits literally fell outside the social order.

Vidhan Sabha: State Legislative Assembly.

Valmiki: A Dalit community in North India.

Zamindari: A tax system used in North India prior to and during colonial rule. This system cemented the hierarchy of peasant society by requiring wealthy landowners (zamindars) to collect taxes directly from cultivators on behalf of the colonial state. The zamindari system reinforced Dalit subjugation.

INDEX

Tables, figures, and maps are indicated by an italic *t*, *f*, and *m*, respectively, following the page number.

People's Power Party. *See* Lok Janshakti
Party (LJP)
Periyar, 51–52, 54–55, 74, 133–34
Gandhi opposition of, 88–89
on intercaste marriages, 78–79
social and political agenda, 54–55
petitioning, 154
collective action, 154
social mobilization, in movement *vs.* non-
movement states, 165, 165*t*, 168, 176
Phule, Jyotirao, and Savitrabhai, 53
policy disruption, electoral mobilization, 173
political parties. *See* parties, political; *specific parties*
politics
cleavages, from social cleavages, 30
equality in democracy, leveraging, 1–2
mobilization, social relations and, 190–91
politics, Dalit, 192–209
brief overview, 192
democratic mobilization and social change, 202
ethnic and multiethnic politics, diverse
society, 202
marginalization and mobilization, 192
participation without mobilization, 193
social movements and political parties, 195
voice without choice, 197
politics of othering, 6–7
poverty, 190
rates, mobilization type on, 154, 156*t*, 163*t*
proportional representation (PR) system, 33–34
Protestant missionaries, 50
protests
collective action for, 154
against corruption, by marginalized, 170–71
electoral mobilization, 168–69
social mobilization, 164–67, 167*t*, 168
against state neglect, 176
Puthiya Tamilagam (PT), 93–94, 93*t*
Tamil Nadu, state assembly elections, 93–94, 93*t*

Rajah, M. C., 51
Ram, Babu Jagjivan, 137
Ram, Kanshi, 66–67, 99, 138, 139–40
Ramachandran, M. G., 89
Ramasamy, Periyar E. V., 51–52, 54–55,
74, 133–34
Gandhi opposition of, 88–89
on intercaste marriages, 78–79
social and political agenda, 54–55
Rashtriya Janata Dal (RJD), 25, 111–12,
111*t*, 201–2
Bihar, 131
Rashtriya Swayamsevak Sangh (RSS), 205
religious conversion, 79, 188–89
banning, Dalits agreeing with, 80*t*, 81
banning, non-Dalits agreeing with, 81, 81*t*

Republican Party of India (RPI), 73, 85
Maharashtra, state assembly elections,
94–95, 96*t*
Uttar Pradesh, 104–5
research design, 21
aims, 25–26
context-driven explanation, 25–26
controlled cross-case comparisons, 25–26
India, factors favoring, 21–22
mechanism-process approach, 25–26
observational study, 216
states chosen, rationale, 11*m*, 22–25, 23*t*, 24*t*
within-case process tracing, 25–26
resource-mobilization theory, 30–31
resources. *See also specific types*
for ethnic group mobilization, 35
symbolic, electoral mobilization and, 132
transfer, social movements, 2
ryotwari, 60

Samajwadi Party (SP), 175
Scheduled Castes (SCs), 10, 11*m*, 13
self-awareness, on Dalit social
mobilization, 124
self-mobilization, 45–46, 194–95
self-respect movement, 51–52, 60
Sen, Amartya, 177–78
Seva Bharati, 65
Shiv Sena, Maharashtra, 135, 150
Dr. B. R. Ambedkar, recognition by, 150
stigmatization, 135
Shiv Sena-Bharatiya Janata Party alliance, 98–99
Singh, Charan, 101–2
single-member-district plurality (SMDP), 33–34
slogans, 138–39
social blocs. *See also specific types*
democratic accountability and, 164, 165*t*, 167*t*
social change. *See also specific types and issues*
democratic mobilization and, 202
social cleavages, political and electoral cleavages
from, 30
social exclusion. *See* exclusion, social
social mobilization, 3, 4
on electoral mobilization, Dalit, 7–8
vs. electoral mobilization, 5
of marginalized ethnic groups, 3, 4
for petitioning, in movement *vs.* non-movement
states, 165, 165*t*, 168, 176
prior, on electoral mobilization, competitive
party system, 45
for protests, 164–67, 167*t*, 168
for society and state, 33
social mobilization, Dalit, bloc voting and, 121–52
benefits, 122
ethnic blocs for ethnic party success, 121–22
explanations, reconsideration, 149